Icons and the Name of God

Icons and the Name of God

by

Sergius Bulgakov

Translated by

Boris Jakim

William B. Eerdmans Publishing Company

Grand Rapids, Michigan / Cambridge, U.K.

"The Icon and Its Veneration" was originally written in Russian with the title
Ikona i ikonopochitanie, published privately in Paris, 1931. "The Name of God" was
originally written in Russian with the title *Imia Bozhie,* published privately in Paris, 1953.

Published 2012 by
Wm. B. Eerdmans Publishing Co.
2140 Oak Industrial Drive N.E., Grand Rapids, Michigan 49505 /
P.O. Box 163, Cambridge CB3 9PU U.K.

Printed in the United States of America

18 17 16 15 14 13 12   7 6 5 4 3 2 1

Library of Congress Cataloging-in-Publication Data

Bulgakov, Sergei Nikolaevich, 1871-1944.
[Ikona i ikonopochitanie. English]
Icons ; and, The name of God / by Sergius Bulgakov; translated by Boris Jakim.
p.   cm.
ISBN 978-0-8028-6664-6 (pbk.: alk. paper)
1. Icons.   2. God (Christianity) – Name.
I. Bulgakov, Sergei Nikolaevich, 1871-1944. Imia Bozhie. English.
II. Title.   III. Title: Name of God.

BX577.B813   2012
246'.53 — dc23

2011039491

www.eerdmans.com

Contents

Translator's Introduction

Divine energy radiates from the icon of Christ, just as it does from the Divine Name Jesus.[1] The icon is not just a picture, and the Name of God is not just a word: they are modes in which this Divine energy radiates into us. These two modes of revelation are present together when we pray before an icon, especially when we venerate Christ on His icon while mentally proclaiming His Holy Name. The Divine energy should be understood in a mystically physical sense: the countenance on the icon shines forth, and this radiation enters our spiritual center, our heart, illuminating it. It is the same with the Name: when we utter it, the Divine energy contained in it enters our heart, deifying us. The two essays offered here, "The Icon and Its Veneration" and "The Name of God," treat these two distinct but intimately related modes of Divine illumination.

In these essays Bulgakov explores the dogmatic underpinnings of

1. Directly applicable here is the doctrine of Gregory Palamas, who distinguished God's essence from His manifested energies, which Palamas saw, for example, in the uncreated light. The icon and the Name are other examples of the revelation of such energies. Here is what Bulgakov says in this connection with reference to the Name of God: "... the Name of God occupies in the ontological hierarchy the same place as the light of Tabor.... One can tranquilly make the following juxtaposition: the Name of God is God, the light of Tabor is God, ... [and] ... the grace of God sacramentally bestowed upon men is God ..." (p. 165 in the present volume).

both the veneration of icons and the glorification of the Name of God. In his discussion of the Name of God, he shows that this Name is an incarnation of Divine energies, a theophany, a Divine revelation that imprints its image in us. He agrees with John of Kronstadt that "the Name of God is God."[2] This is what Bulgakov says: "Since the Name of God contains Divine energy and gives the presence of God, one can say . . . that, practically and energetically, the Name of God is God. More precisely, in the Name of God is present the Power of God, which is inseparable from the Essence of God and in this sense is God Himself" (pp. 159-60).

For Bulgakov, the sanctification of icons is associated with their naming; in other words, an icon stops being a mere religious painting and becomes a holy thing when it is named. Here is what Bulgakov says about the relationship between icon and Name: "A holy icon is not just a picture, a human artifact, a photograph; it is also a bearer of God's power and a holy hieroglyph of the Name of God; and the Name itself, the Name of God, is not just a means of designation chosen on the basis of considerations of convenience, not just an empty 'symbol' . . . it is also a Divine icon in word, a holy symbol whose essence consists in its having two natures. The Name of God is not only a means for designating or invoking Divinity but also a verbal icon, and that is why it is holy" (p. 126).

For Bulgakov there is only one objective basis for resolving both the question of icon veneration and the question of the nature of the Name of God: the doctrine of the Divine energy acting in man and the Incarnation of the Word, a doctrine that has its ontological foundation in the image and likeness of God in man. The fact that the image of God is the image of man and thus of the whole world is what makes possible the icon as originating in theophany, in Divine revelation: "God cannot reveal Himself to stone and in stone but He can reveal Himself to man and in man, and through man (and therefore in stone as well). In relation to both the icon and the Name of God the Divine energy acting in man unites itself with human energy, becomes incarnate in the latter, resulting in the inseparable and inconfusible union of Divine power and hu-

---

2. Bulgakov clarifies that God here is *Theos*, not *ho Theos*, i.e., not God Himself, but Divinity.

viii

man activity, where the latter is the bearer of Divine power as it were" (p. 119).

In "The Icon and Its Veneration," Bulgakov describes in some detail the iconoclastic controversy of the Byzantine period, a controversy that culminated in the decree in favor of icon veneration enacted at the Seventh Ecumenical Council. In "The Name of God," he discusses a more recent dogmatic controversy that is much less familiar: the "onomaclastic" controversy that roiled the Orthodox Church at the beginning of the twentieth century and has still not been resolved. The doctrine that was being disputed — known by such names as onomatodoxy, glorification of the Name, worship of the Name, "Name-of-Godding," and (in Russian) Imiaslavie — stated in a nutshell that "the Name of God is God." The controversy over this doctrine grew very virulent, and the powerful clerics who opposed it resorted at times to armed force to impose their views. Bulgakov accuses these "onomaclasts" of desiring to destroy the Name of God the way the old iconoclasts would break icons into pieces.[3] (In the Appendix to this introduction, I give a brief chronology of the onomaclastic controversy and discuss some of the philosophical and theological implications of onomatodoxy, or Imiaslavie.)

*   *   *

"The Icon and Its Veneration" was written in 1930 and published in 1931. It is situated between the "Little Trilogy" (completed in 1929) and the "Great Trilogy," begun in 1933;[4] like the "Little Trilogy," the essay on icons shows a mode of uniting heaven and earth; like the "Great Trilogy," it attempts to show how this union can be understood dogmatically. The essay "The Name of God" was written in the 1920s; it is the concluding section of the

---

3. Bulgakov points out that even at the time of the iconoclastic controversy the iconoclasts were also called onomaclasts (*onomatomachoi*) (see p. 121).

4. The "Little Trilogy" consists of *The Friend of the Bridegroom* (on John the Baptist), *The Burning Bush* (on the Mother of God), and *Jacob's Ladder* (on the angels); the "Great Trilogy" (On Divine Humanity) consists of *The Lamb of God* (on Christ), *The Comforter* (on the Holy Spirit), and *The Bride of the Lamb* (on the Church). All are available in English translation from Eerdmans.

major work, *The Philosophy of the Name,* which Bulgakov was commissioned to write by the All-Russian Council of 1917-1918 as a comprehensive treatment of the question of the veneration of the Name of God (in response to the onomaclastic controversy). Also included in the present volume is an appendix to "The Name of God": "A Sophiological Interpretation of the Dogma of the Name Jesus." This appendix (which Bulgakov calls a "Post Scriptum") was written in 1942.

Appendix: On the Imiaslavie Controversy

1. *History*

In 1907 the Russian monk Ilarion published a work that was to ignite the Imiaslavie (or onomatodoxy) controversy: *On the Caucasus Mountains.* In this book, Ilarion told his readers that his experience with the Prayer of Jesus led him to believe that "the Name of God is God Himself and can work miracles." The book became extremely popular among the Russian monks on Mount Athos. Inspired by Ilarion, the main proponent of the Imiaslavie doctrine was Antonii Bulatovich, a monk of the Russian Andreyevsky skete on Athos. Bulatovich's advocacy caused a huge stir on Athos and in Russia: many monks and theologians embraced Imiaslavie as a fresh way of communing with the Divine mysteries, whereas many church hierarchs and Tsarist officials considered it to be a dangerous heresy. In 1912 the Holy Synod (the organization that defined church teaching and practice under the Tsar) banned *On the Caucasus Mountains.* In January 1913 a monk by the name of David, who was a supporter of Imiaslavie, was elected as the rector of the Andreyevsky skete on Athos, taking the place of Hieronim, who was an opponent of it. Hieronim did not recognize the results of the election and complained to the Russian Embassy in Greece. The Russian government insisted on reinstating Hieronim. In June 1913 a small Russian fleet consisting of a gunboat and two transport ships delivered the archbishop of Vologda, Nikon (Rozhdestvensky), and a number of troops to Mount Athos. In May and June, Nikon held talks with supporters of Imiaslavie (onomatodoxians) and tried to convince them to change their beliefs voluntarily, but was unsuccessful. On July 31 the Russian troops stormed the monastery. Although the monks were not armed and did not actively resist, the soldiers were ordered to attack them with bayonets and rifle butts. Allegedly, four monks were killed and at least forty-eight were wounded. The onomatodoxian monks had no choice but to surrender. A military transport, converted into a prison ship, took over 600 monks to Russia, setting sail for Odessa on July 9. About forty monks were left in the Athos hospital, judged unable to survive the transportation. On July 14 a steamship delivered approximately 200 more monks from Athos. The rest of the monks signed papers attesting that they rejected Imiaslavie. After interrogation, eight imprisoned monks were returned to Athos, forty were put into jail, and the rest were defrocked and exiled to different parts of the Russian Empire. In February 1914 some of the onomatodoxians were received by the Emperor Nicholas II; this reception was considered a sign that the official view of the onomatodoxians was changing. In May 1914, Makarii, the Metropolitan of Moscow, and the Moscow Synodal Office decided to allow the onomatodoxians to participate in church services without their having to repent; a similar decision was taken by the Metropolitan of Kiev. On May 10 the decision was partially adopted by the Holy Synod that the onomatodoxians were allowed to keep their positions in the Orthodox Church without a formal repentance, but it specified that the teaching itself was still to be considered a heresy. One of the tasks of the All-Russian Church Council of 1917-1918 was to resolve the question of Imiaslavie, but the work of the Council was aborted due to the calamitous events of the time. Pavel Florensky and Sergius Bulgakov were among the theologians who spoke out at the Council in support of Imiaslavie. In 1918 the Holy Synod of the Russian Orthodox Church canceled its previous decision, and no longer allowed the onomatodoxians to participate in church services unless they repented. Even at the present time (as of 2011) the Imiaslavie controversy remains unresolved in the Orthodox Church and there is no accepted doctrine of the Name of God.

2. Theological Ramifications

A number of theologians and religious philosophers defended the onomatodoxians, seeing in their doctrine a continuation of the fully orthodox tradition of the deification of the Divine Name Jesus Christ and associating with this deification the manifestation of Divine energies in the world (the doctrine of Palamas). Chief among these theologians were Pavel Florensky and Sergius Bulgakov.[5] In particular, Florensky stated that if the onomaclasts' assertion that the Name of God is "just a word and nothing more" were taken to its logical conclusion, "this would signify the end of any possibility of sacrament, prayer, even of cult itself; and under the cover of piety it would lead to the most unrestrained positivism."[6] The ultimate result would be the breakdown of "the entire ecclesial order."[7]

The religio-philosophical exploration of the themes raised by the Imiaslavie controversy reached its lapidary culmination in the five theses of Aleksei Losev: "1 — The Name of God is an energy of God's essence. 2 — The Name of God, as an energy of God's essence, is inseparable from the essence itself and is therefore God Himself. 3 — The Name of God is God Himself but God Himself is not His Name: God is higher than all names and is higher than human and angelic knowledge. The Names of God are living symbols of God who is being revealed, i.e., they are God Himself in His revelation to the creature. 4 — The Name of God is not a mere sound and it must be venerated. 5 — In the Name of God man encounters God. The efficacious Name of God has two natures, insofar as human energy too participates here. The proclaimed Name is a place of encounter of Divine and human energies."[8]

---

5. Bulgakov's views of the controversy and his ideas on Imiaslavie are given in the essay "The Name of God" in the present volume.

6. *Bogoslovskie Trudy*, 1977, no. 17, p. 189.

7. *Bogoslovskie Trudy*, 1977, no. 17, p. 189.

8. *Kontekst-90*, Moscow, 1990, pp. 15-17.

The Icon and Its Veneration (A Dogmatic Essay)

1. The History of the Dogma of Icon Veneration

The veneration of icons was legitimized in the Church by the decree accepted in the seventh act of the Seventh Ecumenical Council. In this decree, having confirmed the doctrine of the six earlier ecumenical councils, the fathers proclaim: "We preserve as unalterable all the traditions of the Church, whether written or unwritten. One of these traditions prescribes the making of painted icon images, since this is in conformity with the history of Gospel preaching and serves to confirm that Christ was made man truly, not illusorily, as well as serving for our benefit. On this basis . . . we decree that holy and precious icons be offered (for veneration) in precisely the same manner as the image of the Holy Life-giving Cross, whether they be made of paints, of mosaics, or of some other material, as long as they are made appropriately, whether they be found in the holy churches of God, on sacred vessels, on walls and on boards, or in homes and on roads, and also whether these be the icons of our Lord, God, and Savior Jesus Christ, of our immaculate Mistress the Holy Mother of God, or of the holy angels and all the saints and righteous men. The more frequently with the aid of icons they are the objects of our contemplation, the more those who gaze upon these icons will be motivated to remember the prototypes themselves, the more love they will acquire for them and the more they will be motivated to kiss them, to offer them reverence and veneration, but not at all to offer them that true service, *latrēia*, which, according to our faith, can appropriately be offered only to the Divine nature.... The honor bestowed upon the icon refers to its proto-image, and he who venerates the icon venerates the hypostasis portrayed on it."

As we see from the text of this decree, it does not contain any *dogmatic* definition of icons or any *dogmatic* justification for their veneration; it only legitimizes the use of holy icons and establishes the form of their veneration (reverence and veneration — *timētikē proskunēsis*, but not service, *latreia*). In conformity with this, there is no dogmatic definition in the *oros*[1] of the Seventh Ecumenical Council: it is enforced not by anathematisms but only by ecclesiastical disciplinary punishments (removal of bishops and clergy, and excommunication of laity and monks). It is true that, later, at this same Council, along with other general and personal anathematisms, an anathema is pronounced against those who do not accept holy icons. However, this only belongs to the ritual of the Council; it was not introduced, and even could not be introduced, into the decree itself because it lacked dogmatic content. Thus, it is necessary to establish first of all that the Seventh Ecumenical Council gave us only *the canon of icon veneration*, not the *dogma* of what the icon represents as a fact of dogmatic significance. This absence of dogma was also connected with the general character of the Council, which tended to be "economic" rather than dogmatic. Moreover, the Council was extremely short-lasting and hurried (which is explained by the historical circumstances surrounding it). It lasted only about a month and consisted only of eight sessions (of which only two, sessions 6 and 7, were devoted specifically to the essence of the matter, and even here it was a question not of discussion but of the presentation of a single report, probably given by Patriarch Tarasios himself, in the form of a critique of the theses of iconoclasm). Thus, it can be said that, although the Church legitimized icon veneration, it did not present a dogma of it; and the question of the dogmatic meaning of icon veneration still remains an object of theological discussion. Of course, in this connection we have the whole history, extending over many centuries, of the

1. The decree of the Council. — Trans.

dogmatic struggle for and against icon veneration, even if this struggle has not yielded indisputable dogmatic results. There exists a whole series of patristic writings devoted to this question and demanding respectful and serious discussion. These writings must of course be taken into account in any dogmatic investigation of the question.

We must first examine the history of icon veneration (of course, within the limits set by our task of dogmatic investigation). In this history we first of all encounter the fundamental fact that the icon first appears in paganism. The entire pagan world is full of icons and icon veneration. This is sufficiently attested by the monumental temple-building and sculpture of the East and of Egypt, by the irresistibly beautiful art of ancient Greece, and by the prosaically imitative art of ancient Rome. Paganism was full of representational art, and Israel, during all the epochs of its existence, was surrounded by its own religious art. However, Israel's art was essentially pagan, for it originated in the worship of false gods. Therefore, Israel's icons were *idols*; that is, they were the icons of false gods and in this sense they were false icons; or they were simply fetishes in which was obliterated the very distinction between the image and that which was imaged, between image and proto-image, between icon and deity; and for this reason *latreia*, worship appropriate to deities, was proffered to them. Both forms of the pagan veneration of icons equally made men stray from the service of the true God and therefore constituted a religious temptation, which was the more dangerous, the more enchanting were its artistic images. Israel was besieged by this temptation, and continually gave in to it, according to the testimony of the Holy Scriptures, historical and prophetic. In this sense, according to its *religious* coefficient pagan idolatry was an abomination before the Lord, a spiritual debauchery that was often combined with a bodily debauchery. Judaism's attitude toward idolatry, which initially was communicated to early Christianity as well,[2] could only be expressed in intense and unending struggle.

However, this does not change the fact that it was paganism that first posed and solved the problem of the icon as a sacred image, insofar as it

---

2. Cf. Prof. Hugo Koch, *Die altchristliche Bilderfrage nach der literarischen Quellen* (Göttingen, 1917).

was possible to solve this problem given the religious limitations of paganism. Paganism took as its starting point the conviction, which it seemed to consider self-evident, that the Deity is portrayable in images that, if not adequate, are at least rich with symbolic significance. At the same time, paganism tacitly rejected the apophatic idea that it is impossible to portray the Deity because He is imageless and invisible, an idea that became one of the chief foundations of iconoclasm. This led to a further conviction, which constituted the second foundation of pagan iconography: it was considered that the image proper to the Deity could be known to and portrayed by man, that is, that in a certain sense this image was human in character. This does not necessarily mean that these pagan icons always presented the images precisely of human beings; on the contrary, we know that pagan temples were full of nonhuman images: nightmarish figures of the animal world and of the natural world in general oppressed the human consciousness. However, these were images that were made by man, that passed through the prism of human consciousness and in the end were humanized.

Therefore, what is of chief significance for pagan iconography is not these monstrous idols in which the essence of the image is obscured, but human, or humanlike, icons, which attained their peak in Greek art. The Greek gods in their likeness to men represented the peak of the artistic theology and anthropology of paganism and were also the true revelation of this theology and anthropology. Just as in its highest achievements Greek philosophy manifested itself as a Christianity before Christ, and on this basis also became the natural language of Christian revelation and theology, so the revelation of the art of antiquity in the form of iconography was, in a certain though limited sense, a Christianity before Christ and indisputably served as the prototype of the Christian icon. The pagan, and especially the Greek, world *manifested* man's likeness to God, representing this likeness in ideal images of natural man as the perfect form of corporeality. And these manifestations of beauty were so convincing and irresistible that, after them, there was no need to find or prove anew the *possibility of the icon*. On the contrary, the icon was taken from paganism as something familiar and self-evident by the Christian Church, which of course changed the content of icon images while assimilating the principle of the icon. *Art* was the bridge connecting pagan iconography with Christian iconography. Through the icon, art was raised to religious heights, comparable to those to which ancient philosophy was raised through Christian theology. Pagan iconography bore witness that art has its visions and seeings[3] which contain religious revelation. Religious art complemented theology for the pagan world, and therefore iconographic theology was something that originated in paganism. Moreover, the ideal images of pure humanity that were required also by the Christian icon were already present in pagan art. To be sure, this does not mean that these images were merely repeated by Christian iconography; on the contrary, the latter put its own stamp on them. Nevertheless, this does not diminish the fact that pagan iconography represents, so to speak, the natural old testament for Christian iconography, just as pagan philosophy is the natural old testament for Christian theology. To be sure, these genuine revelations of pagan religious art were made complex and obscured to an extreme degree by the religious ambiguity, if not by the outright demonism, that characterized paganism. Pagan art needed to be exorcised, and this exorcism was performed by Christianity. As a direct result of this exorcism, art as such suffered a loss, but in return it stopped being possessed. For Christian theology pagan iconography already posed the general question concerning the nature of icons of the Deity and whether they are possible, as well as concerning the pathways of art as a special form of the knowledge of God.

Nevertheless, precisely because of the religious temptation it represented, paganism posed such a danger for the chosen nation that the Old Testament's entire attitude toward pagan art was determined by motives of religious pedagogy. Pagan art remained under a religious prohibition for Israel, and all idolatrous tendencies — such as those manifested by kings who began to serve pagan gods — were regarded as a religious fall. The psychological type of the pious Jew in this respect can be clearly seen in the Apostle Paul, who, while in Athens, face to face with the highest achievements of Greek art, became perturbed in spirit "when he saw the city

---

3. There is a play on words here involving *videniya* accented on the second syllable (visions) and *videniya* accented on the first syllable (seeings). — Trans.

wholly given to idolatry" (Acts 17:16). Besides idols he did not see anything there. The making of idols, or of "any likeness," was prohibited by the second commandment, in connection with the first, in the general law of the true worship of God; and at the same time a prohibition was placed on all representational art except, perhaps, architecture and the adornment of temples (the express gift of the Holy Spirit given to Bezaleel and his helpers: Exod. 31:1-10). The denunciations found in the prophetic books, as well as a kind of satire in the description of idol-making in the noncanonical Wisdom of Solomon (ch. 13), only serve to confirm this general observation. The prudence of such an attitude was confirmed by what we know of the life of the Jews then: at every convenient opportunity they tended to succumb to the crudest religious fetishism, to outright idolatry, whose objects did not rise above the level of emblematic images: for example, the bronze snake permitted by Moses as a remembrance of a miracle but which turned into a fetish and for that reason was destroyed by the pious King Hezekiah (2 Kings 18:4); the golden calf; the Teraphim. To the general prohibition that stifled religious art, there was only one exception: God Himself commanded that two cherubim with extended wings be made of gold and placed above the ark of the covenant (Exod. 25:18-22); and this was done by Solomon in the temple together with carved images on the doors and walls (1 Kings 6:23-32). This of course was an exception that was incomprehensible from the point of view of the Old Testament, an exception which, in the eyes of iconoclasts, old and new, did not disprove the general rule. But in essence it did abolish the general rule, thereby leaving it with nothing more than a conventionally pedagogic significance. This image of the two cherubim, which is usually adduced by apologists of icon veneration against Judaizing iconoclasts who insist on the letter of the second commandment, already represents a fundamental recognition of both the rights and the possibilities of religious art, as well as the possibility of portraying the spiritual world with the resources and images of this art, although pedagogically it is limited in quantity. In addition, it is necessary to recognize that to admit the icons of angels did not yet signify icon veneration. Why and in what sense does the Old Testament admit the portrayal of angels? To this question we usually find no answer in the theological doctrine of icons, either from icon venerators or from iconoclasts.

6

From Judaism the Christian Church inherited the prohibition against religious images as something self-evident and having the force of law, and in this sense the Church's initial tendency was somewhat iconoclastic. There were more than sufficient religious-moral and pedagogic reasons for this: the Christian communities were little islands in a sea of paganism, and they could not help being besieged both outwardly and inwardly by the influence of paganism. For Christianity it was clear that paganism with its worship of idols was fatally possessed by demons. And it is on these religious positions that Christianity first encountered paganism as its fundamental enemy, with which it could have nothing in common. This also determined the character of the early Christian apologetics, with its irreconcilable hostility toward paganism, particularly toward the worship of idols. It is interesting to note that this attitude was wholly reproduced among the apologists for icon veneration in the epoch of the iconoclastic disputes (Patriarch Nicephoros, St. Theodore the Studite). For us at the present time, when the battle against idolatry has only a historical significance, the difference between idols and icons is much less clear than what is common between them: the recognition that the Divine world can be represented in images of the human world (and even in images of the animal world and of the whole created world in general) with the resources of art, as well as the recognition that these images are worthy of veneration. Paganism bequeathed to Christianity an already developed idea of the icon as well as the fundamental principles of iconography (planar images with reverse perspective, methods of representation, ornamentation, etc.). In this light it is easy to understand how the icon appeared in the Christian Church and occupied its place in spite of the second commandment's prohibition and as if contrary to this prohibition, which Christianity too accepted implicitly. One can of course see in this the direct influence of paganism, or an "acute Hellenization" of Christianity, similar to that observed in the development of Christian dogma (Harnack). In fact, from Greco-Roman culture Christianity chose and took that which was its *own*, that is, that which belonged to it as a "Christianity before Christ" in the pagan world, in the same way that a magnet attracts iron filings. Here it is necessary to speak not of the influence *upon* Christianity but of the influence *in* Christianity of that which was naturally drawn into it by the force of internal affinity.

Thus, the icon began to occupy an important place in the life of the Church and became a fact of Church tradition before there was any dogmatic reflection on this fact or any doubt that the Deity could be represented (in a relative way) in images and that the veneration of icons was admissible. The Old Testament prohibition was first revoked by the force of fact, and only later did this fact begin to provoke dogmatic reflection and doubt. The history of icon veneration clearly illustrates this. The earliest images (from the Roman Catacombs) have a timid and primitive allegorical-symbolic character (anchor, lamb, dove, fish, vine), to which are added certain typical images of Old and New Testament themes (Noah's Ark, Daniel, Jonah, Moses bringing forth water from the rock, the Good Shepherd carrying the lamb, the wise and foolish virgins, etc.), as well as images of Christ, the Mother of God, and saints. Gradually, icon painting and icon veneration became so widespread in the fourth century that the fathers of the Seventh Ecumenical Council (and St. John of Damascus before them) could already adduce a long series of testimonies from various fathers of the Church (Basil the Great, Gregory the Theologian, Gregory of Nyssa, John Chrysostom, Cyril of Alexandria, Nilus of Sinai, and others), testimonies that include, in part, indications that the utilization of icons had become customary and in part a fundamental recognition of this custom. It is evident that the wave of icon veneration coincided with an artistic "boom" in iconography in the fifth to seventh centuries. Historians also remark on a series of superstitions associated with icon veneration, and in some cases, especially in barbarian lands, it becomes almost indistinguishable from idolatry. In their struggle against icon veneration, iconoclastic emperors, besides by outright heresy and political calculations, could be guided by so-called "enlightened absolutism," a kind of *"écrasez l'infâme"*[4] of the epoch; and in the first place this "enlightened absolutism" was directed against the extremely populous and largely uncultured monasticism, which bore the brunt of the defense of icon veneration.[5] Nevertheless, however aggressively imperial power

---

4. *"Écrasez l'infâme"* ("crush the infamous thing") is a phrase associated with Voltaire. The "infamous thing" is superstition. — Trans.

5. Cf. the later, though perhaps tendentious, testimony in the epistle of the

8

might have engaged in the persecution of icons (by the way, the role of imperial power in restoring icon veneration should also not be underrated), this does not negate the fundamental fact that the Church itself was beset by doubt, or at least uncertainty, regarding the legitimacy of icon veneration; and this led to a bitter dogmatic struggle, whose outcome was far from obvious. In support of their cause the iconoclasts could refer to testimony from Church tradition that was unfavorable to icon veneration, together with the unrevoked Old Testament prohibition as well as the banning of icons in churches by the Council of Elvira at the beginning of the fourth century. But the most important thing consisted of course in the fact that the iconoclasts put forward a series of very serious dogmatic objections against icon veneration, thereby establishing an entire iconoclastic theology. Of course this theology was not fully preserved, but even to the extent one can judge on the basis of extracts adduced for purposes of refutation, it took enormous exertions of theological thought to refute it. The very fact of the iconoclastic Council of 754 (whose acts too have not been preserved), where 348 bishops participated and unanimously accepted its decree[6] (*oros*), indicates how influential and widespread these ideas were. The struggle against iconoclasm required the efforts of such theological writers as John of Damascus and Patriarch Herman even before the Seventh Ecumenical Council, but even this Council did not conclusively eliminate the heresy. It was to raise its head again not only politically (under Leo V, the Armenian, under whom the second iconoclastic Council, that of 815, took place, confirming the *oros* of 754) but also theologically. A dogmatic defense of icon veneration turned out to be necessary even after the Seventh Ecumenical Council, and this defense was undertaken with the same energy as before by St. Theodore the Studite and Patriarch Nicephoros, although there can be varying opinions about how successfully this struggle was waged by them.

Byzantine Emperor Michael II in 824 addressed to Ludovic the Pious and read at the Frankfurt Council ("Mansi" coll. conc. 14, p. 420).

6. Professor I. D. Andreev is right when he says that the proofs of iconoclasm "were chosen masterfully and were superior in terms of precision of expression, consistency, clarity, and power" (see Andreev's essay: "*Sv. Tarasii, patriarkh Konstantinopol'skii*" [St. Tarasios, Patriarch of Constantinople], in *Bogoslovsky Vestnik*, 1899, IV, p. 177).

In general, historically the phenomenon of iconoclasm turns out to be highly complex and not fully clarified. But whatever might be its external causes (e.g., the indirect influence of Islam, or imperial willfulness), one cannot deny the existence on *both* sides of genuine theological thought, as well as of legitimate theological doubt. Therefore in the iconoclastic controversy one must see an expression of a necessary moment in the historical dialectic of the dogma of icon veneration. Iconoclasm was also characterized by a legitimate tendency to counteract the barbarization and superstitions that arose here and there in connection with illegitimate icon veneration, although this tendency sometimes went to the extreme of pneumatomachy (for examples see Heféle-Leclercq, *Histoire des conciles,* vol. IV, 1). But, leaving this problem to the historians,[7] let us instead ask: What constituted the dogmatic essence of the question of icon veneration? What is the main thread that passed through all the particulars of the controversy? If we look with the eyes of the orthodox apologists of icon veneration (in particular the Patriarchs Nicephoros and Herman, and St. Theodore the Studite), we might initially think that iconoclasm was essentially a christological heresy, specifically connected with the diminishment or denial of the truth of the Incarnation. The chief argument of these apologists, constantly repeated by them, was that if Christ was truly made man, then He could be portrayed in images and His images are worthy of veneration; thus, anyone who denies the fact that He can be portrayed in images and that His icons are worthy of veneration, denies the Incarnation and is thus guilty of docetism or some other christological heresy. However, if we turn from this stylized description to the historical reality (even though our knowledge of this reality is insufficient owing to the fragmentariness of the surviving literature), we will see something completely different and discover in the opponents of iconoclasm an arbitrary or even tendentious (because of simplification) deviation from the crux of the matter — we will discover a kind of *ignoratio elenchi.*[8] And, first

7. Besides the works mentioned, see the following well-known works: Schwarzlose, *Der Bilderstreit* (Gotha, 1890); Karl Hase, *Gesammelte Anfsätze zur Kirchengeschichte,* II (1928); Georg Ostrogorsky, *Studien zur Geschichte des Byzantinishcen Bilderstreites* (Breslau, 1929).

8. A fallacious argument in which the conclusion reached or proposition proved is irrelevant to the matter at hand. — Trans.

of all, external history already testifies that, historically, iconoclasm cannot be referred to any specific heretical movement in christology[9] and that, in general, it is not at all a christological heresy. On the contrary, it dogmatically justifies itself by motives of struggle precisely in behalf of orthodox christology, and it is impossible to find even in iconoclasm's polemical arguments any direct evidence showing that it was in fact directly linked with heretical christology.

Thus, the dogmatic opposition of icon veneration and iconoclasm was enacted within the limits and on the basis of orthodox christology, though it was connected with different interpretations of this christology. The following questions confronted orthodox dogmatic thought: How is the portrayability of Christ possible, and is it possible in general? Also: Within what limits is the veneration of Christ's icon admissible? (In connection with this, answers were also sought to the question of the veneration of other icons, though this question received little independent discussion.) The answers to these questions were not self-evident, even if icon veneration had become accepted as something self-evident. These questions were totally *new* in dogmatics and demanded independent discussion, which in fact began with the dogmatic reflections of the iconoclasts. In general, we have the argumentation of iconoclasm as system-

---

9. That is the opinion of Professor A. S. Lebedev, who says: "One cannot find a single fact in the entire history of iconoclasm which would indicate that there was any causal connection between iconoclasm and the earlier heresies which were related to the person of Christ and the operations in Him and which were condemned by the ecumenical Councils. On the contrary, it is easier to see a hostile relationship between iconoclasm and the Nestorian heresy as well as the monophysite and monothelite heresies" (Professor Lebedev, *Istoriya sviatykh vselenskikh soborov* [History of the holy ecumenical Councils], 2nd ed. [Moscow, 1876], pp. 221-22). "In its origin iconoclasm stands outside any connection with the heretical errors of earlier times. It constitutes a wholly original phenomenon, one that is independent of the earlier heresies" (p. 222). In particular, early icon veneration is encountered among heretics as well (the Carpocratians); and, on the other hand, it encounters sharp opposition among the Arians (Eusebius) and Eunomians, as well as among the Nestorians (the Thomists in the East) and the monophysite sects (Philoxenos and Severus). In general, historically the relation to icon veneration was determined by a complex and variable set of causes, which produced these kinds of fluctuations within the limits of the Orthodox Church itself in the course of three centuries.

atized in Act 6 of the Seventh Ecumenical Council, where Bishop Gregory of Neocaesarea read the decree of the iconoclastic pseudo-Council of 754, as well the polemical work of Patriarch Nicephoros against the treatise of Emperor Constantine Copronim, of which, however, only extracts were presented. Doubts concerning the possibility of Christ's icon were already expressed in the fourth century by Eusebius Pamphilus, bishop of Caesarea, in the epistle to the Empress Constantia. As is known, he was an Arianizer, but in this connection one cannot perceive any direct influence specifically of Arianism. Here[10] we have the first, and of course only preliminary, exposition of the dogmatic problem of the icon: Is Christ portrayable as God through the portrayal of His flesh? Is it possible to portray Christ's glorified body as it was in the Transfiguration and after

10. Acts of the Seventh Ecumenical Council, Russian translation of the Kazan Religious Academy, 2nd ed., pp. 255-56: "Since you wrote about some icon, supposedly that of Christ, and desired that I bring such an icon to you, what icon did you mean which you called that of Christ? Did you mean that which is true and unchanging and contains the essence of His nature or represents that nature of His which He assumed for our sake, being clothed in flesh as if in the garment of a slave? But as for His image as God, I myself think that it is not He you are seeking, for you are taught by Him that no one knows the Father except the Son and that no one knows the Son Himself except His Father Who begot Him.... Of course, you are seeking an icon that portrays Him in the form of a slave and in the flesh, in which He was clothed for our sake; but we are taught that it too was dissolved by the glory of Divinity, and that the mortal was swallowed up by life.... Thus, who has the ability to portray with dead and soulless paints and shadows the brilliant and blinding rays of the radiance of His glory and dignity? Who has the ability to portray Him as He is? Even His chosen disciples could not gaze upon Him on the mountain, but fell face-downward, having recognized that the brilliance of this light was unbearable for them. Thus, if the image perceived by them during the Incarnation acquired such glory from the Divinity inhabiting Him, what can we say about His state when, having removed mortality from Himself and having washed off corruption, He exchanged the form of the slave for the glory of the Lord and God — after He had conquered death, ascended to heaven, seated Himself on the royal throne at the right hand of the Father, and reposed in the ineffable and inexpressible bosom of the Father?" These acute questions, read at the Council by deacon Epiphanius, merited a direct response and refutation, but the reply consisted, first of all, of *ad hominem* references to Eusebius' Arianism and, secondly, of patristic testimonies about the autonomous existence of Christ's flesh, which had not become "Divine" (pp. 256-61). However, no direct answer was given to the question of whether Christ's glorified body could be represented in images.

the Resurrection and Ascension? The iconoclasts' fundamental idea is that, in the orthodox understanding of the Incarnation, Christ as the God-Man cannot be represented in images: His Divinity is unportrayable (1 John 4:12), and His humanity, even if it is portrayable, cannot by itself give the image of Christ. If we regard the image of Christ's human flesh as the image of Christ Himself, we assume either that His flesh can be separated from His Divinity and portrayed in this separateness, or that His Divinity is inseparably fused with His flesh, so that God too is portrayed in the image of the flesh. Both assumptions involve fundamental christological heresies: in the first case we have Nestorianism, which separates the natures; in the second case we have monophysitism (the doctrine of Dioscuros, Eutyches, and Severus, as well as of Arius in a certain sense), which fuses the natures into one. "Here the painter has made an icon and called it Christ, and the Name Christ is the Name of God and of man. Consequently, the icon is an icon of both God and man; and consequently the painter fused the natures that cannot be fused, and committed the heinous error of fusion. Those who venerate icons have the tendency toward the same blasphemy" (Acts of the Seventh Ecumenical Council, p. 226). "Venerators of icons separate the flesh from the Divinity and represent the flesh as having its own hypostasis, assimilating to the flesh a particular person, whom, according to their words, they portray on icons. By this they show an addition of a fourth person to the Trinity, transforming the Trinity into a quaternity; and furthermore that which is deified through the assumption they portray as undeified. Thus, in thinking of painting an icon of Christ, they are compelled either to regard the Divine as unportrayable and fused with the flesh, or to regard Christ's flesh as undeified and separate (from the Divinity), and to recognize the flesh as a person having his own hypostasis, and in this case they become, like the Nestorians, theomachians" (p. 230). Thus, the iconoclasts present themselves as staunch defenders of the purity of the christological dogma, supposedly violated by icon veneration. This dogmatic argument is their chief argument, compared to which the Biblical argument (which in particular nevertheless consists in a weighty indication of the prohibition of images by the second commandment in the Old Testament, a prohibition that is by no means weakened by any reference to the depiction of the cherubim on the ark of the covenant), the historical argument, the patristic argument, the liturgical argument, and others have only a secondary and auxiliary significance. The anathematisms at the Council of 754 are expounded accordingly: first a defense is put forward of the orthodox doctrine of the Holy Trinity and of the person of the Lord Jesus Christ and of His two natures; and only secondly is the possibility of representing Him on icons denied.[11]

The basic argument of the iconoclasts, which discloses the aporia of icon veneration, can be represented according to the following schema:

A. *The theological argument.* The imagelessness of God and therefore His unportrayability and invisibility. "No man hath seen God at any time" (John 1:18). According to His Divinity, Christ has no image. That is the major premise.

B. *The christological argument.* Given the inseparability and inconfusibility of the natures in Christ (the Chalcedonian dogma), the image of His flesh is not in any sense an image also of His Divinity, and therefore it is not the icon of Christ. That is the minor premise.

C. *Conclusion.* The icon of Christ contains a triple theological-trinitarian-christological heresy (portrayal of the unportrayable God, quaternization of the Holy Trinity, and denial of the Chalcedonian dogma).

This is the dogmatic dilemma, consisting of two arguments, (1) apophatic and (2) kataphatic, that the icon venerators were confronted with by the iconoclasts, who asserted that this path would inevitably lead to the violation of the propositions of general theology and christology and that it disclosed a dogmatic aporia. This aporia can be removed in two ways: one can either reject it completely by not accepting the two premises, major and minor, in the sense in which they are expounded by the iconoclasts, and then the entire formulation of the question of icons would be altered, *metabasis eis allo genos;* or one can attempt to get around

---

11. I have omitted Bulgakov's very long footnote, which contains an extract from the Acts of the Seventh Ecumenical Council comprising a list of eight anathematisms directed by the iconoclasts against icon veneration. — Trans.

it even while accepting the major premise. The de facto solution chosen by the defenders of icon veneration was the second one: they desired to overcome the aporia not from outside, as it were, but from inside, accepting the major premise as self-evident, but attempting to get around the minor premise. Let us see to what extent they succeeded in doing this.

Let us first say that they did not succeed at all[12] in their attempt at the Seventh Ecumenical Council to fulfill this task by means of refutations of the iconoclasts' theses read by deacon Epiphanius but evidently belonging to the spiritual leader of the Council, Patriarch Tarasios himself.[13] To the christological argument against icon veneration, where the latter is reduced to monophysitism or Nestorianism (the minor premise), the following reply is made: accepted, first of all, is the full force of the iconoclasts' assertion that "Christ is unportrayable and invisible according to His Divinity but portrayable according to His humanity" and that "in one and the same Christ both the unportrayable and the portrayable are perceivable." Here, nothing lessens the general doubt that flows from this concerning the possibility of Christ's icon. Further, the iconoclasts' chief objection against the icon venerators, consisting in the assertion that the latter reproduce either Nestorius' diphysitism or the monophysitism of Eutyches, Severus, et al., is answered in the following manner: "The heresies of Arius, Dioscorus, Nestorius, and Eutyches, since they are opposed to one another, thereby mutually demolish one another, although they are all equally heinous.... If we accept that, according to their words, the Church followed Nestorius, then they are lying when they say that she is in agreement with Eutyches and Dioscorus. But if, on the contrary, we concur that the Church is in agreement with Eutyches and Dioscorus, then in this case they will turn out to be liars, because Nestorius and Eutyches are opposed to each other in their heinousness; and therefore this syllogism of theirs turns out to be groundless" (Acts of the Seventh Ecumenical Council, pp. 223-24). And of course this argument is evasive and totally insufficient. Instead of a direct

---

12. See Professor I. D. Andreev, "*Sv. Tarasii, patriarkh Konstantinopol'skii*" (St. Tarasios, Patriarch of Constantinople), in *Bogoslovsky Vestnik*, 1899, VIII, pp. 46off.

13. See Andreev, "*Sv. Tarasii, patriarkh Konstantinopol'skii*," pp. 470-71.

refutation, this is an indirect one, and one that is wholly based on *ignoratio elenchi*, on evasion of the essence of the question. In fact, all of these heresies, while contradicting one another in one respect, can turn out to be, and actually do turn out to be, in agreement in another respect, precisely in the fact that they all violate the true relation of the Divine and human natures in Christ, which in fact are without separation and without confusion. In Nestorianism this relation is violated by separation; in monophysitism it is violated by confusion. And this resemblance in one thing is not nullified by their differences in another thing. Therefore, it is not surprising that, even after the Seventh Ecumenical Council, the theological work of the dogmatic defense of icon veneration, begun even prior to the Council by John of Damascus, had to continue as before, for the iconoclasts' fundamental dogmatic argument went unrefuted at the Council and was not even really understood. What do we find in these later defenders of icon veneration, in Theodore the Studite and Patriarch Nicephoros?

Initially, along with auxiliary and secondary proofs and in any case ones that were not dogmatic in nature (the significance of icons as aids to remembrance, edification, education, etc.), the defenders of icon veneration put forward the truth of the Incarnation as their fundamental dogmatic argument, thus giving the question a christological formulation. This was the case even before the iconoclastic Council of 754, and even before the Seventh Ecumenical Council. Thus, Patriarch Herman[14] directly linked the icon portrayability of the Lord Jesus Christ with the truth of His Incarnation and appearance in the flesh.[15] We encounter this same argument in John of Damascus,[16] although here it is combined with a series of

14. About Herman see Professor I. D. Andreev, "*Sv. German, patriarkh Konstantinopol'skii*" (St. Herman, Patriarch of Constantinople), in *Bogoslovsky Vestnik*, 1897, V-VII, especially VII, pp. 229-30; G. Ostrogorskii, *Soedinenie voprosa o sv. ikonakh s kristologicheskoi dogmatikoi v sochineniiakh pravoslavnykh apologetov rannego perioda ikonoborchestva* (Relating the question of holy icons to the christological dogmatics in the works of Orthodox apologists of the early period of iconoclasm) (Prague, 1929).

15. See Ostrogorskii, *Soedinenie voprosa*, pp. 37-39.

16. John of Damascus, *Precise Exposition of the Orthodox Faith*, book IV, ch. XVI; *Orations of Defense against Those Who Reject Holy Icons*, First Oration, ch. 8, 18, 21, 22; *Second Oration*, ch. 5, 6, 20.

considerations of another order (about which below), and we also encounter it in Pope Gregory II (Acts of the Seventh Ecumenical Council, p. 18), as well as in Gregory of Cyprus.[17] However, this christological argument is put forward here only in a general form, without any connection with the specific formulation that it received at the hands of the iconoclasts at the Council of 754. Therefore, more important for us are the judgments of the later apologists, who knew the objections of the iconoclasts against the portrayability of Christ, objections based precisely on the dogma of the Incarnation and therefore having a christological character. To be content with accusing the iconoclasts of denying the Incarnation, or of docetism (which, by the way, can be perfectly compatible with the acceptance of the portrayability of Christ's flesh, even if the latter is thought to be illusory), became impossible after the iconoclasts decisively confessed the orthodox dogma of the Incarnation established at all the ecumenical Councils, and accused precisely their opponents of betraying this dogma. Therefore, it was necessary to undertake a substantive analysis of the christological argument in support of icon veneration, thereby accomplishing what, as we have seen, the fathers of the Seventh Ecumenical Council had not done (and of course could not have done because of the short duration of the Council — about a month — and the haste this necessitated). After the canonical institution of icon veneration it was still necessary to develop its theology. This turned out to be the task of the later defenders of orthodoxy in the ninth century — Patriarch Nicephoros and Theodore the Studite. What did they say?

Let us begin with Theodore the Studite (759-826), the great confessor of icon veneration. He wrote three refutations of the iconoclasts, seven chapters against them, a number of letters of dogmatic content, etc. How does he answer the iconoclasts' chief argument, which asserts the unportrayability of the Divine nature and the inseparability in Christ of the portrayable human nature from the Divine nature? Astonishingly, not only do we not find a refutation of this argument in Theodore, but we even find a total acceptance of both of its premises, major as well as minor. First of all, he himself powerfully argues in favor of the unknowability and imagelessness

---

17. See Ostrogorskii, *Soedinenie voprosa*, pp. 43-45.

17

of the Divinity. Christ "according to His Divinity is unportrayable"; in Him "has been accomplished the union of the nonunitable, the mixing of the unmixable, of the unportrayable with the portrayable, of the imageless with that which has an external image."[18] Thus, Theodore wholly accepts the iconoclasts' first, or theological, argument asserting the unportrayability of God, which he also takes to mean His imagelessness, the absence of all form; in general he understands this in the purely apophatic sense of *a privativum*. However, while the iconoclasts not without logic concluded from this that it is not possible to portray Christ on icons, Theodore drew the opposite conclusion, namely that "Christ, who has come in flesh, is portrayable in the flesh."[19] "The property of the Divinity is unportrayability, incorporeality, the absence of external appearance and form; whereas the property of the humanity is portrayability, tangibility, measurability of three kinds. If Christ consists of two natures, He is of course both unportrayable and portrayable."[20] If our Lord Jesus Christ, without any doubt, came in the human image and in our appearance, then "it is just to say that He can be portrayed and represented on icons just as we can be, even if according to His Divine image He remains unportrayable. . . . But if He were not portrayable, He would stop being man."[21] Fur-

---

18. The *Works* of Theodore the Studite in Russian translation (St. Petersburg, 1907), vol. 1, *First Refutation of the Iconoclasts*, pp. 120-21. This idea is included by him even in the anathematisms: "He who does not confess that our Lord Jesus Christ, come in the flesh and portrayable in the flesh, *remains unportrayable according to His Divine nature*, that one is a heretic. [The italics are Bulgakov's. — Trans.] If we begin to assert that the Divinity too is portrayable as a result of the fact that the flesh of the Word is portrayable, and at the same time we do not in one hypostasis distinguish the one from the other according to natural property, whereas in fact the one does not destroy the other in inseparable unity, that one is a heretic" (pp. 132-33). "The property of the Divinity is unportrayability, incorporeality, absence of external appearance and form. By contrast, the property of humanity is portrayability, tangibility, measurability of three kinds. If Christ consists of two natures, then of course He is both unportrayable and portrayable" (p. 159). In his epistle to the iconoclastic Council (*Works*, II, p. 325), Theodore also says that "Christ remains unportrayable according to Divine image" (although He is portrayable according to human image).

19. The *Works* of Theodore the Studite, I, p. 132.

20. The *Works* of Theodore the Studite, I, p. 159.

21. The *Works* of Theodore the Studite, II, p. 325.

ther, Theodore develops his thought predominantly in the direction of the portrayability of Christ's human nature. He indicates the genuineness of Christ's body,[22] from which His portrayability follows. He also links this portrayability with the individual character of the Lord's body, which is not a body in general but possesses its own concrete features.[23]

Thus, Theodore the Studite first of all sharpens the antinomy of portrayability and unportrayability in Christ, attesting that "Christ remains unportrayable when He is portrayed on icons"; "Christ is unportrayable even though He is God who has become man," but at the same time "Christ is portrayable even though He is not just man."[24] His portrayability as man is connected by Theodore with His genuine, natural corporeality,[25] and he concludes: "Thus, it is possible to have an artificial

22. "Was Christ not like us in His image and appearance? Was His body not built of bones? Were His eyes not protected by eyelids and eyebrows? Were His ears not configured with curving channels? Was the sense of smell not adapted in Him for this purpose? Was He not given healthy flowering cheeks? Did He not pronounce words with His lips? Did He not eat and drink?" (The *Works* of Theodore the Studite, II, letter XXXIII, p. 376).

23. "For example, Peter is portrayed only to the extent that he, together with his general profile, differs from other people by having certain particular characteristics, such as aquiline or blunt nose, or curly hair, or good color in his face, or handsome eyes, or something else that distinguishes his external appearance. However, although he is constituted of soul and body, not one property of his soul is reflected in the externals of the image. And how could it be otherwise if the soul is invisible? We find the same thing in relation to Christ. He can be portrayed not in the aspect in which He is just a man, even though He also remains God; but to the extent that He, differing by His personal properties from all those who were like Him, was crucified, and it is in that form He is portrayed. Thus, Christ is portrayable according to His personal being, although He is unportrayable according to Divinity" (The *Works* of Theodore the Studite, I, p. 169).

24. The *Works* of Theodore the Studite, I, pp. 121-22.

25. "In conformity with His nature He is visible and representable, tangible and portrayable; in conformity with His nature He partakes of food and drink, grows and matures, labors and rests, sleeps and is awake, hungers and thirsts, gives forth tears and sweat, in general does and suffers what is characteristic of a mere man" (p. 122). "He [Christ] came out of the womb of His Mother, the Theotokos, having a form; and if that were not the case, He would have been a monster and not One who received the form of a man, O, theomachians! If He came out of the womb having the form of an infant, which is what truly happened, it follows with absolute necessity that He can be portrayed on icons" (*Works*, II, p. 334, letter to Brothers, VIII). "It is a condemnation of them [the icono-

image of Christ, with which He has a resemblance,"[26] and he thus derives the possibility of Christ's icon from what he calls the portrayability of His human nature.

If we compare this theology of Theodore the Studite with the doctrine of the opponents of icon veneration that is already familiar to us, we will easily become convinced that it does not advance the question a single step forward and in essence occupies the same dogmatic position as the iconoclasts (though less consistently than they), while drawing a conclusion therefrom in favor of icon veneration. In fact, Theodore sharpens the fundamental antinomy of the icon with an even greater power than do the iconoclasts, this antinomy representing an aporia that has not yet been overcome in the theology of icon veneration: Christ as God is unportrayable and unimageable, although He is portrayable and imageable in His corporeality. From this antinomy the iconoclasts drew the conclusion that the icon of Christ, or in general any image of Him, is impossible. By portraying the portrayable in Him, His human corporeality, and giving this image out to be the icon of the integral Christ Himself, Who has one hypostasis in two natures, we separate these natures and give out the image of the merely human nature, more precisely the image of His body, to be the image of Christ, i.e., we leave ourselves open to being accused of the nature-separating diphysitism of Nestorius or of the monophysitism of Arius, Eutyches, and Severus. Without any embarrassment, Theodore poses the antinomy in order to step over it, without removing or overcoming it. He is helped in this by the ambiguity of his understanding of the *portrayability* of the Lord's body: that is, for him this portrayability is indisputable in the sense that the living body of the Lord in His earthly life could be seen, touched, and therefore portrayed as such: *that is how* He was seen not only by believers but also by nonbelievers, not only by the disciples and the myrrh-bearers but also by the high priests and the soldiers who crucified Him. However, it appears that one cannot conclude from

clasts] if the Mother of God is portrayable on icons, but the One who was born of Her, and was nourished at Her breasts, and experienced all of the things related to His bodily existence, is not portrayable; or if the eyewitnesses and servants are portrayable, but the One whom they served and with whom they conversed, is not portrayable" (p. 335).

26. The *Works* of Theodore the Studite, I, p. 177.

this that Christ's body is portrayable on icons in His concrete spirit-bearingness, i.e., as the body of Christ Himself, even if it is portrayable in His physical corporeality (as would be depicted on an anatomical chart). One can even say that this task could be more readily fulfilled by those who didn't believe in Him, since for them it would not have differed in any way from the general task of portraying any man in general. But such a portrayal of any man in general, or more precisely, of the human body, could in no way be an accurate portrayal of Christ as God and man — without separation and without confusion. This impossibility of an accurate portrayal was what was asserted by the iconoclasts. Therefore, the concept of portrayability and unportrayability contains a terminological ambiguity, where one sense takes the place of the other *(quaternio terminorum).* The great defender of icons and confessor of icon veneration, Theodore the Studite, served icon veneration with his entire life, with the great exploit of faith, but even he did not overcome the theological arguments of the iconoclasts, and the question remained suspended in the air.

From Theodore's theses there follows not the portrayability but precisely the unportrayability of Christ, who in His Divine hypostasis unites two natures, only one of which is portrayable, while the other is unportrayable. Theodore himself could not fail to see this aporia, and he tried to get around it by distinguishing the image from the proto-image (about which below). However, before one can make any such distinction one must still demonstrate the portrayability of Christ in the inseparable and inconfusible unity of the two natures, one of which is portrayable, while the other is not.

Things are not much different in the case of the second great defender of icon veneration who acted after the Seventh Ecumenical Council, namely Patriarch Nicephoros. In general, we do not find in him any new elements in the development of the controversy. He too asserts the unportrayability of the Divinity[27] while affirming the portrayability of the

---

27. 'We portray Christ not to the extent He is God and not to the extent we erect icons to Him, but to the extent we use the icons, to the extent He was man and came into the world" *(Works of our saintly father, Nicephoros, archbishop of Constantinople,* [Russ. trans.] 1904, Part I, p. 49).

human nature. Like the Studite, Nicephoros links the portrayability of Christ with the genuineness of His human flesh: "The icon of Christ is His likeness; it is like His body, gives us the image of His body, represents His appearance, shows through imitation much of how He acted, taught, and suffered."[28] "What say you, who proclaim unportrayability (of the Lord's body) and allow the absurdities of docetism? The One Who was wrapped in swaddling clothes, Who lay in the manger, Who sojourned in the cave — is this One portrayable or not? The unportrayable is not found in space; if it is not in space, it is not a body; if it is not a body, it cannot, with greater reason, be a man. Thus, Christ did not become man; He did not assume our nature and was not subject to the sufferings that are usual for our body. . . . I ask you: is the portrayable One portrayable or not?" "If Christ was made incarnate, He abides in space and is portrayable, for space serves as the limit of content."[29] "We represent Him in an image not to the extent He is portrayable but to the extent His nature is subject to representation in an image."[30] "Following Paul and confessing in Christ two images, manifesting for us two natures, we recognize the man of passions Who is like us, having an external appearance and being portrayable."[31] "Why can there not be conceived in application to it (to the person of Christ) the antithesis of the portrayable and the unportrayable?"[32] "The Word not only cannot be portrayed when the flesh is portrayed, but it is unportrayable even when it is present in the body, which is united with it substantially and without separation."[33] "Since the Word economically assumed the suffering of the body, and since this body is called the body of God the Word, it follows that the icon and likeness too of His assumed body relates to it as His own."[34] These and similar judgments are not so much developed as repeated in the treatises of Patriarch Nicephoros. In

28. *Works of our saintly father, Nicephoros, archbishop of Constantinople*, Part II, p. 174.

29. *Works of our saintly father, Nicephoros, archbishop of Constantinople*, Part II, pp. 188-89, 130.

30. *Works of our saintly father, Nicephoros, archbishop of Constantinople*, Part II, p. 131.

31. *Works of our saintly father, Nicephoros, archbishop of Constantinople*, Part II, p. 69.

32. *Works of our saintly father, Nicephoros, archbishop of Constantinople*, Part II, p. 73.

33. *Works of our saintly father, Nicephoros, archbishop of Constantinople*, Part II, p. 75.

34. *Works of our saintly father, Nicephoros, archbishop of Constantinople*, Part II, p. 92.

general, there is nothing new in these treatises compared to the ideas of Theodore the Studite.

In the works of John of Damascus (prior to the Seventh Ecumenical Council), together with some very valuable thoughts, we find the following thought about God's unportrayability, where in explaining His representation on icons, John is guilty of conscious anthropomorphism (or psychologism), i.e., he deprives icons of ontological significance: "Icons are the seeing of that which is invisible and imageless but that which is portrayed bodily because of the *weakness* of our understanding [but it is precisely this weakness that the iconoclasts fought against!]), for Holy Scripture too attributes images to God and to angels, and about the cause of this the very same Divine man (Dionysius) teaches us. For in one thing only, *in adaptation to us* (who are incapable of ascending to rational contemplations and require appropriate and understandable aids), can one indicate the reason why images are justly attributed to the imageless and forms to the formless."[35] In images "are represented appearances, forms, and features of the invisible and bodiless, portrayed *bodily* because of the weakness of our understanding both of God and of the angels, since we cannot perceive the bodiless without images appropriate for us. For in one thing only, *in adaptation* to us (who are incapable of ascending to rational contemplations and require appropriate and understandable aids), can one indicate the reason why images are justly attributed to the imageless and forms to the formless."[36] There is no doubt that such relativism, if it is taken as the sole basis for the veneration of icons, is more of an argument against icon veneration than for it. The iconoclasts' passionate urge to edify consisted precisely in a struggle against such concessions to weakness and in a defense of spiritual religion.

John of Damascus' second argument, too, misses its mark: "In antiquity, God, bodiless and without appearance, was never represented in images. But now, when God came in the flesh and 'dwelled among men,' I represent in images God's appearance. I venerate not matter but the Cre-

---

35. *First Oration in Defense*, XI, Works of St. John of Damascus [Russ. trans.], p. 32. Cf. *Precise Exposition of the Orthodox Faith*, book IV, ch. XVI, p. 321.

36. *Third Oration in Defense*, XXI, p. 401.

ator of matter, Who became matter for my sake, chose to live in matter, and through matter accomplished my salvation. I venerate not as I venerate God. No, for how can that be God which has existence out of the nonexistent? But *God's body, too, is God.*"[37] Here, John of Damascus makes the same supposition that the iconoclasts accused the icon venerators of making: that is, he first reduces the body to nothing more than matter (which, of course, is not completely accurate), and then he asserts that "God's body, too, is God." Of course, such an imprecise and ambiguous expression can naturally be interpreted as Eutychianism, the doctrine according to which the human nature is swallowed up and dissolved in the Divinity. However, this does not exhaust John's doctrine of icons. This doctrine has more powerful elements, which we will touch upon below.

We arrive at the general conclusion that the defenders of icon veneration did not gain a theological victory over their opponents. This did not prevent the triumph of icon veneration, whose truth was attested by the Seventh Ecumenical Council, which was recognized as ecumenical (though not until after a long struggle and many doubts) by the whole Church. But, as was the case before the Seventh Council, icon veneration entered the practice of the Church through the guidance of the Holy Spirit, but without dogmatic definition; and in essence it remained without dogmatic definition after the Seventh Council and remains without it to the present day. The Byzantine East seemed to have exhausted its strength in the many-centuries struggle with the iconoclasts and revisited this question neither in the decrees of the Church nor in theology. Before us at the present time this question arises again. It is remarkable that this has turned out to be the fate of this question in the West as well. Over the many centuries of the brilliant blossoming of scholastic theology, in which countless questions, both trivial and of paramount importance, were discussed, the question of icon veneration was not posed at all; and this *indifference of western theology* to the question of the dogma of icon veneration is an astonishing fact, which, I think, has its original source in the peculiarities of Catholic theology. But in Protestantism too, which has again raised the banner of iconoclasm (as well as in sectarianism), we fail

---

37. *First Oration in Defense,* XVI.

to find an in-depth dogmatic exploration of the question. In its attitude toward icons Protestantism adheres to an Old Testament type of prohibition of icons and in general to a rationalistic, abstract pneumatomachy. It does not rise to the level of the iconoclastic theology of the seventh century but rather regards icon veneration as nothing more than a kind of idolatry and superstition. Nor in the Catholic reaction, in the Counter Reformation, do we find any attempts to advance the question dogmatically (in addition, it is usually ignored by the Catholic dogmatic handbooks[38]). Although the Council of Trent *confirmed* the necessity of icon veneration, this Council represented not a step forward in the development of the doctrine of icon veneration but rather a step back compared to the Seventh Ecumenical Council. Below, we will touch upon the relevant decree of the Council of Trent.

A dogmatic reexamination of this question is long overdue. This must begin, of course, with a reexamination of the initial formulation of this question. Until now the dogma of icon veneration has been investigated wholly as an aspect of christology, as one of the conclusions of the latter. However, as we have seen, this question cannot be fundamentally resolved within the limits of christology, for any such attempt leads to insuperable aporias. The question must be transposed to the domain of general theology and anthropology in their interrelation; and this interrelation is given by sophiology (which, to a certain degree, includes christology). It is thus necessary to show, first of all, that, in its essence, the dogma of icon veneration is a sophiological problem.

2. Antinomy of the Icon

We have seen that the chief difficulty in the doctrine of the icon consists in the fact that two things are recognized at the same time: (1) the imageless-

---

38. If we do not count the splendid articles *"Images"* and *"Iconoclastes"* in *Dict. de théol. cath.* VII, and in *Dict. d'arch. chret.* Characteristic is the absence of an independent examination of this question by Thomas Aquinas in *Summa theologiae* and his judgment in the question of the veneration of Christ's image: III-a. q. 25.

ness and therefore unportrayability of the Divinity and (2) His "imaging according to us" through the in-humanization and therefore His portrayability. What we get is a kind of antinomy. And this real or imaginary antinomy leads, further, to real or imaginary aporias in the doctrine of the icon, to aporias that were not removed or overcome in the dogmatic controversies over icon veneration in the seventh to ninth centuries. The iconoclasts were the ones who indicated the existence of this antimony, and from it they drew a negative conclusion — *against* the admissibility of icons in general. By contrast, the icon venerators, placing the main accent on the Incarnation, drew an affirmative conclusion in favor of the portrayability of Christ's flesh and thus in favor of Christ's icon. If we accept both of these premises that lead to the antinomy, we find that it is the iconoclasts, not the icon venerators, who were right, for the dogmatic logic was clearly on their side. The icon venerators could avoid a clear aporia only at the cost of obvious inconsistency and one-sidedness; and in actual fact their doctrine manifested a breakdown of equilibrium with respect to the inseparability and inconfusibility of the two natures in Christ, as formulated in the Chalcedonian dogma, in the direction of mono- or diphysitism. By portraying Christ's human flesh in the capacity of the icon of the Savior and by recognizing at the same time the absolute imagelessness and unportrayability of the Divinity, they took *pars pro toto*, the part for the whole. In other words, in the capacity of the portrayal of the *whole* Christ, the God-Man, uniting in Himself the Divinity and the humanity, they took the icon of His humanity alone, if in general it could be separated from His Divinity. And given such a position the iconoclasts' attack could not be defended against, which was clearly attested by the unceasing dogmatic battle in the course of two centuries, both before and after the Seventh Ecumenical Council, and both in the East and in the West. This battle never ceased; it only quieted down and stopped drawing attention to itself, ceding its place from the ninth century onward to new dogmatic controversies over questions separating the eastern and western churches (primarily regarding the papal primacy and the filioque). Meanwhile, the political situation in the East was becoming more and more precarious: the emperors had no time for dogmatic disputes; while the West, in essence, had never been interested in the dogmatics of icon veneration. Of course, truth triumphed in the Church guided by the Holy Spirit; that is, in practice, icon veneration was victorious. However, this does not by any means signify that, with the acceptance of this practice, the Church had also accepted the dogmatic doctrine of icon veneration that was developed during this epoch by its defenders as well as by its opponents, and in reality had an iconoclastic origin. We repeat: the Church has a *canon* of icon veneration, but she does not know a generally accepted *dogma* of icon veneration — she has not defined a dogmatic doctrine of icon veneration, which therefore could not be put into the *oros* of the Seventh Ecumenical Council. For the wisdom of the Church, guided by the Holy Spirit, is more perspicacious than her individual members, more perspicacious, in particular, than the theologians of icon veneration of the eighth to ninth centuries, and even than the fathers of the Seventh Ecumenical Council; and in general this wisdom manifests itself in the ability to distinguish theological opinions from church decrees. *And by no means are we obliged to accept these opinions,* for in their logical development they actually lead to iconoclasm; and moreover, in and of themselves, they are unsound. This is what we must first show, before turning to a positive solution of the problem.

First of all we must regard as incorrect the initial antinomy that is uncritically accepted by both sides. It consists in the opposition between the invisibility and therefore the imagelessness (or formlessness) of God and the visibility and therefore the imagedness of man — an antithesis that enters into the definition of the interrelation of God and man. One can show that, in general, such an antinomy does not exist at all, for the two terms that are supposed to constitute the antinomy here are *not actually situated in one and the same logical plane.* They belong to different conceptual series, and therefore they do not constitute an antinomy and in general should not be put together. The first term of this pseudo-antinomy belongs to general theology and is included in the theological antinomy, whereas the second term belongs to cosmology and is included in the cosmological antinomy. To unite them in one antinomy is the same thing as to put together yards and pounds simply because both of them are measures (though of course they measure totally different things). This will become clear if we examine the antinomies of different order that are mixed together here.

The first term of the antinomy of the icon, the assertion that God is invisible and imageless, belongs to the so-called apophatic (negative) theology[39] developed by the neoplatonizing Pseudo-Dionysius but also typical of the whole of patristic theology. The idea behind this theology is simple and clear: Divinity as the Absolute, i.e., the nonrelative, remains beyond any correlation, distinction, definition. Divinity as the Absolute is *not who, not what, not this kind;* it does *not even exist,* for existence too is already a relation. It remains beyond the distinction of subject and object, of person and state. It cannot be expressed except as the negation of all definition, as NO, as *a privativum,* by a mute mystical gesture as it were. About this Divine Nothing it is said: "No man hath seen God at any time" (John 1:18; 1 John 4:12; cf. 1 Tim. 6:16). And what is especially important here is that the Divine Nothing is not even God, for God is already a correlative concept that presupposes the world. The Divine Nothing is, so to speak, the absolute God in Himself and for Himself, who is totally inaccessible to objectifying thought, which is based on the opposition between the knower and that which is known, between subject and object, in general on a certain conscious distinction or relation. The Divine Nothing is conceived artificially, so to speak, by a certain illegitimate judgment (to use Plato's expression); it is posited by thought, not through judgment but only through negation. In our thought this imaginary idea (using a mathematical expression) is a product of metaphysical abstraction, and in our life it is a product of mystical dying or submergence into the mystical night. But this is by no means a *religious* idea, for it does not belong to religion, which is *connection, religio,* interrelation. All religions, including revealed religion (both Old and New Testaments), know the *God* who is revealed in the world and is correlated with the latter. But the Divine Nothing is the Absolute *outside* of creation and *outside* of religion. At the same time the postulate of apophatic theology concerning the unthinkability and ineffability of Divinity constitutes, as it were, a necessary *background* for the idea of God. This postulate contains the mute testimony that He is not only God, i.e., the absolute-relative, but also Divinity in

---

39. See my book *The Unfading Light,* the section on Divine Nothing (Negative Theology). [Published in Russian in 1917. — Trans.]

28

Himself, the Absolute above all relation. This expresses the unsearchability and inexhaustibility of God's being, the bottomless ocean, unapproachable light, and unfathomable darkness of Divinity.

However, with this absolute NO of Divinity is antinomically joined the absolute YES; with absolute nonrelativity is united relation in the absolute itself, i.e., *absolute relation,* distinction, definition. In this is expressed the *life* of the Absolute, which is not abstract like our concepts, but lives concretely. God, as the absolute relation in Himself, is the Holy Trinity, the trihypostatic Person, the Divine triunity. Negative or nonrelative Absoluteness is just as unconditional and primordial in Divinity as the absolute relation. For human reason this correlation of NO and YES is antinomic, an identity of opposites *(coincidentia oppositorum).* This is an impassable boundary for reason; the cherub's flaming sword blocks the path of thought, bearing witness that this place is holy: "put off thy shoes from off thy feet" (Exod. 3:5).

It would be incorrect and impossible to rationalize or remove this antinomy, which is ideal-real (for in God all things are ideal-real), by resolving it in process, in becoming, which would be accomplished in Divinity as it were, developing in a certain ontological sequence. As a result of such rationalization of the antinomy it would be supplanted by genesis and we would get the *history* of God in Himself, which would be reduced to the *origination* of God from some pre-God or super-God, ontologically preceding God. Here the apophatically negative Divine Nothing is replaced by a positive Nothing; it is understood as Nothing, or as some divine *me on,* which can and must become defined, which can and must leave its meonal state. In NO arises YES; the Divine Nothing is transformed into a Proto-God *(Ur-Gottheit)* or Proto-freedom, which through self-definition becomes the God Who is in the Holy Trinity. By the same token the Holy Trinity is understood here as the personalistic moment in the impersonal Proto-God. Such considerations have nothing in common with apophatic theology. On this path of peculiar mystical rationalism, which removes the antinomy, there enters, following Plotinus, German mysticism in the person of Eckhart and especially in the person of Boehme with his followers in this question. We find the same thing, but now in the domain of metaphysical rationalism, in the doctrine of Hegel and in a certain sense in the doctrines of Schopenhauer and Hartmann. But the absolute relation in God, i.e., the Holy Trinity, *does not arise* in God as His secondary self-definition; it is just as primordial and absolute in God as His absoluteness. One can say that *Ur-Gottheit* and *Gott* are equally primordial and pre-eternal, that they are interpenetrating and identical. In God there is no process but there is life, i.e., eternal actualization, eternal act, *actus purus* in the eternal mobility of the Absolute. This is the first antinomy — the *theological* one — in our thought about God: God in Himself as Absolute and therefore nonrelative and God as Absolute Relation — God Who is beyond all definition and God Who is in the Holy Trinity. The very dogma of the Holy Trinity stands on the sharp point of the primordial theological antinomy. However, this is the first antinomy, not the sole one.

Let us now pass to the next antinomy, the *cosmological* one. God has His absolute relation within the Absolute, i.e., He is the Holy Trinity. But He also has an absolute-relative relation. The latter is God's being *outside* Himself, in His relation to the world, to creation. The self-existent God is both the Creator of the world and the world's Providence. For our thought this correlation in God leads to an antinomy. In fact, God Who is in the Holy Trinity has the whole fullness of life within Himself; He is all-blissful and self-sufficient in the sense that this fullness cannot be completed by anything and does not have anything outside itself. God does not need anything and cannot receive anything into Himself that He does not have; and in this sense there is no place in God for any process. But at the same time into the fullness of the absolute relation enters not only God's relation to Himself but also His relation to not-Himself, i.e., to the world. But since there is nothing, and can be nothing, that could have a relation to God and be not-God, this relative being of the world, too, is a Divine being, though one that is placed by God *outside* Himself, i.e., in *nothing*, in absolute nothingness, *ouk on*,[40] which is summoned to being by God's power, i.e., in creation. (Creation is nothing that came to *be*, having been filled with Divine being.) This establishes the absolute-relative relation in God, precisely as the Creator to creation. Clearly, the Divine genuineness

---

40. See the section "Creaturely Nothing" in *The Unfading Light*.

of this relation in God requires that both terms of this correlation possess full reality and autonomy, i.e., not only the Creator but also creation, not only God but also the world. God is correlative to the world, and therefore to that extent He presupposes the world not for His own fulfillment but as an object of His love (see John 3:16). "God so *loved* the world"[41] that the Lamb of God was "foreordained before the foundation of the world" (1 Pet. 1:20), i.e., in eternity. Thus, within the limits of the doctrine of God as absolute relation is indicated a new antinomy, an antinomy no longer between the Absolute and the Absolute-Relative, though it is within the limits of the Absolute-Relative, in the two forms of this relation. That is to say, on the one hand, God in Himself, who is in the Holy Trinity, abides higher than any relation outside Himself; He is filled with Himself and closed within Himself. On the other hand, God goes out of His fullness outside Himself; He posits Himself as Creator, creating the world and thereby thrusting Himself into the flux of the becoming of temporal, emerging being. In virtue of the genuineness of this world and of the world process, God Himself as Creator and Providence to that extent is becoming with the world (cf. Solovyov's "becoming Absolute"). In the fullness of His trinity God does not need the world and does not need to receive anything from the world's life, but at the same time, because of His love for the world, God creates it, seeking in it other, creaturely hypostases in the union of the love of the Holy Trinity. Thus, it turns out that God does not need the world but that, in creating it, He seeks it. The first proposition is logically incompatible with the second; and we get an antinomy that, however, ontologically signifies a self-identity. It is essential to have in view that the first antinomy cannot be regarded as the *ground* of the second; and conversely, that the second is not the *consequence* of the first; no causal relationship can be established between them.

The doctrine of God's creation of the world leads us to the doctrine of God's revelation in the world. And on this further path we encounter a new antinomy: the sophiological one. Here is what it consists in. Between God as Creator and the world there exists an impassable abyss, making their un-

---

41. "*Dieu est fou de l'homme,*" according to Schelling's expression. [Literally, "God is crazy about man." — Trans.]

mediated correlation impossible. The creature cannot withstand its Creator, cannot look at His Face, cannot bear His approach. "Thou canst not see My face: for there shall no man see Me, and live" (Exod. 33:20), God tells Moses. The creature remains hopelessly and totally enclosed in its own creatureliness and separated from God by its nothingness out of which it was created by God; the creature's being is extra-Divine. But at the same time the creature exists solely by the power of God and, consequently, in God: "in Him we live, and move, and have our being" (Acts 17:28). Outside of God the creature would return to its nonbeing: "Thou takest away their breath, they die, and return to their dust. Thou sendest forth Thy spirit, they are created" (Ps. 104:29-30). The creature abides, therefore, in extra-divine Divine being (panentheism), both differing from God and not differing from Him. The interpenetrability of God and the world that is revealed and accomplished in the deification of the world and in the Incarnation represents with equal power both of these poles of the relations of creation: the world is the not-God existent in God; God is the not-world existent in the world. The metaphysical "place" of creation is, therefore, the actual interpenetrability of God and the world, and the just-as-actual distinction between God and the world is defined antinomically.

The nature of an antinomy consists not only in the fact that it co-posits two propositions that seem opposite to each other when examined abstractly, but also in the fact that it establishes their actual identity. If one measures antinomy with the yardstick of rational logic (which does not by any means exhaust the logos of being and the world of reality, but only describes the latter in its own way), it leads to contradiction, i.e., to inconceivability, to a logical dead-end, before which logic steps back in perplexity and can do nothing more than confirm the hopelessness of the situation. An antinomy attests to the equivalence of the contradictory propositions, as well as to their inseparability, unity, and identity. In this sense, an antinomy is a logical leap over the abyss, but it thereby also becomes something like a bridge over it. It expresses the connection of God and the world both in their distinction and in their unity; it expresses a certain divine *metaxu*[42] (to use Plato's expression): God in creation, Who is

42. Intermediary or bridge. — Trans.

the Divine Sophia. God turns His face toward the world by His Wisdom: "O Lord, how manifold are Thy works! in wisdom hast Thou made them all" (Ps. 104:24). "The Lord possessed Me [Wisdom] in the beginning of His way, before His works of old" (Prov. 8:22). Sophia is Divine life in its pre-eternal content, as God's self-revelation and glory, as *Deus revelatus* in relation to *Deus absconditus*. Sophia does not differ from the unisubstantial nature of Divinity; She is this nature not only as act but also as eternal Divine fact; She is not only power but also the effect of power, not only breadth but also depth. In Her, God knows and sees Himself and loves Himself; He loves not with the personal love of mutuality, which constitutes the pre-eternal love of the three hypostases; rather, He loves *His Own*, His Own Divinity[43]; His Divine life is worthy of love. Sophia, therefore, is the Divinity of God or the Divinity in God, and in this sense She is also the Divine world prior to its creation. For creation God is Sophia, for in and through Her He is also revealed both as the personal trihypostatic God and as the Creator. The world is created by Sophia or in Sophia, for there is no other principle of being, and can be no other. Consequently, the world too is Sophia, but a Sophia who is *becoming*, creaturely, existent in time. The world, created on the basis of Sophia, is destined to achieve a state in which, in it, "God will be all in all,"[44] i.e., in which it will become perfectly sophianic. However, this fullness refers only to the final and perfect accomplishment. Thus, on the one hand, the world is pre-eternally inscribed in the Divine Wisdom, having in the latter its higher, heavenly reality, its "proto-images," *proorismoi* (according to the teaching of the Church fathers). And one can say that the sophianicity of the world is an axiom of cosmology. But on the other hand just as real are the asophianicity and even the antisophianicity of the world immersed in itself, into its own half-being. The world is sophianic and antisophianic at the same time; and this constitutes its antinomy, which expresses its life. In the world there is nothing truly existent that is not a holy hieroglyph of a heavenly proto-image. This is what the Apostle Paul is referring to when he says, "The in-

---

43. See our essay "Hypostasis and Hypostatizedness," in the *Collection in Honor of P. B. Struve* (Prague, 1925).

44. See 1 Corinthians 15:28. — Trans.

visible things of God, His eternal power and Divinity, are, from the foundation of the world, *visible* in the things that have been created" (Rom. 1:20).[45] But at the same time the world has its own life; it exists in its own way, in a different manner from its eternal proto-images in the Divine world, in the Divine Sophia. And this antinomy is resolved in movement and in the world process; one can say that it itself is the process (cf. Hegel's fundamental intuition: *Der Widerspruch ist das Fortleitende*[46]).

The sophiological antinomy is consistently and completely disclosed in the christological one. The fundamental christological dogma of the Fourth Ecumenical Council dealing with the two natures and the one hypostasis in Christ (in relation to which the Sixth Ecumenical Council's decree concerning the two wills and energies is only a particular expression of the same general idea) is expressed antinomically and represents a disclosure of the sophiological antinomy with reference to christology: in Christ the two natures are united in one person without separation and without confusion, without division and without mixing. This means that the Creator and creation, the eternal and the temporal, the noncreaturely, Divine Sophia and the creaturely Sophia are united in one being and in one life, and that this is accomplished in such a way that each retains Her independence and Her metaphysical distance *(without confusion)* from the other without being deprived of the mutual connection *(without separation)* derived from the ontological identity. Here we have a new *coincidentia oppositorum*, a union of principles mutually negating and excluding each other (for the Creator is not creation, and vice versa) but also coexisting in Christ. The christological antinomy expresses here with maximal clarity the general sophiological antinomy — the unity and ontological identity of the distinct and opposite principles of the Divine and the creaturely: the Creator descending into creation with the Birth of Christ and the Incarnation; and creation ascending to the Creator with the Ascension of Christ in the flesh and His sitting at the right hand of the Father.

The fundamental sophiological antinomy is expressed, further, in a

45. This verse is translated from the Russian Bible used by Bulgakov. The italics are his. — Trans.

46. Contradiction leads the way forward. — Trans.

whole series of particular antinomies in the general doctrine of God. Thus, eternity and time are antinomic: God is eternal and in this sense supratemporal, but for the world God is revealed in time, just as Christ's coming into the world and His Ascension from it occurred in time. Further, God's supraspatiality and omnispatiality, or omnipresence, are antinomic: the Creator's freedom from all limitation and from the outside-locatedness of space on the one hand and the spatial conditionedness of God's action in the world, in particular in the appearance of Christ, on the other.[47]

Here, for the sake of clarity, is the schema of the three above-expounded antinomies in their logical sequence and interrelations:

I. **Theological antinomy (God in Himself)**
    THESIS: God is the Absolute and, consequently the pure NOT, the Divine Nothing. (Apophatic theology)
    ANTITHESIS: God is the Absolute-in-Itself self-relation, the Holy Trinity. (Kataphatic theology)

II. **Cosmological antinomy (God in Himself and in creation)**
    THESIS: God in the Holy Trinity has all fullness and all-bliss; He is self-existent, unchanging, eternal, and therefore absolute. (God in Himself)
    ANTITHESIS: God creates the world out of love for creation, with its temporal, relative, becoming being, and becomes for it God, correlates Himself with it. (God in creation)

III. **Sophiological antinomy**
    (Divine Wisdom in God and in the world)
    THESIS: God, unisubstantial in the Holy Trinity, reveals Himself in His Wisdom, which is His Divine life and the Divine world in eter-

---

47. In essence, we find a sophiological antinomy also in the doctrine of Gregory Palamas on the unknowability of the Divine essence, *ousia*, and the knowability of the Divine "energies," *energeia*. Here, the "energies" are identical in nature with God and in this sense they are God, as well as the uncreated foundation of creation.

nity, fullness, and perfection. (Noncreaturely Sophia — Divinity in
God)

ANTITHESIS: God creates the world by His Wisdom, and this Wisdom, constituting the Divine foundation of the world, abides in temporal-spatial becoming, submerged in nonbeing. (Creaturely Sophia — Divinity outside of God, in the world)

The *antinomy of the icon* — uniting the portrayability and the unportrayability of God, and in particular of the Lord Jesus Christ, the God-Man — represents a particular case of the general sophiological antinomy. This antinomy lies at the very basis of the dogma of icon veneration, and it is the first thing that must be disclosed and shown here. The nature of antinomy consists in the identity and inseparability of opposite things, in *coincidentia oppositorum*, and the antinomy of the icon consists in the fact that God is unportrayable, for He is inaccessible to the creature's knowledge, is transcendent in relation to the creature, while at the same time being portrayable, for He reveals Himself to the creature, His image is inscribed in the creature, and "the invisible things of God . . . are visible in the things that have been created" (Rom. 1:20)[48] in the creature, as St. Paul, the apostle of antinomic theology, tells us with divinely inspired audacity. This visibility of the invisible, this portrayability of the unportrayable, is what the icon is.

Before turning to a further examination of the doctrine of the icon, let us return to the initial thesis that is shared by both the iconoclastic and the icon-venerating theologies, namely to the opposition between the unportrayability and imagelessness of God and the portrayability of man (more precisely of the human body), on the basis of which some claimed to prove the impossibility of Christ's icon while others claimed to prove just the opposite. Do we have an actual antinomy here, in which the two terms are not just joined together externally but are internally connected without separation and without confusion, as *coincidentia oppositorum*? No, we do not; and that is the crux of the matter. Here we have not an antinomy but a mere contradiction, the joining together of two mutually

48. The King James Version has been modified to conform with the Russian version used by Bulgakov. — Trans.

alien propositions that do not belong to the same logical series. The first proposition refers to negative theology and says that God is unknowable and unportrayable, i.e., that He is the Divine Nothing, the absolute NOT, of apophatics. As we know, this proposition belongs to the first or theological antinomy. It can be joined into an antinomy only with its own antithesis; and it can be so joined with nothing except this antithesis, namely with the doctrine of God as the Absolute Person, the Holy Trinity. In no wise can the apophatic NOT, the Divine Nothing, be directly placed into a correlation with creation (in particular, with man), because from the Divine Nothing there is as yet no conceivable path to creation. We must, in the series of antinomies, pass through the cosmological antinomy and reach the sophiological antinomy, which expressly represents the relation of the Creator to creation. Meanwhile, the second part of the antinomy of the icon in the theology of iconoclasm and icon veneration, its antithesis, belongs to the cosmological antinomy: it has in view the creature, the human essence in its relation to God who is revealed in creation. Thus in the argument we find joined together two propositions in the capacity of the thesis and antithesis of one antinomy which actually belong to two different antinomies. They are therefore incompatible and represent an external joining-together of two ideas that do not belong together and from which no conclusion can be obtained. And no conclusion is obtained.

In fact, if we stop at the first thesis of negative theology, we would have to accept that, in general, the human nature does not have any relation with Divinity and therefore with the portrayal of Divinity, and that the iconoclasts are right. There is no conformity between God and man, and there is no icon of Divinity in the human form and can be no such icon. The error here consists not only in joining together things that cannot be joined and are absolutely different, but also in the fact that the thesis of apophatic theology, which is purely negative and cannot in its all-engulfing negativeness be joined with anything, is applied here as positive, i.e., is joined together with a second thing. The erroneousness of taking the apophatic NOT for a special form of positive ontic definition, i.e., for an *expression* of a state preceding all particular being, has already been shown in the example of the doctrine of Boehme and Hegel. But here the same error is repeated, just in another way. The pure NOT of apophatic theology, God in the apophatic definition, does not have any relation to the world, and therefore there is no connection between the two premises of iconoclastic theology; and from this no conclusion can be drawn — either for or against icon veneration. The apophatic NOT is a darkness in which all images are extinguished, and therefore only the Old Testament prohibition remains in force: thou shalt not make any idol for thyself, or any likeness — and therefore any image.[49]

But on their side don't the iconoclasts have the testimony of Holy Scripture? Do they not refer (strangely, together with the icon venerators) to the text: "No man hath seen God at any time" (John 1:18)? And does this text not have a totally apophatic meaning, which is exactly how the iconoclasts understood it? However, the problem is that they break this text in two, as a result of which even the first part of it, which they cite, loses its true character, i.e., its antinomic character. This is the full text: "No man hath seen God at any time; the only begotten Son [variant reading: God], Which is in the bosom of the Father, He hath revealed Him [*exēgēsato*]."[50] In other words, what we have here is not abstract apophatics (into which this text is transformed when only half of it is cited) but an expression of the third or sophiological antinomy, which consists of two contradictory but mutually linked propositions: the thesis "God (in Himself) is invisible" and the antithesis "God (in the cosmos) is revealed by the Son." We have a similar antinomy, though not as clearly expressed, in the First Epistle of John (4:12), with the thesis "No man hath seen God at any time" and the antithesis "If we love one another, God dwelleth in us." We can also refer to the antithesis the first words of this epistle: "we have heard . . . we have seen with our eyes . . . the Word of life" (1:1).[51] Thus, in the Word of God we find not an apophatic doctrine of God's unknowability but an antinomic affirmation

49. Cf. Deuteronomy 5:8. — Trans.

50. The King James Version has been slightly modified. — Trans.

51. We find the same sort of antinomic (not apophatic) meaning in 1 Timothy 6:16: "[God dwells] in the light which no man can approach unto; Whom no man hath seen, nor can see" (thesis). Before this, in 6:14, we hear of "the appearing of our Lord Jesus Christ" (antithesis). Also, in 2 Peter 1:16-17 we read: "we made known unto you the power and coming of our Lord Jesus Christ . . . [we] were eyewitnesses of His majesty. For He received from God the Father honour and glory" (antithesis).

of both His invisibility and His visibility, i.e., the affirmation that "His invisible nature, namely, His eternal power and deity, has been clearly perceived in the things that have been made. So they are without excuse, *ta aorata kathoratai*" (Rom. 1:20).[52] This sophiological antinomy, which further becomes a christological antinomy (and then a pneumatological one), is the precise formula of God's *revelation* in the world. Revelation presupposes, on the one hand, that which is revealed, as a certain inexhaustible mystery, surpassing all knowledge; and on the other hand it presupposes the unceasing disclosure of this mystery, the visibility of the invisible, the portrayability of that which surpasses all images, the word about the inexpressible. And here both terms of the antinomy are necessary for the idea of revelation: if there is no mystery and depth, if the object of revelation is completely knowable and exhaustible by a one-sided act of cognition, then we have knowledge, not revelation. But on the other hand if the mystery is not known, not revealed, not disclosed, it simply does not exist for man, for the unknowability of the mystery in revelation is correlative with the knowledge of it. The transcendent becomes immanent without losing its transcendence, just as, conversely, the immanent permeates the transcendent, though without overcoming the latter; this interpenetrability of the two, this transcendent-immanent correlation of theirs, is the antinomic formula of the world's sophianicity. The one Divine Sophia, the pleroma of the world, is in God's eternity and constitutes the entelechy of the world, shines in and shapes the world. The one Sophia exists in immobile eternity and in temporal becoming: She is *to ontos on kaito gignomenon*, the given and the task to be accomplished, the beginning and the end.

If apophatic theology is taken as the fundamental premise of the doctrine of the icon, it of course eliminates the very possibility of the icon. This conclusion contained both the strength of the iconoclasts and the weakness of the icon venerators who attempted to get around its inevitability. In fact, if in general Divinity is higher than any image and absolutely unportrayable, it is clear that *no* image of the human body, and in particular no image of Christ's flesh (even if it is actually portrayable), can have any rela-

---

52. The King James Version has been modified to conform to the Russian Bible used by Bulgakov. — Trans.

tion to the icon of Christ as the God-Man, and that He as God, even though He has been made man, remains unportrayable. The apophatic argument totally annihilates the complementary, or positive, argument. In the light of the apophatic argument the portrayal of the flesh can have *no* relation to the image of Divinity, as the iconoclasts indicated: icon veneration here really would be sarcolatry (veneration of the flesh), i.e., in essence it would be idolatry, which is prohibited in the Old Testament.

Now, after this critical excursus, which brings us to a totally negative conclusion regarding the iconoclastic and icon-venerating theologies of the eighth to ninth centuries, let us now turn to a substantive examination of the question. What is the icon? Is the icon possible? And how is it possible?

3. Art and Icon

The icon is, first of all, an object of art. Therefore, the question of the icon is part of the general problem of art as a special form of the knowledge of Divine things and of revelation. God is revealed not only through thought in the contemplation of Divine wisdom and in theology but also through beauty in productions of art that offer visions of Divinity. Naturally, the iconoclasts were also opposed to art in general. The iconoclastic Council of 754 condemned not only icon veneration but also art (this constitutes perhaps an even more pernicious aspect of this sophiaclastic doctrine than the iconoclasm itself). This Council proclaimed that "Against the dogma that is most needful for our salvation, i.e., Christ's economy, *blasphemes the art of painting which does not have a foundation in it,* and this art undermines these six holy divinely gathered ecumenical Councils" (Acts of the Seventh Ecumenical Council, p. 221; the italics are Bulgakov's). A response was given at the Seventh Ecumenical Council in the epistle read by the deacon Epiphanius: "No reasonably thinking man will condemn art if it yields something useful for the needs of this life; one need only have in view the goal and the means by which the work of art is made: if it is made for piety, it must be accepted, but if it is made for something shameful, it is detestable and must be rejected" (p. 223). Thus, in defending icons, the Seventh Ecumenical Council was also compelled to defend art. However, the fathers of the Council confined themselves to this brief judgment: they gave no further attention to the religious justification and understanding of art. Nevertheless, if we are to understand the icon, which, after all, is first of all a work of representational art, we must begin precisely with the Council's brief clarification. And so, what is art? What exactly does it do, and what is it based on? According to the most preliminary definition, representational art deals with the *image (eikōn)* that it reproduces. And so, what is this image, or "icon," in the most general sense?

Clearly, an image is a correlative concept: it is correlative to the thing of which it is the image, i.e., to the proto-image or original. And the nature of the image must first of all be understood on the basis of its relation to the proto-image. Between the image and the proto-image there exists both an identity of sorts and a substantial difference, the result of which is resemblance. The apples drawn by Apelles, which birds (apparently very dumb ones) attempted to eat because of their amazing resemblance to real apples, will never become real, but will always remain only their image. The boundary separating the image from the proto-image is the *reality* of the latter and the *ideality* of the former. Things can have real and ideal being in the image and in actuality. And all that exists has its images, is infinitely reflected in these images as if photographed, and, through these imprints, can be read in the memory of the world (the akashic records[53] of the occultists). These images are not repetitions of being, which remains one and unique (reality does not repeat itself); rather, they are its ideal repetitions. The ideal thought-image of being is reproduced, and this reproduction is so limitless that one can say that everything speaks about itself for the whole world, imprinting its image in numberless repetitions of itself throughout the whole universe. *Everything in the world* (i.e., in *real* being) has its ideal thought-image and thus is naturally imaged (by the way, pho-

---

53. "The akashic records" (*akasha* is a Sanskrit word meaning "sky," "space," or "aether") is a term used in theosophy to describe a compendium of mystical knowledge encoded in a nonphysical plane of existence. These records are described as containing all knowledge of human experience and the history of the cosmos. The concept originated in the theosophical movements of the nineteenth century. Bulgakov uses the German term (Akasha-Chronik) which is usually associated with the anthroposophy of Rudolf Steiner. — Trans.

tography of all kinds, whose possibilities are probably just beginning to be realized, is only an obvious instance of this universal imageability of things, of their ideal self-repetition). Real being fixes a thing in space and time, whereas the ideal thought-image is free of this fixation and is not limited by space and time. About it, as having ideal being, one can say that it does not exist but has significance (in German: *Gilt*).

Let us take a further step in disclosing what an image is. The lack of ontological independence characterizing an image consists not only in its dependence on reality or the original but also in its dependence on the subject or the bearer of the image. The fact is that although a "natural image" belongs to a thing as the latter's word about itself, as its imaging of itself, this word sounds and this image is imaged in or for someone as its possessor or subject. The image arises in its bearer, in its addressee, as it were, for an image without address does not exist. The subject reflects the image *in himself;* he is the living screen onto which are projected the beams sent by the thing. This constitutes the inevitable subjectivity of the image. This subjectivity signifies not that the image is not characterized by an objective foundation in a thing (this in no wise lessens its objectivity) but that the image necessarily presupposes an idealization connected with the subject as its creative bearer. The image becomes visible for the one seeing, lighting up in him. But who is the one seeing? Such a subject of idealization in the world is man, the logos of the world; and in this sense one can say that all the images of being that find themselves in man are thereby *human* not in the sense of "weakness and adaptation," i.e., bad anthropomorphism (as in John of Damascus), but as a result of the dominant position of man in the world as the eye of the latter, as the ideal mirror of it, and therefore in the anthropological sense.[54] One can add that the angels know the world in its ideal proto-images, and that this is determined by the angels' general relation to the world[55] as well as to man, i.e., by their angelo-humanity.

54. Some might point out that the knowledge of images can be accessible (though to a very limited degree) to animals as well. To this, one might object that it is accessible to animals only to the extent they are humanlike, for man's nature includes the capacities of the animal world.

55. See my book *Jacob's Ladder: On the Angels* (Paris, 1929). [This work has been translated into English by T. Allan Smith (Grand Rapids: Eerdmans, 2010). — Trans.]

Thus, man is a being who sees images, *zōon eikonikon*, and who also creates them, *zōon poiētikon*. First of all, man receives into himself the images of being and reflects them, so to speak, to the extent they themselves ask to enter him; but he also creatively assimilates and reproduces them. Therefore, man's mirroring of images should not be understood in the sense of passive, indifferent reflection. Man actively participates in this iconization of being (just as he actively and creatively realizes the knowledge of being, or logicization). *In and through himself* he finds the icons of things, for he himself is in this sense the *pan-icon* of the world. All that has reality is imageable for man, in man, and through man, who in himself not only finds the thought-images of all that exists but also has the ability to express these images, to reproduce them, to impart to their ideal being a certain reality — in short, he has the ability to create *icons* of the world. This creative ability not just to see but also to reproduce ideal images of the world in "matter" (whatever it might be: paints, marble, bronze, fabric, etc.) constitutes representational art and is a manifestation of man's artistic nature. As one who sees images (*zōon eikonikon*), man is an artistic being, and every icon of a thing, i.e., every reproduction of its image, is a work of art that creates icons of the world and of man, of the world-man. For this reason, controversies over icon veneration imply, in essence, either an acceptance or a rejection of art, pronounce a judgment on art. The character of the icon depends on the character of art. As *technē*, every particular art has its special laws, but here we are discussing not these special characteristics of the particular arts but the fundamental principles that determine the tasks of art and the ontological premises that make art possible.

The first temptation we encounter in defining the tasks and nature of representational art is the temptation of interpreting its tasks naturalistically or photographically in the sense of the apples of Apelles, which impart to reality the possible power of illusion ("they look real," "it looks like it's alive"). But photographic naturalism of all sorts is not yet art. Insofar as such naturalism contains elements of art, the latter is expressed here in the *manner* in which the imaged or photographed thing is "taken," i.e., it is expressed in a determinate or premeditated stylization, which already overcomes naked naturalism. Alternatively, photography can be viewed as nothing more than a sort of transcription, as material that art can employ but which itself is not yet art. As for pure naturalism in art, it is first of all a utopia, because art can never (and of course should never) overcome the chasm separating the ideal image of a thing from its reality. The ten thalers in Kant's famous example[56] will never become real however well they might be drawn. In the best case what we have in naturalism is either a counterfeit, i.e., a deception, or a self-deception, i.e., a hallucination accompanied by the loss of the sense of reality, by the obscuring of the basic intuition of *being,* as a result of which thought-images are equated with reality. Moreover, the fundamental task of art as the iconization of being is betrayed and thereby negated by naturalism: art does not seek to complete reality, or create alongside it a new being (that would be sterile luciferism); rather, it desires to reveal the word, idea, or thought-image of reality. Consequently, the task of art lies not in the real but in the ideal domain — not in the domain of being but in the domain of meaning. Furthermore, as naturalism understands it, the task of art is contradictory and anti-artistic. In actual fact, naturalism signifies the fidelity of art to the object, the accurate reproduction of the object in its given state. But such a *single* natural image of the object simply does not exist; instead, it is divided into an infinite cinematographic reel of images, and even the natural image that we see with our eyes is always a synthesis unconsciously performed by us — it is an image of images. The illumination changes; the shape changes as a result of foreshortening depending on the "take"; the coloration changes depending on the interrelation with the surrounding objects — changes ensue depending on the inexorable limitations of the resources of representation; in short, *panta rēi,* "everything flows," in the visual images of things. Therefore, even the most orthodox naturalism involves an inevitable artistic arbitrariness, a stylization, a "take." In short, it involves not the passive mirror-reflection that naturalism is so proud of, but creative activity, however defective it might be — in other words, it involves art. One can say that a naturalistic fidelity to things would signify the self-blinding of the eye that should see

56. Bulgakov probably means "100 thalers" — a reference to Kant's comparison of 100 real thalers and 100 imaginary thalers in his refutation of the ontological argument. — Trans.

the ideal thought-image of a thing but instead limits itself solely to the matter that expresses this thought-image: naturalism is enslavement to the matter of a thing, but this is the negation of creative activity, not art.[57] Of course, there can exist a whole domain of representational technique that does not expressly refer to art but pursues certain practical goals. The chief task in this domain is fidelity to nature, i.e., naturalistic accuracy, in the production of pictures for practical use, such as anatomical, botanical, and zoological diagrams and all kinds of schematic drawings. But this is not art. Art penetrates the skin of things in order to see beneath it their thought-images, their ideal form, which shines through their whole being. Their natural image simultaneously shows, reveals, and realizes this form; it is the immediate image of the real being of this form, but at the same time it obscures this form, for the real image of things is inadequate to the ideal form — it is not the *artistic* image of things. Art seeks to reveal things in their true being, to give them a more artistic expression than they have in reality, in nature. Such a pretension would be absurd if art were not grounded in a special relation to things, a relation peculiar to art. It is precisely in the icon of this thing that art, by

57. It is necessary to admit that among the defenders of icon veneration (with the sole exception of John of Damascus, in whom this naturalism is combined, as we shall see below, with a sophianic interpretation of icons) we find *only a naturalistic* conception of art, which in advance prevents one from understanding the essence of the icon and thus defending it systematically. This must be said in particular about Theodore the Studite. He attempts to prove the portrayability of Christ by asserting that His body consisted of a number of definite human members that are portrayable, as if the icon is a kind of anatomical chart. Here in his interpretation of the icon he even goes beyond naturalism when he asks the iconoclasts: "In their view, what is the physical foundation and the cause of such unportrayability? Did not Christ take upon Himself our image? Was His body not made up of bones, and so on?" (*Works*, II, p. 376). If we follow to its conclusion the Studite's naturalistic logic we would have to say that the best icon of Christ is a photograph. The image not made by hands which, according to tradition, is a miraculous imprint of the Savior, cannot be regarded as a passive photographic-like image (in spite of its visible likeness to such an image) precisely because it was an act of His miracle-working will. The so-called Shroud of Turin (if its authenticity is accepted) comes closer to being this kind of image; but it is not an icon of Christ and is not regarded by anyone as such, although for those who believe in its authenticity it is an object of great holiness, which clothed the body of Christ and preserved the imprinted traces of this body.

creating an *ideal* image, liberates the image from reality, as if isolating it from natural being and thus separating out the pure, unadulterated, nonreflected image of the thing. (In this sense, art is also the artistic interpretation of the world, analogous to the scientific one, for analogous operations are carried out in science: by means of abstract concepts and artificial experimentation a phenomenon is isolated out of the complexity of the world.) Thus, art is first of all a certain *seeing* of the idea of a thing in the thing itself, a special seeing of the thing that is realized in the work of art, or in the icon. Therefore, at the basis of the icon lies the capacity of noetic seeing. But what does this seeing see, and where does it look?

It looks at the thing, but through the thing and beyond the thing. It sees in the thing its super-thing or proto-thing, its noetic image, or idea. It deciphers the cryptogram of being, through which the thing is transformed into a certain hieroglyph of meaning, and thus artistically generalizes it. For ideas are general and, in this sense, logical, whereas things as realities are singular and alogical. But of course in order to understand the task of art *in this way*, it is necessary to *believe* it when it claims that it knows this world of noetic beauty, of the ideal proto-images of things. In relation to these proto-images the thing itself is only an icon or mold, although it is from this mold and, so to speak, on the occasion of it, that icons in the proper sense arise. That is how one should understand a judgment that frequently recurs in the writings of the holy fathers, namely that all proto-images have their images, a judgment that is most powerfully expressed by Pseudo-Dionysius: "Truly, visible icons are the seeing of the invisible."[58] "They [sacred symbols] are products and representations by visible images of divine traits and ineffable and elevated contemplations."[59] According to John of Damascus' definition, "every image is a revelation and showing of the hidden."[60] If these images did not exist and there were no noetic seeing of them, art would be objectless and contentless, or it would be limited to copying by hand. Kant famously said that things without

---

58. From the epistle to John the Divine, as cited by John of Damascus (*Third Oration,* p. 416).

59. From the epistle to Titus, as cited by John of Damascus (*First Oration,* p. 361).

60. *Third Oration,* XVII, p. 400.

concepts are blind and concepts without things are empty; we can adapt his statement for our purposes and say that things without proto-images are blind (naturalism) and proto-images without things are empty or abstract (schematism).

Every thing is concrete; it is an intergrowing of the proto-image with "matter" — *hulē*. Besides being the natural icon of the proto-image, the thing is also the proto-image of its artificial icon. The creative act of art in the iconization of a thing consists, first, in the seeing through it of its proto-image and secondly in its expression by the resources of art. Thus, art expresses the meaning of a thing, its name, its idea. The icon of a thing in this sense is the hieroglyph of its ideal proto-image not in the sense of the repetition or copy of a given thing but as the imprinting of the actual proto-image, which has real being in the world in the imaged thing. Though this thing is the original for its icon, it itself is not, strictly speaking, the icon's proto-image. The artistic appearance of the thing (of the original) bears witness about the ideal proto-image, which exists not in the cosmic reality but *higher* than the latter. This appearance speaks not only about the spatial-temporal, material being of a thing but also about its ideal being. In short, if one wishes to express this idea in the language of the history of philosophy, one will of course refer to the Platonic ideas, i.e., the noetic heavenly proto-images of all creation, proto-images that are not abstract concepts extracted from things (the Aristotelian *koina epi pollōn*) but concrete, existent thought-images, possessing in themselves the energy of being and actualizing themselves in the latter as the internal entelechies of things. Here of course we encounter the fundamental aporia of the doctrine of ideas, an aporia discovered by Plato himself: Do *all* things have their ideas, and do things that belong to nonbeing have their ideas? What is the relation of ideas of the abstract and of the concrete, of man and Socrates, and so on and so forth? It is not part of our task to attempt an answer to this most difficult question of philosophy. For our purposes it is sufficient to confine ourselves to the indication that everything that is portrayable, i.e., every icon of every thing, expresses the *idea* of the thing or at least its *ideational* nature, i.e., its relation (even if negative) to true being; for evil too, nonbeing, is the ontological parasite of good, i.e., of ideational being — evil belongs to the latter like its shadow (and even darkness itself exists only in relation to light).[61]

In theological language the philosophical doctrine of ideas as the proto-images of the world signifies the sophianicity of the creature, which has its proto-image and foundation, its idea and entelechy, in the Divine Sophia, the pan-organism of ideas. In developing this doctrine we can use as our foundation the teaching of John of Damascus, who, following Pseudo-Dionysius, connected the doctrine of icons with the doctrine of proto-images (although he himself did not sufficiently develop this theme). Here are his words: "There exist in God images and plans of what will be accomplished by Him, i.e., His pre-eternal and never-changing council. . . . *These images and plans (paradeigmata) are predeterminations (proorisomoi),* says St. Dionysius, *for in His council is sketched everything that is predetermined by Him and unchangingly exists before its being.* Likewise, if one desires to build a house, he will first sketch it in his mind and form its image."[62] This is a special form of *image,* a special concept of it.[63] Unfortunately, though John of Damascus expounds his doctrine of the world's sophianicity precisely in his orations on icons, he does not apply it further to clarify the iconization of the world.

---

61. For Christian theology the doctrine of ideas is related to the doctrine of angels, who are the personal bearers of ideas of earthly being in the spiritual, heavenly world. This relation is explored by me in *Jacob's Ladder,* to which I refer the reader. But for the question of icons this aspect of the doctrine of ideas does not have any significance.

62. *First Oration in Defense of Icons,* X, p. 351. [The italics are Bulgakov's. — Trans.]

63. *Third Oration,* XIX, p. 401: "The second kind of image is *thought in God* about that which He will create, i.e., His pre-eternal council, remaining always equal to itself, for Divinity is unchanging and without beginning is His council, in which that which is decided before the ages is accomplished at the time predetermined and assigned by Him. *For the images and examples of that which will be created by Him are the thoughts about each of these objects,* and in Dionysius they are called predeterminations, since in His council is inscribed and imaged that which is predetermined by Him before its being and will be accomplished without fail." [The italics are Bulgakov's. — Trans.] The sophiological significance of this doctrine is indicated by me in my book *The Burning Bush,* excursus III (on the patristic literature). [*The Burning Bush* (Paris, 1927), subtitled "An Essay in the Dogmatic Interpretation of Certain Features in the Orthodox Veneration of the Mother of God," has been translated into English by T. Allan Smith (Grand Rapids: Eerdmans, 2009). — Trans.]

Thus, representational art, i.e., the iconization of things, is rooted not in their subjectively anthropomorphic adaptation to the weakness of human perception (which is what even the defenders of icons believed) but in the objective anthropocosmic foundation of the world, in those sophianic proto-images of the world in conformity with which the Wisdom-created world exists.

This is the source of the fundamental deficiency of the naturalistic understanding of art, as well as of the symbolic and emblematic character of art. Art attests to the images of being, and this testimony is not a deception (not even one that elevates us)[64] but a tale told in the language of the world about pre-eternal being; it is testimony of creaturely sophianicity about the noncreaturely Sophia. This testimony cannot be exhausted by or limited to one or another work of art, and there cannot even be just one perfectly adequate expression of an idea. In other words, the artistic testimony about the idea of a thing cannot be fully identified with this idea but is only its icon, not the proto-image itself. Therefore, one and the same artistic theme or thought-image can be expressed in different ways. The whole world is a palette for the artist in his search for and expression of forms. However, in distinguishing things and proto-images, *naturam rerum* and *ideas rerum*, one cannot separate them. The proto-images, having their pre-eternal foundation in the Wisdom of God, exist in things. From this follows the recognition of a certain identity between the proto-image and the world's being, between noncreaturely and creaturely Sophia. These are two forms of the being of one principle — its being in eternity and in time, in significance (*Geltung*) and in becoming. The icon of a thing attests to this identity. It reveals the eternal proto-image in the proto-image of the thing (the original) by imparting to this ideal proto-image independent being as it were alongside the thing. However, the icon is inseparable from the proto-image, which exists both in ideal and in empirical reality. Thus, in iconization we distinguish not two, but *three* items, i.e., not only the original and the image, the thing and the icon of the thing, but, beyond that, also the intelligible proto-image, in relation to which the thing itself is an icon. Consequently, the artistic icon is the icon of the real icon of the

64. Reference to a line from Pushkin. — Trans.

49

ideal thought-image. If there were no ideal proto-image, things would be empty and would admit only a photographic mirror-image, random and deprived of ideal content. If there were no real proto-image, or original, the ideal nature of things would remain beyond the capabilities of creaturely vision and inaccessible to the latter. But an artist sees in and through a thing its idea and portrays precisely this idea in true being, not obscured by the empirical. In a thing he reads its name or idea, and by means of artistic hieroglyphics he pronounces and repeats this name, so that it receives an independent expression alongside the thing as the image of the proto-image. In iconization the idealization of the thing occurs. The image is an altero-being of the idea, which has been detached as it were from its reality. The thing testifies about itself; it speaks itself not only in itself but also in this altero-being of itself, in its images, which represent a kind of rolling echo of its being in the world.

This cosmic echo resounds in man, who is the eye and ear of the world. All the thought-images of being, the icons of being, are contained in man before being fixed in the images of things; in their multi-unity they are seen in him. Man sees them outside himself but through himself, and in this sense he finds them in himself and expresses them for himself. If knowledge is remembrance (anamnēsis), then art is a tale told about remembrance. Man is a contracted world,[65] the anthropocosmos. In their substance the icons of the world have a human character, just as art itself does. Analysis of the icon leads us to the idea of all ideas — to *humanity*. What is humanity?

4. The Divine Proto-Image

The holy fathers bear witness to the proto-images of the world in God, which of course do not remain in separation and multiplicity but enter into the one all-embracing Divine Proto-image. How can one express the relation of this Proto-image to the trihypostatic Divinity? We know what the hypostatic Image in the Divinity is: it is the Son, "the brightness of His

---

65. A concept associated with Nicholas of Cusa. — Trans.

glory and the express image [*charaktēr*] of His hypostasis" (Heb. 1:3).[66] It is "the image of the invisible God [*eikōn tou Theou aoratou*], the firstborn of every creature" (Col. 1:15). In this text the relation between the Father and the Son is defined as the relation between Proto-image and Image; and what is most remarkable is that this is the relation between the Proto-image and the Image of the *invisible* Image of God, Who is therefore revealed and visible in this sense.[67] What significance can be attached here to this revealedness or visibility of the Father in the Son, which is the arche-image and proto-image of all images?[68] In the Holy Trinity God the Father is "invisible" (transcendent). He reveals Himself in the Son, the hypostatic Word, the Word of all words and the Image of all images. In Him is revealed the content of God's life; in Him are shown all the possibilities of all things in God, and then in creation, in the universe, of which He contains the ideal thought-image. Thus, about Him it is said: "All things were made by Him; and without Him was not anything made that was made" (John 1:3), as well as: "For in Him [*en autō*] were all things created . . . all things were created by Him [*di' autou*], and for Him [actually, in Him: *eis auton*]: And He is before all things, and by Him [*en autō*] all things consist" (Col. 1:16-17).[69]

66. The translation in the King James Version has been modified to conform with the Russian translation used by Bulgakov. — Trans.

67. In John of Damascus (*Third Oration*, XVIII, p. 400) we read: "The first natural and unchanging image of the invisible God is the Son of the Father, showing in Himself the Father. For 'no man hath seen God at any time' (John 1:18). And again: 'Not that any man hath seen the Father' (John 6:46). And that the Son is the image of the Father, the Apostle speaks about this: 'Who is the image of the invisible God' (Col. 1:15). Also, to the Hebrews: 'Who being the brightness of His glory, and the express image of His person' (Heb. 1:3). And that He shows in Himself the Father, about this in answer to Philip's words: 'shew us the Father, and it sufficeth us' (John 14:8), the Lord says: 'Have I been so long time with you, and yet hast thou not known Me, Philip? He that hath seen Me hath seen the Father' (14:9). The Son is the natural, unchanging image of the Father, like the Father in all things except unbegottenness and fatherhood."

68. "Who was the first to make the image? The Lord Himself first begot the Only Begotten Son and His Word, His living and natural Image, the unchanging reflection of His eternity" (John of Damascus, *Third Oration*, XXVI, p. 403).

69. The King James Version has been slightly modified. — Trans.

The relation between the Father and the Son, Proto-image and Image, is a relation between the inexpressibility of mystery and the expression of revelation, with the two being identical but also different: consubstantial and equally real but heterohypostatic. That Paternal Word which the Father has (for He Himself begets the Son) is His own image, but this image is hypostatic: it is the Son, begotten and being born. *Eikōn*, image, here signifies the disclosure, the revelation of the Father in the Word, the Father's Thought, the Idea of ideas, which also has hypostatic being. Thus, the Divine Image resembles every image in that It manifests the Idea, the Word of Its Proto-image, the Father, and in this sense It is His ideal thought-image. And just as an image exists inseparably from its proto-image, so the Son is the image of the Father, shows the Father.[70] However, this image itself has hypostatic Divine being, its own reality, something that is usually not proper to images. The reality of the Image-Word in the Holy Trinity is accomplished by the Holy Spirit, proceeding from the Father upon the Son and reposing on the Son. The Holy Spirit is the hypostatic love of the Father for the Son and of the Son for the Father, and this love is the accomplishing power. The Holy Spirit is the hypostatic life of the Father in the Son and of the Son in the Father, for the Divine life is precisely hypostatic love. The Holy Spirit is the accomplishing, life-giving hypostasis; in and through Him the Son receives reality for the Father and the Father receives reality for the Son: the Holy Spirit is the reality of the Father for the Son and the reality of the Son for the Father; He is the hypostatic reality.[71] He actualizes the Son for the Father and, through this, for Himself as well; He reveals the Son to the Father. In this sense in the patristic literature He is sometimes called the *Image of the Son*, and through this is defined His participation in the revelation of the Father in the Son or in the imagehood of the Son in relation to the Proto-image, the Father: the Holy Spirit *accomplishes* the Image of the Father in the Son,[72] and therefore the Image of the

---

70. Relevant here is John 14:8-9: "Philip saith unto Him, Lord, shew us the Father, and it sufficeth us. Jesus saith unto him, Have I been so long time with you, and yet hast thou not known Me, Philip? He that hath seen Me hath seen the Father; and how sayest thou then, Shew us the Father?"

71. ". . . the Spirit searcheth all things, yea, the deep things of God" (1 Cor. 2:10).

72. John of Damascus, *Third Oration*, XVIII, p. 400. "The Holy Spirit is the image of

Son is not the Son alone in separation but the Son overshadowed by the Holy Spirit proceeding from the Father. In other words, the Father, the Proto-principle, the Proto-image, is revealed in the Son and in the Holy Spirit, in this biunity with hypostatic differentiation.

From the *biunity* of the Image of God, in which the Father is revealed in the Son and in the Holy Spirit,[73] it is necessary to pass to the *one* imagehood itself, or to the content of the Image, for which the Proto-image is God Himself Who is in the Holy Trinity. About this Image it must first of all be said that, ontologically, in essence, It does *not* differ from the Proto-image: the Image is identical in essence to the Proto-image; It is equi-eternal and equi-divine. The one Image of the trihypostatic Divinity is not a creaturely or extradivine principle; rather, It belongs to the Divinity; It is the Divinity's life, which is actualized in the triunity of the three separate hypostases. About this Divine Image, the *icon* of the Holy Trinity in itself, one can say that it too is God (though only *Theos*, not *ho Theos*),[74] *for in God there is nothing non- or extradivine. This icon of Divinity in Himself is His self-revelation, the absolute content of Divine life, in the Word of all words* ("All things were made by Him"), accomplished by the life-giving Spirit. In this sense the icon of Divinity is the living and life-giving Idea of all ideas in their perfect all-unity and perfect all-reality, and therefore it is the Divine world, or the world in God, before its creation. In other words, this Divine icon of Divinity, His self-revelation in Himself, is that which, in Biblical language, is called Hokhmah, Sophia, the Wisdom of God (in the patristic language it is called, less precisely, *paradeigmata* and *proorismoi,* proto-images and predeterminations of all creation). She Herself bears witness

---

the Son: 'no man can say that Jesus is the Lord, but by the Holy Spirit' (1 Cor. 12:3). Thus, we know Christ the Son of God and God through the Holy Spirit, and in the Son we contemplate the Father, for by nature the Word is the herald of the mind and the manifestation of the Spirit. Likewise, unchanging too is the image of the Son, the Holy Spirit, differing only by procession, for the Son is begotten but not proceeding."

73. This is what the doctrine of the filioque is applicable to: not to the hypostatic procession of the Holy Spirit from the Father and the Son (*a patre filioque*, which violates the one principle in the Holy Trinity) but to the disclosure of the One First-principle, the Father, in two hypostases *in spiritu filioque.*

74. "Only God, not the God." — Trans.

about Herself by the Holy Spirit: "The Lord possessed Me in the beginning of His way" (Prov. 8:22). But this Icon of Divinity, which is the Proto-icon of all icons, is itself the Proto-image in relation to the creaturely world, which was *created by Wisdom*, i.e., on the basis of and according to Wisdom, and in this sense the world itself is the creaturely icon of Divinity. The difference between the Icon of Divinity in Divinity, which Icon at the same time is the Proto-image for the created world, and the latter is that this Icon is perfectly adequate to Divinity. Therefore, there is no *ontological* distinction in It between the Proto-image and the Image, whereas the world is inadequate to its Proto-image. The creaturely world is created out of nothingness and must yet be perfected in its being: it abides in becoming and the Proto-image is actualized in it in the process. At the same time it is identical with its Proto-image in its ontological theme, so to speak. The ideas or proto-images of the Divine world are *seeded into* the creaturely world entelechically, i.e., in the capacity of foundation and goal, original given and task to be accomplished, as inner entelechy. The sophianicity of the world contains precisely this thought about the identity as well as the distinction between the Proto-image of the world and its image. The creaturely world is the icon of the Divine Sophia, an icon sketched in nonbeing and receiving reality only in becoming.

In general, all *iconicity* is based on this relation between the trihypostatic God and His Image, the Wisdom of God, which is the world's Proto-image in Divinity Itself, and on the relation of the world's Proto-image to the world as its creaturely image. These relations must permeate the whole doctrine of the icon. (This also corresponds to Gregory Palamas's distinction between the *ousia*, the hidden essence of God, and the *energeia*, the revelation of God, His Sophia.) God is revealed to the world in Sophia, Who is the Image of God in creation. Therefore, the God Who is correlative to creation is not the imageless, invisible, unknowable, and therefore unportrayable God; rather, He is the revealed God *Who has His own image*, and this Image of God is the Proto-image of creation which is sketched in the latter. In this sense, in the doctrine of the icon one must take as one's starting point *not the apophatic thesis* of God's invisibility and imagelessness but the *sophiological doctrine* of His imagedness and of the co-imagedness of the world to this image. God sketched His image in the creature, and this

Divine image is therefore imageable.[75] This removes the iconoclasts' principal false premise, namely that God is imageless and unportrayable, a premise that the icon venerators too accepted out of carelessness and misunderstanding.

Let us go further. Man is the world's head, i.e., its ontological center. Therefore, the creation of the world is the gradual creation of man, whose appearance on the sixth day, in the fullness of creation, completes and exhausts the latter. Man is the eye of the world, the contracted world, the microcosm, even as the world is the world-man, the anthropocosm. It is precisely in man that the image of God shines out in the world. From this it follows that the proto-image of the world, Sophia, is the co-image of man, is human. In other words, the Divine Sophia is the pre-eternal Divine Humanity. The thought that man bears the image of God contains as its basis the inverse thought that humanity is proper to the image of God. We have the true appearance of the earthly Adam in the Heavenly Adam, in the Word of God, which could become human only by virtue of this co-imagedness of God and man. Therefore one can say that the very Image of God in God is the Heavenly Humanity, and that the Proto-image according to which the anthropocosm was created is precisely this Heavenly Humanity. And man is the image of this Proto-image; the earthly Adam is the image of the Heavenly Adam, as the creaturely Sophia, the living Icon of Divinity.

The truth that man is created in the image of God, i.e., that he is the creaturely image of the noncreaturely Image of God, the Divine Sophia, is proclaimed by the Word of God[76] in the tale of the creation of man (Gen.

---

75. "The fact that man is created in the image and likeness of God shows that the making of images too is, in some sense, a divine work" (Theodore the Studite, *Works*, I, p. 178). Unfortunately, this theme does not receive further development here and disappears in the apophatic doctrine of the Divine invisibility.

76. This truth is disclosed by John of Damascus in the doctrine of various types of images (*Third Oration*, XX, p. 401): "*The third type of image is created by God by imitation, i.e., man.*" "God created man in His *image and likeness*. And Adam saw God and heard the sound of His feet as He walked in the evening, and he hid in paradise. And Jacob saw and wrestled with God. It is clear that God appeared to him in the form of a man. And Moses saw as if the back of a man; and Isaiah saw Him as a man sitting on a throne. And Daniel saw the likeness of a man and as if the Son of Man come to the Ancient of Days" (*Third*

1:26-27; Prov. 8:22-31). Man is the living icon of Divinity, an icon created by God but not made by hands; humanity is the image of God. Therefore, in visions of the Old Testament, in particular in the prophet Daniel's vision of the Son of Man (Dan. 7:13) as well as in the prophet Ezekiel's vision of glory (Ezek. 1), i.e., even before the Incarnation of the Son, God appears in the image of man. This image is worthy of veneration in man; censing is performed before it as before an icon of Divinity insofar as this image is not distorted by sin, by which it has become obscured after having once shone in Adam.[77] It is in this sense that, already after the creation and not only after the redemption, men are called gods: "Is it not written in your law, I said, Ye are gods?" (John 10:34). Humanity has an obscure sense of its Divine image, even though the latter has been darkened. From this came the pagan anthropomorphism that led to idolatry: the representation of gods in the human image. In the art of antiquity this icon creation attains true heights of sublimity. This icon creation is direct artistic testimony about man's likeness to God, a testimony that religiously justifies its general task. In antiquity's icon veneration two questions were clearly posed: What does the image of God in man consist in, and if this image of God is portrayable, how is it portrayable? Those who limit the image of God in man to his spiritual nature, in distinction to or even in opposition to his bodily nature, thereby cut man in two, limiting his humanity to the soul alone and relegating the body to the animal nature. If they are consistent, such limiters of the image of God must come

---

Oration, XXVI, pp. 402-9). "Do we not bow to one another because we are created in the image of God? For, as the magnificently eloquent Basil who is well versed in Divine things says, honor offered to the image passes to the proto-image. The proto-image is that which is imaged, that from which the impression is made" (*Brief Exposition of the Orthodox Faith*, book IV, ch. XVI, p. 320). In the rite of burial composed by John of Damascus we sing: "I am the image of Your ineffable glory, though I bear the sores of transgressions." [The italics in this note are Bulgakov's. — Trans.]

77. Cf. the above-cited words of John of Damascus (*Third Oration*, XXVI, pp. 403-4). There are no grounds to see in this solely an anticipation of the Son of God Who is to come in the human image (p. 404); on the contrary, His very coming should be viewed in connection with the presence of the image of God in man in virtue of his creation and not only in virtue of the Incarnation. Therefore the Son of Man too wields judgment over the entire human race, and at the Last Judgment He judges it with a human judgment.

to believe that the image of God in man is unportrayable and that man himself is therefore unportrayable (and thus they must of course arrive at the most radical iconoclasm). Man as a spiritual being remains invisible and unportrayable for such limiters of the image of God, while the human body is for them the animal principle in man, that which in him is *lower* than humanity. For them the human body is nothing more than a collection of bones, muscles, nerves, etc., and in this sense the portrayal of man is conceived purely naturalistically, like the depiction on a physiological or anatomical chart.

Not much higher is the value placed on the body by those who see in it only matter *(hulē)*, which receives and gives a place for man's psychical life. From this, strictly speaking, there does not yet follow any conclusion in favor of the portrayability of the image of God in man, because "matter," at least according to its philosophical (as well as physical) concept, is that "difficult" formless form of being which is conceived (according to Plato's expression) as a certain illegitimate judgment and whose unique definition is *me on,* the nonexistent. Even if one sometimes encounters a more positive attitude toward matter, from such a recognition of matter it of course does not follow that it is portrayable as such.[78] To this platonizing understanding of matter it is necessary to oppose an understanding according to which the body is not matter at all, i.e., not solely matter, an understanding according to which the body does not get its reality from matter alone. The body is a form manifested in matter and governing the latter; it is an actualized thought-image, ideal-real being.[79] Now the ques-

78. John of Damascus, *First Oration,* XVI, p. 354: "I do not worship matter; I worship the Creator of matter Who became matter for my sake and chose to abide in matter, and through matter worked my salvation, and I will not stop venerating the matter through which my salvation has been accomplished. . . . I venerate and respect the other matter through which my salvation has been accomplished. Do not blaspheme matter, for it is not contemptible" (cf. *Second Oration,* XIII, p. 380). "I worship the Creator of matter Who became matter for my sake . . . for 'the Word was made flesh' and it is clear to all that flesh is matter and the creature" (XIV, p. 381). Of course, the interpretation of the body as matter is clearly insufficient, and it is rather difficult to draw from this a conclusion in defense of icon veneration.

79. See the doctrine of the body in its distinction from matter in my book *The Unfading Light* (Moscow, 1917), Section II.

tion arises: Is it correct to limit the significance of the body as form, as thought-image, to animality alone and to see in it only a phenomenon of the animal principle, or should one see in it the image of God, the revelation of man's spiritual nature in his corporeality? Is the body not the image and instrument of the spirit? The eye exists because the soul is an eye; the ear exists because the soul is hearing; the brain exists because the soul is thought and seeing; the legs exist because the soul is movement; the hands exist because the soul is activity, and so on. And the body as a whole, as the most perfect appearance of beauty and harmony (a beauty and harmony that the art of antiquity knew and revealed), is a revelation of the God-like spirit. There is no doubt that this is the case. The human body is the perfect work of art of the Divine Artist, the Wisdom of God, whose "delights were with the sons of men" (Prov. 8:31). Would it diminish creation and the Creator if one did not see in the body as well, just as one sees in the spirit, the image of God in man, a palpable appearance of the spiritual principle living in man? Man is one and whole; he is not dismembered into parts, into body and soul, but is incarnate spirit or spirit-bearing flesh. The original Adam too, clothed in God's glory of which he was deprived after the Fall (Rom. 3:23), manifested in his integral being the image of God.

Just as in God, in His self-revelation, we distinguish the revealed God Himself from His Divine Icon, the Wisdom of God,[80] where, moreover, the Proto-image and the Image in God are inseparable as well as distinct, so in man the spirit living in him and the spirit's palpable appearance in bodily form are distinguished from each other, but again without separation. The body as form does not exist without spiritual content; without such content it is not a body. It is a body precisely as the form of the spirit, as a revelation and icon not made by hands, which is the basis of all icon creation, of the iconization of man. The body as such exists only in its spiritualization. There is no face without an expression — that is clear to everyone. However, not only the face but the whole body has an "expres-

---

80. In this sense the Wisdom or Glory of God can be regarded as the body of Divinity. See my essay "The Eucharistic Dogma," in *Put'*, 1930, I-II. [This essay is available in B. Jakim's English translation in *The Holy Grail and the Eucharist*, 1997. — Trans.]

sion": it expresses or reveals the spirit living in it. Only in abstraction is it possible to see in the body only "matter," or nothing but anatomy and physiology; and within its own limits and in its own place such abstraction can be fully justified. But, in essence, such an understanding of the body is a slander against it, a slander originating in blindness, owing to which the icon of Divinity is not seen in it.

However, a question naturally arises: Why was a religious understanding of the body, as well as imagery of the latter, proper only to paganism, whereas such imagery was prohibited for the chosen nation? In the light of this idea of the spirituality of the body how should one understand the second commandment and all the Old Testament prohibitions? We can find the reason for this in original sin, which obscured man's image and, having removed his glory, clothed him in "coats of skins."[81] The human body, having become thick with flesh and animal in nature, became incapable and unworthy of manifesting the image of God, since it was afflicted by sin and distorted by passions. Such were the images of idols as well: the Divine image, indestructible in man, shines in the idols *through* a mask of sin and *in opposition to* the latter, but nevertheless the direct object of the image is not the face but the mask.[82] These human passions are depicted in idols; idols are icons of passions and sin and are unworthy of veneration. Thus, the Old Testament prohibition refers to the untruthfulness of the human image that appeared as a consequence of man's loss of the purity of his humanity. Nevertheless, as we have pointed out, this did not prevent Old Testament theophanies in a *human* image, which of course was free of sinful distortion. This is made particularly

81. Genesis 3:21. — Trans.

82. In this passage there is a play on the words *lik* and *lichina*: *lik* can mean face, countenance (the common word for which is *litso*, which can also mean person), but it can also mean person (the usual word for which is *lichnost*), innermost personhood. *Lichina* means mask, false semblance. Throughout the text, when referring to the portrayal of Christ or of saints on icons, Bulgakov uses the word *lik*, implying that their innermost personhood, their real "faces," have been captured on the icon. I have translated *lik* in various ways depending on the context, sometimes as person, sometimes as innermost personhood, sometimes as countenance. In short, the reader of the Russian text has to keep in mind four different words: *lik, litso, lichnost, lichina*. — Trans.

clear by the fact that in the Old Testament, alongside the prohibition of humanlike images, it was commanded that sculptural gold images of angels be made.[83] What meaning can we attach to this apparent contradiction, which for some proves that human images were prohibited while for others it proves just the opposite? The portrayals of the angels — and this is the crux of the matter — contained *human* images, in virtue of the *cohumanity* of the angels.[84] Of course they differed from human images in some of their particular traits, traits that expressed their specifically angelic nature (wings, the absence of gender, a youthful appearance), but these traits did not change the human character of the image itself (just as in general the Old Testament angelophanies were in the human image). Thus, even though the religious reproduction of the human image, the icon of humanity, was prohibited directly, it was prescribed indirectly, in the icons of angels. Why? The reason is obvious: in the portrayals of angels the human image was not darkened by sin. Thus the human image could be portrayed here, although of course it could not be portrayed in its fullness, since after all this was an image of spiritual beings without bodies, even if these beings were cohuman. This image was purer than that of man and therefore in a certain sense it was more human than the merely human image. Such is the paradox of the Old Testament veneration of icons. The portrayal of angels had a symbolic, emblematic significance: in the negative sense it attested to the masked nature of the image of God in man inasmuch as he was darkened by sin. In the positive sense it was, so to speak, an icon of an icon, although this latter icon (the original, true humanity) had not yet been restored.

But it *was* restored through the in-humanization of God, through the Incarnation of the Word, which was accomplished so that "the image corrupted by passions could be renewed." Christ, the one sinless new Adam, restored in His humanity the true human image, which is also the true image of God. The Lord appeared as truly man, and in Him appeared the true man, the new Adam. He has the true human image, which is also the image of God, the living icon of Divinity not made by hands. This is the true

83. See Exodus 25:18-22. — Trans.
84. See my book *Jacob's Ladder: On the Angels.*

significance of the Incarnation for the dogma of icon veneration.[85] Contrary to the opinion of past and present defenders of icon veneration, the foundation of iconography and of icon veneration does not consist in the Lord's assumption of the human body in its natural portrayability. Having assumed this body, the Lord removed from it the veil of sin, thereby manifesting its genuine image in its true humanity. This is how the icon venerators usually reasoned: even though, in and of itself, the human body is portrayable because it is flesh (because of its "materiality"), nevertheless, as such, it is unworthy of being portrayed and venerated because it has no relation to the image of God. It became worthy of veneration and portrayable on icons as the image of the Lord's human nature only because, in the Incarnation, He put on Himself this fleshly body as a sort of garment and thereby sanctified it. Against this the iconoclasts justly objected that, in such an *external* interpretation of the portrayability of Christ's humanity, the icon of this body could not be regarded as the icon of Christ.

Whatever the case may be, the fathers of the Seventh Ecumenical Council, all the holy fathers, and the defenders of icon veneration all agree that the Incarnation has a fundamental and decisive significance for the question of the icon. This is a truth recognized by the catholic consciousness of the Church. However, the further development and application of this idea in the doctrine of icon veneration are far from indisputable and are subject to verification and refinement.

In order to understand the essence of the icon one must start with the fact that the Word's Incarnation revealed that which was already given in man's creation. Man as such, according to his creation, already has the image of God; man is the living icon of Divinity. He stopped being this icon as a consequence of original sin, but this original iconicity of his is restored in him by virtue of the Divine Incarnation. The human nature was manifested as the icon of Divinity after it was manifested in Christ. Christ, the new Adam, was revealed in our humanity as true man; and in Him, in

---

85. This idea is clearly expressed in "the rite of the sanctification of an icon of one or many saints" in the Trebnik. [The Trebnik is a liturgical book containing descriptions of observances and prayers. — Trans.]

His humanity, our humanity found itself in its truth. In the fullness of his spiritual-corporeal being and therefore in his flesh, man, according to his very creation, is the icon of Divinity. Christ as true man in His humanity is the icon of Divinity; and in Him and with Him all humanity, which through Him regained itself, reacquired the image of God.

In assuming the creaturely human nature of the Old Testament Adam, the New Testament Adam assumed, not an image alien to Himself, not an image that was like an external garment, but His own image which He, as God, has in man. His humanity is at the same time the image of His Divinity, according to the very creation of man, who has for himself the Proto-image in the Heavenly Humanity of the new Adam. Christ in His flesh assumed His own image of the Heavenly Adam, His own icon. His Divine image is therefore perfectly transparent in His humanity. The icon-oclasts' chief error, which the icon venerators too were guilty of, consisted in really separating *in relation to the image* the two natures in Christ. According to their doctrine, being invisible, Divinity does not have an image, while humanity is impenetrable for Divinity and is not the image of the latter; and therefore the image ("portrayability") belongs only to the human body. However, in reality, even though *He has two natures,* Christ has *one and the same* Divine image, but He has it *twice* or, more correctly, *doubly.* According to His Divinity He is the Image of the Father and at the same time the Proto-image of all that exists, as well as being the Proto-image of man, who precisely for this reason is His image: "The first man is of the earth, earthy: the second man is the Lord from heaven [*ho deuteros anthrōpos eis ouranou*]. . . . And as we have borne the image [*ten eikona*] of the earthy, we shall also bear the image of the heavenly" (1 Cor. 15:47-49). Man in Christ is the direct image of His Divinity, for the Latter Itself possesses a human image. That is why creation too, created in the image of God, bears the image of man. Therefore the iconoclasts were wrong in their starting premise (which was fully shared by the icon venerators, by Theodore the Studite et al.) that Christ's Divinity is unportrayable because It is imageless; in reality, It has Its image in man and is therefore portrayable.[86]

---

86. In general, unportrayability, understood as imagelessness or formlessness, is er-roneously regarded as a consequence of God's perfection. The opposite is more likely to

Here, pious thought is impeded by the fear of recognizing directly and decisively that creaturely man himself as a god by grace is the image of God and that therefore the icon of Christ's humanity is *not just* the icon of His body without relation to Divinity but is *in general* His icon, precisely as the image of His Divinity in the creaturely nature. Christ has His image, one and identical, doubly: invisibly for creaturely eyes according to His Divinity and visibly according to His humanity. The existence of the *image* does not necessarily signify that it is visible to creaturely eyes, for the image can be both visible and invisible. Such is Christ as "the image of the invisible God" (Col. 1:15): He remains invisible for humanity *until He comes,* i.e., until He becomes visible through His humanity in the Incarnation. The same Image that is existent in the bosom of the Holy Trinity penetrates the visible world and puts Its imprint on this world, manifesting itself in the human image.[87]

According to the christological dogma we have one hypostasis with unity of life in the case of two natures. With regard to the icon both the iconoclasts and the icon venerators argued as follows: according to His human nature (or, more correctly, according to His bodily nature) Christ has a visible image and is portrayable, whereas according to His Divine nature He does not have such an image and is unportrayable. Therefore, *with regard to the image they separated the natures and thus limited the power of the image* in order to rescue it in some way, to keep from rejecting it completely. But the image belongs *not to the nature* of Christ in its duality but to His hypostasis in its unity. Having *one hypostasis,* though in two natures, Christ also has *one image,* though it is disclosed *doubly,* in the two natures: invisibly and spiritually in one nature and visibly and bodily in the other nature. In other words, this image is unimageable by us according to its Divinity but imageable or portrayable according to its humanity. In the humanity it is visible and all that is visible is portrayable, or can have its

---

be true: it would signify imperfection. God is the Form of forms, the Image of images, the Idea of ideas, and it is erroneous to think that limitlessness and formlessness *(apeiron)* in the sense of imagelessness, chaos, abyss, would correspond to God's majesty.

87. Angels also have a human image in conformity with their cohumanity, but in conformity with the spirituality of the angelic nature this image is spiritual, i.e., invisible for man with the exception of certain special, extraordinary "appearances" of theirs.

icon. Therefore the icon of Christ too is possible precisely according to His *visible* human image, which, however, is identical with His invisible image, the Divine one. And just as in defining the interrelations of the two natures in Christ, orthodox theology teaches about perichoresis, the mutual penetration or permeation of the natures in spite of all their separateness, so also with regard to the Image of Christ which is imprinted in His Divinity and humanity, we must recognize a certain kind of perichoresis. The latter is expressed in the clear shining of Christ's Divine image in His human image. We have a certain anticipation of this in the Lord's Transfiguration: on Mount Tabor the disciples saw the Lord with changed image: He was *transfigured*. What does this mean? It means that, though He retained His own human image, this image became *transparent* for His invisible Divine image: "O Christ God, Your disciples beheld Your glory to the extent they could see it."[88] The *glory* is precisely the spiritual Divine image of Christ; and the *glorification* of His body, its appearance in glory, is precisely His body's transparence for Divinity; it is the very same perichoresis about which we spoke above. The Lord's body, which was glorified after the Resurrection, now unchangeably retains the features of this glorification. The glorification is precisely such an identification of Christ's two natures in the *unity* of the image with preservation of the separateness between His heavenly eternal humanity and His creaturely humanity, of one humanity in biune being. In the correlation of Christ's *two* natures with the unity of His Divine image we have the same thing as in the correlation of Divine and creaturely Sophia, or of the Divine and created world. Sophia is one, and this oneness establishes the identity of the two worlds in their foundation, although this oneness and identity does not remove the inexorable difference between them: the creature, even if deified ("God is all in all"), cannot become God; it is identified with Him only by the grace of deification.

Not only was the visible image of God in Christ's humanity accessible to perception, being seen by His contemporaries, but it is portrayable in general, i.e., its *icon* is possible. Here we come to the very essence of the question of the icon's nature.

---

88. From the kontakion of the Feast of the Transfiguration. — Trans.

5. The Content and Limits of the Icon

The icon of Christ portrays His human image, in which His Divinity too is imaged. Therefore, most directly this icon is a human image and as such it is a type of portrait. That is why in discussions of the icon it is first necessary to ask oneself what it is that the human image represents in general as a picture or portrait. It is perhaps first easier to say what it does not represent. It does not represent that which both sides in the iconoclastic controversy took it to represent: it does not represent a naturalistic portrayal of individual parts of the body in their combination, i.e., something like a collection of anatomical or physiological photographs.[89] Such an understanding is tantamount to a rejection of art. Art sees the thought-image or idea that shines through a thing and constitutes the ideal content or foundation of the latter. In this sense the portrayal of a human being too (let us conditionally call it a *portrait*) deals first of all with the ideal form of the human body, with the image of humanity, and then with the individual features that we have in the given image. A portrait is artistic testimony about this thought-image and its fixation with the resources of art. In this sense it portrays not the external features of the person but his *innermost personality* as seen by the artist, and this seeing of the innermost personality that is revealed in the proto-image or original is conveyed not in abstract contemplation but concretely, the artist showing how it exists in the original. And in this way the portrait of a given person is obtained.

This portrait resemblance thus combines the reproduction of individual features of the person's body (his hair, figure, etc., which is usually the only thing the icon venerators had in view) with his innermost or spiritual personality. It would be a mistake to think that the resemblance consists in the hair, nose, and warts; it extends far deeper. The chief difference between man and all the things of this world, even including the animals, is

89. In addition to numerous judgments in the patristic literature (some of them presented above), here is what we find in the apologia for icon veneration read by deacon Epiphanius in the sixth act of the Seventh Ecumenical Council: "The icon is like the proto-image not according to essence but only as a reminder and according to the position of the portrayed members. When he paints the portrait of some man, the painter does not try to portray the soul" (p. 223).

that man is a bearer of spirit, that his body is the vessel as well as the instrument and form of the spirit living in him, and this unity of spirit and flesh cannot be torn asunder. Man cannot be portrayed without this spirit-bearingness of his. Therefore to regard portrait images as nothing more than reproductions of the members of the human body and of their positions (which was the understanding of both sides in the iconoclastic controversy) is not only to deny art but also, in essence, to deny the icon. The body cannot be regarded as nothing more than flesh and bone, separately from the spirit living in it: without the latter it does not even exist as body. It is not only the vessel and instrument of the spirit inseparable from the latter, but it is also the image of the spirit. The body of every man is the icon not made by hands of his spirit, and the portrait of a man is the artificial icon made by hands of this icon. In it is portrayed not only the body but also the spirit living in the body, or (which is the same thing) the visible bodily image of the invisible spirit and of its states. Of course, the task of art consists precisely in seeing the *innermost personality* in a person and even in any masks covering the person, and in bearing witness about this innermost personality in the images it creates.[90] And in this sense there exists a qualitative difference between a photograph, however perfect it might be, and an artistic portrait, however imperfect it might be.[91]

Thus, the human portrait can be characterized by quoting Pseudo-Dionysius' phrase that "the icon is the seeing of the invisible," for in it is portrayed the invisible spirit living in the visible body. But this also leads to the fundamental aporia of the portrait, an aporia that marks the limits of the portrait. This aporia has two sides: first, every portrait is the por-

90. For this reason, of course, totally incorrect is the above-presented judgment (expressed at the Seventh Ecumenical Council) that "when he paints the portrait of some man, the painter *does not try to portray the soul*." To the extent this is true, he is simply not an artist.

91. Photography can have significance for the artist as a complement to what can be directly seen by the human eye; beyond that, it can also involve art expressed in a skillful "take," so that photography can be a particular tool of art, like the palette or the brush in the hands of a skillful master. In opposing photography to art, our intention is to distinguish the passively representational, naturalistic reproduction of the instantaneous state of an object from its actively perceptual seeing and imaging.

trayal of a particular individual who in his individuality differs from the rest of humanity as a certain personal and unrepeatable *modus* of the latter; but at the same time he is an icon of humanity in general, for a man is a generic being, and the genus lives in every individual. The aporia here consists in the impossibility of precisely capturing and conveying this correlation and inner interface of the individual and the genus, and in the resulting unintended and inevitable exaggeration of one or the other of the sides. Secondly, every portrait is the icon of an icon, an artificial reproduction of the natural image not made by hands of the spirit, which is what the body is. To what degree is the spirit portrayable? Even the creaturely human spirit, which, though creaturely, has a divine origin as breathed into the body out of God's lips, has, in its likeness to God, unsearchable depths and is not exhausted by any of the particular revelations of its life. Consequently, even though every one of the natural icons of the human spirit is true in its iconicity, it nevertheless is not adequate and not exhaustive. One and the same spirit is revealed in different states and thus in different images: in childhood, in youth, in old age, in falls and in ascents, in decline and in bloom.[92] And even if we ignore differences in the degree of artists' penetration into spiritual reality, the portrait inevitably remains one-sided in character. It is always *pars pro toto*, capturing only *one* of the phenomena of the phenomenology of spirit, which it takes as the adequate image of this spirit. From this there follows the inevitable *relativity* of every portrait and therefore the multiplicity, in principle, of portraits. Man in his life manifests an uncountable number of icons of his spirit, rolling the infinite movie reel, as it were, of his phenomenology. Thus, every portrait too, however perfect it might be, is not unique and exhaustive; it is not the direct icon of the integral spirit as such but is only one of its manifestations. However, the integral spirit is palpable in each of its manifestations, for it is indivisible. Therefore, every icon, having a particular significance, at the same time retains something that is general.[93]

92. In this sense, about the creaturely, human spirit too it can be said that it has an ousia and energies, which are distinct from one another but also identical.

93. Here, let us compare the revelation of the Divine spirit with that of the creaturely spirit. The Divine spirit has the absolute and adequate icon of its being — this is the Divine Sophia. The perfect spirit is characterized by fullness and actuality of life with per-

From this we get the following remarkable feature of the portrait: every portrait requires a *name*. A nameless portrait, even given the greatest portrait "resemblance" (which, of course, refers only to a single definite moment of life and is evanescent as time itself), does not yet have the ultimate anchoring point in itself. This point is given only by a name: only a name completes, validates, and therefore itself *enters* as a means of representation into the image. The name *correlates* the image with the original, the icon with the proto-image; it *unites* a given icon with the multi-icon spirit. (In similar fashion, the name itself is given to its bearer, which prior to this naming was multi-named or nameless.) A name expresses the individuality itself — the spirit living and being revealed as the *subject* of its own states, present in all of them and not identified with any of them, for it is not exhausted by them. In this sense the name is a hieroglyph of the person, a symbolic representation of the invisible in the visible, while the icon is, in a certain sense, a hieroglyph of one of the states of this person, one of the self-revelations of the latter. The naming of an icon means that the latter has been included among the set of manifestations of this spirit, of which there can be an indefinite number. Therefore, one and the same name is given to different and multiple portraits of one and the same person, all of them being threaded on him as it were, or fused by him as if into a single movie reel of images. Of course a portrait-icon must be convincing of itself even before being named, independently of the naming. In spite of its inevitable one-sidedness, the portrait-icon nevertheless bears witness about its original: it contains a real *pars pro toto*, because the soul is indivisible and one. But at the same time this ineradicable difference between part and whole remains. Therefore, we do not feel tranquil and content until the image receives a name, which is the icon of the subject itself as the bearer of all of its states[94] and therefore the original of all of its icons.

---

fect immobility and unchangeability of the latter. This is *actus purus*, which belongs to eternity. By contrast, every creaturely spirit in its life discloses itself in its likeness to God in infinite *process*, or becoming, and therefore its entire being is characterized by sophianicity and unceasing sophianization, but Sophia Herself in Her unchanging eternity does not belong to it.

94. The development of this idea refers already to the doctrine of the name, to the theology of the "glorification of the name." I have expounded the philosophical founda-

Let us now directly consider the icon of Christ. In certain respects this icon does not differ from the human icon in general. Like the latter it is a human image in which the spirit living in the person is revealed. Particular icons of Christ portray either particular events of His earthly life (e.g., icons of feasts, different portrayals of events in the Gospels) or His image, which corresponds to the portrait image in general. But of course those general limits that have force in relation to all icons acquire here a particular force. And this refers first of all to the portrayal of the body itself, of the Savior's human nature. He was the perfect man; in His person He showed the true image of humanity. One can say that His body is the *absolute* (in the sense of perfection) human body. But perfection of any kind is very difficult to portray for human art, which has at its disposal only relative resources, only gradations of light and shade as it were, and uses distortion to convey individual form. For individuality in our sinful world is necessarily a distortion, a relativity, a certain monstrousness and defectiveness on the one hand and an excessiveness on the other, a dissonance awaiting resolution. It is only with the aid of a harmony of dissonances that an individual body becomes portrayable.

But the Savior's body is *not* individual in this sense, because it is *pan*-individual, or *supra*-individual, or absolutely individual. In His light there is no shade; in His harmony there is no dissonance; in His type there is no distortion; and therefore the usual representational resources of art are powerless here. Nevertheless, to man, in this case to the artist, it is given to have his vision of Christ, and he seeks His image (it may be that representational art — consciously or unconsciously — does not even

---

tions of the "glorification of the name" in a special work on the name in general and on the Name of God (in manuscript). The first chapter of this work has been published in German in *Festgaben an Mazaryk* (1930): "*Was ist das Wort?*" [Part two of the present volume, "The Name of God," is a chapter of this work. The "glorification of the name" (Imiaslavie in Russian; also known as onomatodoxy) was a highly controversial dogmatic movement that arose at the beginning of the twentieth century and was condemned by the Russian Orthodox Church but supported by Bulgakov and other theologians. Put succinctly, and at the risk of oversimplification, the basic thesis of the movement's adherents was that the Name of God is God. See the Translator's Introduction for a discussion of this movement. — Trans.]

seek anything else). As pan-individuality, the person (*lik*)[95] of Christ, though it cannot be equated with any particular individuality, nevertheless contains all individualities; or, conversely, every human person (*litso*) in virtue of the latter's humanity participates in Christ's human person (*lik*), which is why it is possible to say that, in essence, all humankind in its humanity is one person (*lik*), the *universal person* (*lik*), Christ. This reveals a possible approach to the human portrayal of Christ, though it remains inadequate, inevitably taking on a personal, psychological coloration,[96] but nevertheless in some sense it does correspond to its task. Therefore the image of Christ is always present before the eyes of art. This image is painted by both believers and unbelievers (and perhaps the psychology of unbelieving painters attests more clearly to how deeply this Image is implanted in the human soul[97]). In seeking the true image of *man*, the artist unintentionally finds Christ in this humanity.[98] Therefore the religious art of antiquity too, insofar as it revealed beautiful humanity, unconsciously created the icon of Christ before Christ, and here this art paralleled the philosophy of antiquity, which was a Christianity before Christ.

Thus, Christ in His humanity is *portrayable* as He is seen by man through various subjective prisms, although He is *unportrayable* in His truth and glory, for, to achieve this, the portrayer must not only be like or akin to the one portrayed but he must even be his equal. However, for the justification of art this *portrayability* alone is sufficient if through it too the ray of Christ's humanity can be revealed, even if only in reflection, as it

95. See previous note on *lik*, etc., p. 59. — Trans.

96. It is known from the history of iconography that Christ's face on icon images has reflected the ethnic traits of the countries in which they were painted, though these traits were not always externally and crudely expressive of nationality: we find Greek, Russian, and western ethnic representations (and among the latter we find Italian, German, Dutch, etc. representations).

97. See, for example, N. N. Krimsky's account of how he painted his "Christ in the Wilderness."

98. This feature of Christ's person — His universal humanity and in this sense His ordinariness and impersonality as it were, which in actual fact, however, reveals the depth and rich content of every person — was expressed by Ivan Turgenev in his remarkable prose-poem, "Christ."

glides over all things and shines in the persons [*lik*] of Christ's saints, for even in their individual images saints have something of Christ's person in them (about this, see below). But the icon of Christ is the portrayal not only of His perfect humanity but also of His Divine Spirit — it is the icon of the Divinity Itself. We already know that, in general, the human body cannot be taken separately from the spirit, whose vessel it is: the image of the body is also the image of the spirit. Therefore the icon of Christ is not only the image of His human body, as it was considered to be by the iconoclasts, but also the icon of His Divinity (which the icon venerators did not fully understand, instead seeing in the icon of Christ only the image of His humanity or, more precisely, even only of His body). It is precisely on this point that the problem of the icon becomes maximally acute: How can Divinity be portrayed, and can It be?

God is revealed to us multiply and multifariously — in a word, He is revealed by acts and in images. The Word of God, insofar as He was revealed to man and "dwelt among us,"[99] is *portrayable,* although of course He can never be adequately and perfectly portrayed. However, this condition is not necessary for *portrayability:* for portrayability it is necessary that images of the incarnate Word, icons of Christ, be not empty but have in them a reflected ray of Divinity. But this flows directly from the general fact of God's revelation to man, from the co-imagedness of man to God and therefore from a certain humanity of God. From this it follows that *God is portrayable* for man in this humanity of His. Therefore the true and full postulate of the icon of Christ consists in giving not only a human image of Christ (a historical portrait, so to speak, analogous to other pictures of great men and historical figures that secular artists, both believers and unbelievers, have painted) but also an image in which Christ's Divinity would be portrayed. In the icon the God-Man is portrayed. But this task goes beyond art into the religious domain; or, more correctly, it unites the two domains. From the icon painter this task requires not only art but also religious illumination, vision, and this is possible only in the union of his artistic and religious life, i.e., *on the ground of the Church.* Thus, iconography arises as an *art of the Church,* uniting all the creative tasks of art with the experience of the

99. John 1:14. — Trans.

71

Church.[100] The icon is a work of art that knows and loves its own forms and colors, understands their revelation, governs them, and is obedient to them. But the icon is also a theurgic act in which the revelation of the supramundane is attested in images of the world and the revelation of spiritual life is attested in images of the flesh. In the icon God reveals Himself in man's creative acts; in the icon the theurgic act of the union of the earthly and the heavenly is accomplished. Thus, iconography is both a feat of art and a religious feat, full of prayerful and ascetic intensity (which is why the Church recognizes a special category of saints, that of icon painters, in whose persons art itself is canonized as a path of salvation).

From this follows another feature of icon painting. As an art of the *Church,* it lives not only in the general tradition of art with its schools but also in the Church tradition that is expressed objectively in the iconographic canon. What is this canon? First, it is necessary to reject the false and distorted interpretation of it. The canon contains, first of all, a disciplinary principle for icons, a sort of spiritual censorship, together with requirements of a formal and prohibitory character. These requirements of censorship are variable, corresponding to the character of the epoch and the level of ecclesial development. Of course, this is not what constitutes the canon as a Church tradition. It contains a certain ecclesial vision of images of the Divine world expressed in forms and colors, in images of art — it contains a witness to the iconographic creativity of the Church in her sobornost. The canon contains both visions (i.e., "types" of icons of specific content) and seeings,[101] i.e., specific types and means of the treat-

---

100. This is not understood by some artists, who, highly skilled, easily take to icon painting without thinking about the religious side of this work. It is even less understood by many Orthodox, who, with a complete lack of artistic skill and inspired solely by piety, attempt to paint icons (though, because of their total artistic incompetence, they would never think of trying to paint regular paintings). Here we might also mention the "mass production" of icons by various "daubers" who, trying to satisfy popular demand, constitute a scourge for icon painting as an art. This explains that "crisis of the icon" which is affecting the whole world and Russia in particular, and which started long before the Revolution. Iconography *as a creative activity* is the most sublime and difficult form of church art; that is what both casual artists and unskilled daubers should take into account.

101. See note on p. 5 on visions and seeings. — Trans.

ment of images, the symbolics of forms and colors. This is the treasure-house, as it were, of the Church's living *memory* of these visions and seeings, *the Church's inspiration in her sobornost,* and as such it is a species of church tradition existing alongside other species of it (e.g., the patristic literature, the liturgical tradition, etc.). On this basis the tradition-hallowed icon is, in its own way, just as authoritative a source of religious wisdom as the other, above-mentioned examples of tradition; and therefore, in seeking support in church tradition, theology has the right and obligation to make use of this source.

Like the church tradition in general, the iconographic canon should not be understood as an external rule and invariable law that demands passive, slavish subordination to itself and reduces the icon painter's task to nothing more than a copying of the original. Such an "Old Believer"[102] legalistic interpretation of the canon is, first of all, unrealizable and, secondly, false. It is unrealizable and utopian because copying (if it is not just a question of a "mass production" of icons, which is not copying at all but a more or less crude distortion or parodying) is a creative artistic act in which the copier reproduces in himself a master's work, enlivens this work, and enters into its life. Therefore, artistic copying is a creative activity bearing the mark of individuality. Let us take for example Andrei Rublyov's "Trinity." Of course this icon can be repeated artistically, but that would be, strictly speaking, not a copy but the finding with contemporary resources and in the contemporary consciousness what was once found by the master. Of course, art, which can accept such repetition in free and sincere creative acts and find it worthy and even important, should not confine itself to such repetition, for that would be to denigrate itself. It could not even do so if it wished, because the nature of art is creative freedom, not copying, which is possible for art only in the capacity of a manifestation of such freedom. Art is in unceasing motion, for it is alive. To transform art into nothing more than copying is impossible; there can be no true copying of works of art for the sake of non-art, for their "mass production." Thus, the only tool available for the "Old Be-

---

102. The Russian Old Believers were characterized by slavish adherence to the letter of Scripture and ritual. Bulgakov uses the term metaphorically. — Trans.

liever" approach to the icon original is color photography. Of course, the latter has now become very important for the history of art and the popularization of the latter, but it cannot replace icon painting. And, in any case, the whole utopianness of the "Old Believer" attitude toward the icon would be clearly demonstrated if it turned out that this attitude confined all the possibilities of icon painting to the photographic reproduction of certain supposedly classic originals. This would also be idolatrous in relation to these originals, which alone supposedly possess the property of iconicity. But, moreover, to limit the task of art to the mere copying of existing originals is also religiously false, for this distorts the idea of church tradition. In particular, as far as the religious *content* of one or another icon is concerned, the history of the icon already attests that a unique *life* of the icon exists in the Church. In this life, certain themes and styles of icons of particular content are brought to the surface, while others go out of circulation, but in any case the possible content of the icon can never be regarded as exhausted or as not admitting change or growth. In particular, it is sufficient to note that the glorification of new saints leads to new icons. The same thing is accomplished by the glorification of new miracle-working icons, which previously were not known and not disseminated. Further, it is also important to establish that, though the existence in the Church of icons of a specific content already bears witness to the church tradition in favor of a certain ecclesial certitude and authoritativeness of their content,[103] *new* icons with a *new* content are, in principle, nevertheless possible, and in fact come into being. The life of the Church is never exhausted by the past; it has a present and a future, and is always moved by the Holy Spirit. And if the spiritual visions and revelations attested in the icon were possible in the past, they are also possible today, and will be possible in the future. And it is only a question of *fact* whether creative inspiration and audacity will appear in a new icon. Was not such audacity manifested in the act of Andrei Rublyov, who painted on an icon

103. Nevertheless, certain important people in the Church do not take this into account if one or another icon does not suit their prejudices. We have a clear example of this in the attitude of certain influential church circles (our contemporary sophiamachians) toward icons of Sophia, the Wisdom of God, which are ancient and worthy of veneration or in any case possess the authority of church tradition.

his vision of the Holy Trinity[104] and thereby touched upon the most mysterious and holy object of Christian faith? Was not a similar inspired audacity manifested in the icon of St. Sophia of Novgorod or in various cosmic icons of the Mother of God? To prohibit new icons in advance in the "Old Believer" manner would be to deaden icon painting (and indirectly to encourage either idolatry or a purely imitative approach to icon painting). But even leaving aside the question of the possibility of *new* icons, one must understand that old icons too are necessarily always painted anew.[105] The fact of the matter is that the originals are only abstract schemata, and though there are artistic prototypes for these schemata, these prototypes are of course not indisputable or at least not unique. But in art not only *what* but also *how* has significance. The realization of a given type or original, if it is to be religiously artistic and not just a product of purely imitative craft, depends on the creative perception of the original, on its independent treatment, resulting in a variation of the original that (and this is the most important point) is not even intentional, but is spontaneous and inevitable. The canon is not an external law (which is even impossible here) but an inner norm that operates by virtue of the fact that it is convincing and to the degree it is convincing. In this respect the iconographic canon does not differ from the rest of church tradition, which too is not an external law but has a creative life that is ceaselessly being renewed and continually being enriched in this renewal. This also describes the life of the iconographic original. Since this original too is

104. It is known that Rublyov's "Trinity" differs from similar icons of this type, in that it does not include the figures of Abraham and Sarah who receive their unknown visitors and offer them food. Thus, that which had usually been the portrayal of a particular episode in Old Testament history clearly became, in the hands of Rublyov, an audacious icon of the Holy Trinity. This is perhaps the most obvious example of how an icon painter who takes tradition into account nevertheless transforms it creatively, thereby himself entering into the church tradition by his creative act. That which originally could have appeared to be bold novelty is for us now part of the canon, the correct relation to which Rublyov himself establishes by his own example, which, however, is not unique. One can find an archeological essay on icons of the Holy Trinity in *Seminarium Conda covianum* (N. Malitsky, *'K istorii kompozitsii vetkhozavetnoi Troitsy* [On the history of the composition of the Old Testament Trinity] [Prague, 1928]).

105. What Bulgakov has in mind is the creative "copying" of existing icons. — Trans.

not a law but a "catholic"[106] vision, this "catholicity" includes every member of the Church whose relation to the original is not willful but creative. And, through the accumulation of these infinitesimally small changes, new originals arise, actualizing the life of tradition in the iconographic canon.[107]

The canon is also important for safeguarding the asceticism in iconography to which naturalism is inimical. The style of the icon is diametrically opposed to the ideal of Apelles' apples, to the portrayal of immediate corporeality itself (to which, strangely, the icon-venerating fathers reduce the icon). The icon should have nothing that stimulates sensuality or that even evokes images of the sensual world. Though an icon is a thought-image of the world and of man, this thought-image is taken so supramundanely that, for sensual perception, the icon image turns out to be abstractly schematic, arid, dead. In it one does not hear the voice or smell the fragrances of this world. We find ourselves here in the pale realm of Goethe's "Mothers" (in the second part of *Faust*), or in a kind of mountainous world on high with a rarefied atmosphere. This does not hamper but even facilitates the ideal realism of the icon, as well as the elevated artistry of its symbolism, composition, rhythm, and coloration. But all these images of fleshly being are dematerialized, so to speak; they are taken outside of their actualization in the flesh of the world, as it were. This constitutes the chief distinction and even oppositeness of orthodox iconography (as well as of its artistic prototype in Egyptian iconography and in

106. Referring to the sobornost of the Church. The Russian word is *sobornyi*. — Trans.

107. It is not part of our task to analyze the meaning of the iconographic canon with respect to its artistic elements (elements of composition and painting) or with respect to certain essential characteristics of icon style (the absence of a third dimension, reverse perspective, etc.). This subject still awaits its competent religious-artistic investigator who could disclose the religious meaning of the icon's artistic symbolism, its phenomenology and language, so to speak. Instead of this, until now we have had only interpretations of the icon's theological content, its aesthetic registration in the "Old Believer" manner, or its archeology. [Pavel Florensky offers an analysis of icon reverse perspective in his famous essay, written in 1919: *Obratnaya perspektiva* (Reverse Perspective), available in English translation in *Pavel Florensky: Beyond Vision: Essays on the Perception of Art*, ed. Nicoletta Misler, trans. Wendy Salmond (London: Reaktion Books, 2002). — Trans.]

Greek sculpture) from the western naturalism of the Renaissance. Personal images, losing their character of portraits, are thus transformed into "originals." This also constitutes the distinction between religious pictures from the life of Christ and icons of Christ.[108]

All the same, the existence and validity of the canon attest that the icon of Christ (and of course other icons too by virtue of connection with this icon) is not only a work of art with its individual character, but also an ecclesial vision with its catholic[109] nature, in which the person does not die but is included in the higher catholic multi-unity of the Church. Therefore, in a certain sense one can say that icons of Christ, though they are painted by individual painters, belong, properly speaking, to the Church. This property of belonging is disclosed in a new aspect in the sanctification of icons.

6. The Sanctification of Icons and the Significance of Such Sanctification

As we have seen, the portrait, the picture of every man, necessarily requires naming: the thought-image of form needs to be completed by the *name-image* of idea. But this necessity of naming and this connection between image and name apply in the highest degree to the image of all im-

---

108. From the point of view of dematerialization, even if all naturalism in the icon is eliminated, specific difficulties exist for *sculptural* images, which in principle can be allowed on the basis of the general decrees of the Seventh Ecumenical Council and which from ancient times have predominated in the practice of the western church, though they were never excluded in the eastern church, in Orthodoxy. First of all there is the fact that sculpture, in any event, has to do with three dimensions, from which iconography liberates itself by planar imagery. In addition, the very palpability of the forms is already naturalistic, and this feature is intensified when the statues are portrayed as wearing garments. Nevertheless, sculpture too, without losing its three-dimensionality, can find in its artistic resources the possibility of idealizing images, which liberates them from the fleshliness of naturalism. We find this already accomplished, in its peculiar manner, in the art of antiquity, and to an even greater extent in medieval Christian art; and of course this is not excluded for our contemporary age either.

109. Catholic in the sense of sobornost. — Trans.

ages — to the portrayal of Christ, whether on a religious picture or on an icon. In portraying any human person we inevitably confine ourselves to the periphery of the spirit, to the outer coverings of the latter, which, though revealing the spirit to some extent, are powerless to exhaust its depths; in the portrayal of Christ we have the same thing, but to a degree that surpasses all understanding. One can say that no portrayal of Christ, however powerful, sincere, and skillful, can come even remotely close to completely fulfilling its task, to revealing the Divine spirit of the hypostatic God the Word. In the first case, that of the human portrait, we stand before the unfathomability and therefore the transcendence of all creaturely spirits, who are immanently revealed in life. Here we have the chasm that separates God and man, the Creator and creation, the Divine spirit and the creaturely spirit. From this one can by no means draw the conclusion that Christ's Divinity is, in general, unportrayable. If one did draw such a conclusion it would then be necessary to conclude that the icon of Christ is impossible and that the iconoclasts were therefore right. No, Christ *is portrayable* in His divine-human essence and therefore He *can be portrayed*, but He *cannot be portrayed* in an absolute and exhaustive manner. He is portrayed, so to speak, in His appearances, in the same way that Moses saw *God's back parts* but not His face (Exod. 33:23). Nevertheless, this too was a genuine theophany, after which Moses' face shone (34:35). Christ's portrayal too can be a true icon of Christ (or at least a religious picture from His life). But if this is to be accomplished, the appearance must be correlated with the *One Appearing*. But this means that this appearance must be named. Therefore the naming, the inscription of the Name, constitutes an essential element of the portrayal. It is the name-subject to which the predicate, i.e., the image, refers. The icon as a whole is held together by the naming, by the copula *is*; this portrayal *is* Christ; it belongs to Christ. It is this mute, indicative *is* that actualizes the iconicity in the icon. There can be an indeterminate number of artistic-symbolic predicates, i.e., portrayals, for human art is always seeking to embody the image of Christ, but in all these portrayals there lives one Name: all the predicates refer to one subject and are united with the latter by the copula *is*.

Let us remember that the icon contains an antinomy. This antinomy does not consist in God being unportrayable and only man being portrayable, as the theology of the seventh to ninth centuries held. These propositions are not correlative, and it is impossible to prove the legitimacy of the icon on their basis. The actual (sophiological) antinomy that is contained in the icon consists in the fact that God, who is revealed in creation and has His proper image in the latter, remains, as the Creator, transcendent for creation, inaccessible for creation in the depths of His being. The revelation is true and real, but it is not exhaustive; the images are inseparable from the Proto-image but inexorably differ from it. This antinomy is livingly resolved in becoming, in process: the life of the creature contains the ongoing revelation of the Creator; it contains creaturely eternity in its participation in Divine eternity, in deification. In iconography this antinomy is resolved in the naming of icons, in the unification of name and image. An icon is a named image, a *word-image*, a *name-image*.

From this it is clear how closely and indissolubly iconology is connected with onomatology, how closely icon veneration is connected with onomatodoxy, and the icon itself with the Name. But the theological doctrine of the Name of God had not yet arisen at the time of the Seventh Ecumenical Council, and for this reason alone the dogma of icon veneration could not have reached completion at that time. But the question of the dogma of the Name has been posed in our time,[110] and the two dogmas — of icon and Name, of image and Proto-image — are inseparably interwoven in contemporary theology.[111]

A proper name, in contrast to "common" nouns, expresses in general not a property but an entity, not a predicate but a subject. A proper name is the verbal icon of a hypostasis, of a person, while all its images are different predicates of it. From this follows the necessity of naming every picture in general, or at least every portrait. The Name Jesus is the pre-eternal icon of His hypostasis, which itself is the hypostatic image of

110. Bulgakov is referring to the Imiaslavie controversy. See Appendix to Translator's Introduction. — Trans.

111. To explore the theology of the name is not the purpose of the present essay. To the extent it is necessary to discuss some of its elements, I rely on the conclusions of my (unpublished) work on the Name of God together with the general teaching about word and name. [The second part of the present volume, "The Name of God," is a chapter of this "unpublished" work. — Trans.]

the Father. The Divine Name Jesus expresses the ineffable person of the Lord, of the Father in the Son through the Holy Spirit, and in this sense the Name Jesus is inseparable from the Lord's being, and in it the Lord Himself is present by virtue of the *connection* between the image and the Proto-image (though the identity of the two does not follow from this). Therefore the naming of an image is a kind of consecration of it to the Proto-image, an essential assimilation of it to the Proto-image, as well as its overshadowing by the Proto-image, the realization of its idea, the actualization of the image.

Of course, such naming in and of itself in this sense can have different degrees of reality and power — ranging from subjective pretension to a certain essentiality. There is a whole range of nuances between pretentious daubing, which masks itself with some loud name, and the greatest intensity of art that aspires to communicate to the image maximal saturation with reality, to give the portrait its own life by means of artistic magic. (Examples of this are Leonardo da Vinci's "Mona Lisa," which aspires to be, by the will of the artist, not just a portrait but an incarnation; and the demonic reality of Gogol's "Portrait.")[112] In essence, naming is the anchoring of an image to reality, to a certain ontic point.

But is it permissible to apply such audacious naming to the icon of Christ and His life? If one accepted the premises of the doctrine of icons of the eighth to ninth centuries, one would have to answer in the negative, but on the basis of the considerations we have presented above, a completely affirmative answer can be given to this question: yes, it is permissible, because Christ as the God-Man has a human image. In this image He has included His earthly human life and, in and through the latter, *all* human life. For this reason artistic christology must by no means be confined to and exhausted by the Gospel history with its archeology. (This history too has its limits, for within what historical frame can one situate the portrayal of the Lord's Transfiguration, the Ascension, the walking on water, the temptation in the wilderness, the raising of Lazarus or the daughter of Jairus, and so on?) Strictly speaking, the Gospel history as

---

112. A reference to Nikolai Gogol's story (published in 1835) about a terrifyingly life-like portrait. — Trans.

such represents in general only one of the possibilities of the artistic portrayal of Christ. The religious art of the past and present (and of course of the future), not confining itself to this frame, portrays Christ in His humanity in our life as well. And of course it is correct in doing so. The right to do so is given to man by the in-humanized Christ Himself, who lives in His humanity. The portrayal of Christ in humanity is an inexhaustible theme of artistic piety and creative contemplation; it is artistic thought about Christ, christology in images, which is just as necessary as christology in words and ideas.

However, in the naming of icons of Christ, in this anchoring of the image to the Proto-image, we distinguish two possibilities: that of nature and that of grace. Every human naming of an icon or of a picture, no matter how grounded and sincere it is, inevitably remains only *human;* in other words, it is, in a certain measure, subjective and anthropomorphic, remaining more a desire and a thought than a reality. Man does not have the power to impart to naming the force of Divine reality; this can be done only by the Church, which names icons by the power of the Holy Spirit, and this is the *sanctification* of icons. An icon fully becomes an icon only when it is sanctified. Sanctification places an impassable boundary between a mere religious picture, no matter how sublime it may be in its religious content and artistic achievement, and an icon, however modest it might be in this respect. Sanctification is a sacramental rite of the Church in which "this icon is sanctified by the grace of the Holy Spirit";[113] the power of this rite or its content consists in the act of ecclesial naming, which is precisely contained in the sanctification. The sanctification is the ecclesial identification of the image with the Proto-image, which is accomplished through the gracious and efficacious naming of the icon.

Therefore, it is necessary to distinguish the ordinary human naming of a religious picture or icon from its ecclesial naming, or sanctification. The naming of an icon is necessary for its completion,[114] as well as for the pos-

---

113. From the Orthodox rite of the blessing and sanctification of icons. — Trans.

114. In the patristic literature we repeatedly encounter statements indicating the importance of the naming of icons as a testimony to the connection between image and

sibility of its sanctification. A named but as yet unsanctified icon is only the project of an icon, as it were. And human naming cannot take the place of sanctification, i.e., of ecclesial naming, although this was believed at the time of the Seventh Ecumenical Council and certain adherents of onoma-todoxy affirm this even today (believing that this lends an even greater glorification to the Name Jesus). The awareness of the necessity of sanctification was not immediately reflected in the practice of icon veneration in the form of different rites of sanctification for different icons, and, what is particularly interesting, the Seventh Ecumenical Council did not yet know the special sanctification of icons.[115] The later practice, which established the

---

proto-image, though nowhere does this idea receive dogmatic clarity. Here is what Theodore the Studite writes: "By nature Christ is different from His image, though according to their inseparable naming they are one and the same" (*Works*, I, p. 127). "A name is the name of that which is called by it, and as if a certain natural image of the object which bears it: in them the unity of veneration is inseparable" (p. 129). "The resemblance of the proto-image and the image is indicated only with respect to the name; equally [affirmed] is the identity of veneration, and not of matter" (p. 141). "The icon of Christ, as well as that of the Theotokos, are called by the same Names as Christ and the Theotokos; therefore, those who demand the denial of icons also demand the denial of the one whose icon it is. . . . The image and its proto-image are characterized by the fact that the image and icon are called by the name of the proto-image, and if the one is denied, the other is denied too, since they exist together" (*Works*, II, p. 362, letter XXI). In addition, this is what we find in Patriarch Nicephoros (*Works*, I, p. 270): "Christ, our God, having become man, received a name that designates both of the united natures, both the sanctifying Divinity and the sanctified humanity, so that one word designates the dyad of the united natures as well as the hypostatic union from them of one person."

115. See Act 6, pp. 235-36. Bishop Gregory read the following objection of the iconoclasts: "And there is also no holy prayer sanctifying icons that could transform them from ordinary objects into holy ones; instead, they permanently remain ordinary things without any special meaning except that which the painter communicated to them." The response read by deacon Epiphanius contains a recognition of this fact: "Over many such objects which we recognize as holy no holy prayer is read because, by their very name, they are full of holiness and grace. Therefore, we regard such objects as worthy of veneration and kiss them. This goes for the image of the painted cross . . . as well as for icons: in designating the icon by a particular name, we refer its honor to the proto-image; in kissing it and reverently bowing down before it, we receive sanctification. The same thing holds for holy vessels. Therefore [concludes the counter-objection] either the iconoclasts must recognize all these things as ordinary and not worthy of honor, since they 'do not

necessity of icon sanctification,[116] made up for the incompleteness of the Council's decree, which, since it did not know sanctification, did not distinguish holy icons from all other religious pictures. Sanctification also has significance for the dogmatic doctrine of icon veneration, which we will now explore.

7. The Veneration of Icons

One of the most difficult questions in the doctrine of icons is that of their veneration, i.e., of their iconicity, but this question was left unresolved in the eighth and ninth centuries. What are the limits of this veneration and its true foundations? What fundamentally distinguishes the icon from the Holy Gifts of the Eucharist on the one hand and from idol images on the other?

As we already know, holy naming is necessary for the iconicity of an icon, and this naming is sanctification. Of course, this naming is connected with the image, which in a certain sense is also a hieroglyph of the name. There could not be an icon that consists solely of the inscription of the name: the name is correlative with its bearer and the naming of the

---

have a holy prayer that sanctifies them,' or they must recognize holy icons too as holy and sacred and worthy of veneration."

116. At the present time this practice is common to both the eastern and the western churches. In the Russian Church the rite of icon sanctification, besides the appropriate prayers, also necessarily includes sprinkling with holy water with the pronouncement of words of blessing (we have this in the Catholic *rituale* too); in the Greek Church the sprinkling with holy water is replaced by the anointing of icons with holy myrrh, or in the most recent practice the icon is kept for forty days in the church and after blessing by the priest is handed over to the faithful. However, in the most recent edition (1800) of the Greek Pidalion it is established, with reference to the Seventh Ecumenical Council (see above), that for icons inscription alone is sufficient and sanctification (which is regarded as a Latin custom) is not required (see S. V. Troitsky, *Ob imenakh Bozhiikh i imiabozhnikakh* [On the names of God and the Name-of-Godders] [St. Petersburg], pp. 129-35). But this false opinion, which even within the Greek Church itself was incapable of abolishing the sanctification of icons, was a result of the Greeks getting carried away in the polemic with the Catholics, and of course it does not have any dogmatic significance.

icon is correlative with the content of the image. But holy naming, or sanctification, has reality in a double sense: it not only affirms a certain identity of image and proto-image in relation to its ideal thought-image or form (which is usually called "resemblance"), but it also imparts to this image a certain life, realizes it. It enables the image to participate in the being of the proto-image; it makes the icon the place of the proto-image's special, gracious presence; it *identifies* the image with the proto-image in a certain manner. Now it is necessary for us to find the dogmatic measure of this identification and with that measure to more precisely determine and delimit it. What is clear to us, first of all, is the negative limit that distinguishes an icon in the precise sense, i.e., a named sanctified image, from an unsanctified image, or a religious picture. Of course, it cannot be denied that even such pictures, in and of themselves, are sacred and worthy of veneration to some extent (as it was recognized in the sixth act of the Seventh Ecumenical Council). The image as such is correlative with the proto-image and is sanctified by it. Thanks to this relation of the image to the proto-image, it possesses a certain *natural power*. Such power is clearly possessed by certain sacred pictures that decorate the interiors of churches; these pictures do not have the significance of icons and they are not venerated like icons (by the placing of candles and kissing). To a lesser extent this power is also possessed by pictures *outside* of churches that have a sacred content. It is possible that, in certain cases, such pictures had this power to a greater extent in the period when the Church had not yet established express sanctification and therefore connected the whole power of iconicity with the content of images (we find this in the epoch of the Seventh Ecumenical Council). At that time icons were directly sanctified by the reception of the Church, by virtue of the efficacy of the image itself and by the hieroglyph of the name with the *direct* power of the latter.[117] However, now, when the boundary of separation has become

117. We have already seen that, at the Seventh Ecumenical Council, as justification that icons are not sanctified, reference was made to "the image of the life-giving cross, though no special prayer is said for its sanctification" (Acts of the Council, p. 235). Evidently the iconoclasts too (though inconsistently, of course) recognized the Holy Cross as worthy of veneration, and this too without sanctification. Below we will touch upon the question of the cross in more detail. It is true that the sign of the cross as such pos-

84

clearly manifest and along with the image we have a special sanctification of the icon and know the power of this sanctification, it is not possible to erase or blur this boundary. And therefore we must say that *not* every image, *not* every icon, possesses the power of iconicity; only sanctified icons possess this power, and therefore it is *not possible* to venerate unsanctified icons in the same way one venerates sanctified icons.

The distinction between a natural image and a sanctified image, between a religious picture and an icon, nevertheless remains qualitative in character. Sanctification mysteriously changes the nature of the icon, imparts meaning and power to it, gives it a special relation to the proto-image of the kind that the image as such does not have solely by virtue of natural connection with the proto-image. This act of sanctification can be expressed as follows: the sanctified icon becomes the place of *the presence in the image of the One who is imaged,* and in this sense the sanctified icon boldly identifies itself with Him. The sanctified icon of Christ is, for us, Christ Himself in His image, just as He is also present for us in His Name. The icon is the place of Christ's *appearance,* of our meeting with Him in prayer. In praying before the icon, we pray directly to Him; in kissing it, we kiss Him; in bowing down before it, we bow down before Him. This does not in any way diminish His sitting at the right hand of the Father, or His omnipresence, or His closeness to us in spirit apart from any icon. But He chose to appear to us also in visible form on His holy icon. It is here that there arises before us the question of the interrelation of the icon and the Holy Gifts of the Eucharist, or more precisely the question of the interrelation of the Lord's presence in His icon to His presence in the Holy Gifts. And this question arises in all its acuteness in the theology of the iconoclasts.

As is known, in denying the icon of Christ the iconoclasts opposed to it in the capacity of the only true icon the Holy Gifts, the Eucharistic body and blood of Christ (which is why the sanctification of the Holy Gifts received among the iconoclasts the significance of the sanctification of this

---

sesses immediate holiness, a sanctifying power, though it possesses this power "in the name" of the Holy Trinity, said out loud or implied silently. On the contrary, in the capacity of the icon of the Crucifixion the cross is in fact sanctified, like any other icon.

icon). This erroneous idea[118] was justly refuted by the fathers of the Seventh Ecumenical Council (Acts of the Council, pp. 232-34). Truly, though a certain resemblance can be found between the icon of Christ and the Holy Gifts, this resemblance serves only as a basis for distinguishing them. What they have in common is the fact that, in both the holy icon and in the Holy Gifts, we have appearances of Christ on earth, although these appearances are totally different in character. In contrast to His abiding among His disciples during His life, after His Resurrection and Ascension the Lord only appears to His disciples, and the manner and character of these appearances differ depending on their purpose. The way in which the Lord appeared before the Ascension to the disciples whom He allowed to see and touch His body is different from the way in which He appeared in the heavens to the Apostle Paul, who heard His voice (Acts 9:1-7). And both of these modes of appearance are different from the way in which He appears mysteriously in the Holy Gifts for the communion of the faithful, and all three are different from the way in which He appears in His holy icon so that we may pray to Him.

From the fact that the icon and the Holy Gifts are both equally modes of Christ's appearance, so to speak, it does not by any means follow that these two modes are identical. In the Holy Gifts the Lord is present essentially and really *(praesentia realis)*, though He is present apart from His image, mysteriously. (For that reason, the transformation of the Gifts into an icon of Christ, which we have in the Roman Catholic adoration of the Holy Gifts, is a violent abuse of the latter.) By contrast, in the icon we have Christ's visible image, but without reality, without essential being. The

---

118. This idea is already expressed in the treatise of Constantine Copronim (Patriarch Nicephoros, "Refutation of Mammon," *Works*, II, pp. 100-193): "The bread that we receive is an image *(eikōn)* of His body, manifesting *(morphazon)* His flesh as being transformed into an image *(topon)* of His body." Something similar was also read at the Seventh Ecumenical Council (Act 6, pp. 231-32): "Thus, the holy Eucharist serves as the icon (image) of His life-giving flesh. This icon must be prepared with prayer and reverence. . . . Christ instituted that in (His) image be brought the chosen matter, i.e., the essence of bread not representing the image of man, in order that idolatry not be introduced. Consequently, just as the natural body is holy because it is divinized, so holy too is that which is such by institution, i.e., His holy image, since through sanctification it is divinized by grace."

power of the Holy Gifts consists in their identity and real unity with the Savior's body and, because of the indivisibility of His being, with Him Himself. The power of a holy icon consists in the identity of the thought-image in the icon to its Proto-image, but only as an image, not as a reality. True, in order to be embodied, this image requires matter (board, paints, plates, marble) in which it exists for us. However, the matter does nothing more than receive and give a *place* for the image; it itself is not the image, which is present ideally[119] in the icon, though the latter is a material thing (therefore, when it is erased, the icon becomes void and only the board remains). The only role played by the matter here is that of a means of representation, which is why we can have different types of matter as far as icon creation is concerned. Of course, in the capacity of places of the appearance of Christ, both icons and the Holy Gifts are worthy of veneration (which is why we pray before the Holy Gifts at the liturgy). But this does not abolish the essential difference between them. And one can say (and this is something Roman Catholics do not feel) that one cannot pray to the Holy Gifts in the same way that one prays to an icon. In praying before an icon and contemplating the image, we are ascending in our thought to the Lord Himself, whereas in praying to the Holy Gifts we have before us the Lord Himself as if we no longer require the ascent in our thought toward Him though His image is not present before us. He gives Himself as heavenly food, heavenly bread for partaking and inner union with Him. Therefore, veneration of the Holy Gifts is both greater and less than the veneration of icons, and in general cannot be equated with the latter.

In accordance with this, though we can speak of the presence of the Lord both in the Holy Gifts and in icons, we understand this presence in different senses: in the Holy Gifts His presence becomes efficaciously palpable in the union with Him through communion, while in the icon it is

---

119. The essence of this distinction is not fully captured by the terms of the Seventh Ecumenical Council, *latreia* and *timētikē proskunēsis*. (This problem was never posed in Catholic theology in spite of the widespread practice of *adoratio*.) Thus, a crude mixing was the basis of those superstitious abuses of which the iconoclasts sometimes justly accused the icon venerators, e.g., the accusation that paint was scraped off icons and sprinkled into the holy communion, or that the Holy Gifts were sanctified and placed for communion on icons.

recognized through prayer, where in His icon the Lord approaches the one praying to Him. In accordance with this, the sanctification of the Holy Gifts differs from that of icons not only, so to speak, in its specific weight (for the sanctification of the Holy Gifts is the greatest sacrament, whereas the sanctification of icons is only a sacramental act) but also in its meaning: in the sacrament of the Eucharist the bread and wine are *transmuted* into the very body and blood of Christ, whereas in the sanctification of icons there is absolutely no transmutation of matter or, in general, any change in the essence of the icon. But, in icons, the Church powerfully *identifies* the image with the Proto-image. In this sense one can, perhaps, even speak of the transformation of an image drawn by the human hand into an image that is truly the image of the Proto-image. The "matter" here is not the physical materials used but the image made by human hands. Through sanctification this image becomes one not made by hands; it becomes like the image of the Savior that was imprinted according to His will in the cloth for King Abgar.[120] By virtue of this sanctifying sacramental act, which has its dogmatic foundation in this tradition of the image of Christ not made by hands, we have in the icon a special mode of the appearance of Christ on earth after His Ascension, alongside His mysterious appearance in the Holy Gifts. Apart from the purely spiritual communion with Christ, by the power of the Holy Spirit the Lord offers Himself to be partaken of in the Divine Eucharist and to be seen in His image on the icon, which possesses the special genuineness and efficaciousness of Christ's image.

In the sense of such efficaciousness, every sanctified icon is, in principle, a *miracle-working* one, insofar as it contains the presence of God, even if this presence is not always palpably manifested. And only in the sense of a particular palpable manifestation of this power, which is united with one or another icon by the will of God, are icons glorified as miracle-working. It is natural that in the decree of the Seventh Ecumenical Council, which, as we have seen, did not know the sanctification of icons as a special ac-

---

120. Reference to the legendary "Image of Edessa," an image of Christ "not made by hands." Legend has it to be the first icon, and it is often associated with the Shroud of Turin. — Trans.

complishing act, we do not have a clearly expressed teaching about the *power* of icons. The decree confines itself to indicating the significance of icons with respect to the remembrance of the proto-images and the awakening of love for them.[121] The Council of Trent, as we have noted, underscored to an even greater extent the significance of remembrance while rejecting even more decisively the power of the icon as a place of God's special presence. And this was a step back in the dogma of icon veneration, a step that in essence subverted the latter. It becomes even more significant if we consider the fact that the Council of Trent did not have to concern itself with accusations of idolatry of the sort that the iconoclasts leveled against the orthodox. In any case, on this issue (in contrast to all the other issues, where the Council confirmed with extreme force the entire Medieval Catholic dogmatics) the Council imperceptibly made substantial concessions to the Protestants, thereby weakening icon veneration in the Catholic Church.

In order to deflect completely the accusations of idolatry, the fathers of the Seventh Ecumenical Council sought a dogmatic expression for the special form of icon veneration that would distinguish it from the veneration of God Himself. The dogmatic terms used here were service, *latreia*, with respect to God; and reverent veneration, *timētikē proskunēsis*, with respect to icons. "Kissing, veneration, and reverence, but in no wise that true service which in our faith is appropriate to the divine essence alone ... because the honor bestowed upon the icon refers to its proto-image and one who venerates the icon venerates the hypostasis of the one portrayed on it" (Acts of the Council, p. 285). Therefore, the distinction here is connected with the ideality of the image, in contrast to the reality of the proto-image. However, this consideration can be complemented by the further consideration that the image itself on the icon acquires a certain reality, i.e., that it becomes the place of the gracious presence of Christ, listening to the prayer offered to Him. And precisely this *positively* grounds the "reverent veneration"

---

121. There are certain indirect grounds to conclude that the Council meant a special *power* of icons, namely that the principal analogy given in the decree for the veneration of holy icons indicates the image of the Holy Cross, which has an immediately sanctifying power, "unfathomable and invincible."

(through kissing, bowing, the lighting of candles, censing) that characterizes icons but that is of course impossible in relation to religious pictures or in relation to icons before they are sanctified. Reverent veneration[122] is based on the connection between image and Proto-image, on a certain identity between the two, but the distinction between image and Proto-image limits this veneration, distinguishing it from the veneration of *latreia* offered to the Proto-image itself. The veneration of *latreia* is appropriate to the Holy Gifts too, as the mysterious appearance of the Lord Himself; however, for the sake of accuracy it must be added that, though it was left unarticulated at the Seventh Ecumenical Council, the concept of *latreia* as the veneration of God does admit further definition within its own limits. The *latreia* that is offered to the Holy Gifts is of course nevertheless different from the veneration of the Lord Himself (cf. Matt. 28:17: "And when they saw Him, they worshiped Him"; Rev. 1:7: "Behold, He cometh with clouds; and every eye shall see Him . . . and all kindreds of the earth shall wail because of Him"). However, this distinction lies beyond the doctrine of the icon.

If the correct correlation between image and Proto-image is violated, one gets, on the one hand, merely a religious picture, or a kind of portrait painting of subjectively anthropomorphic character that does not possess objectivity and power, and on the other hand one gets fetishism and superstition bordering on idolatry. The idol can be regarded as a kind of fable-creation in images[123] (according to the Apostle Paul, "we know that an idol

---

122. For Theodore the Studite this relation between image and Proto-image is such that veneration of the image is accomplished relatively *(schētikōs)*, according to unity of naming *(onomatikōs)*, in virtue of resemblance *(omoiomatikōs)*, but not in virtue of essence or nature *(ousiodōs* or *phusikōs)*. Therefore, this relation is a relative, reverent veneration *(schētikē proskunēsis, timētikē)* (*Works*, II, letter 65, to Nacratius, p. 423; letter 85, to Athanasius, p. 446; letter 151, to Severianus, p. 527). In Patriarch Nicephoros we find the following distinction between image and Proto-image: "The icon is a likeness of the proto-image, imprinting in itself by resemblance the external form of that which is portrayed but differing from it, given the distinction of substance, with respect to matter: either the icon is an imitation and reflection of the proto-image, differing from it with respect to substance and material, or it is a work of art, created in imitation of the proto-image but differing from it with respect to substance and matter" (*Works*, II, p. 55).

123. "But the idol is an image of that which does not have actual existence" (*Works*, II, p. 55). Thus, St. Nicephoros limits idols to the domain of fantasies.

is nothing in the world" [1 Cor. 8:4]), but an icon, or any other thing, can become an idol if one has an idolatrous attitude toward it (according to the Apostle John: "Little children, keep yourselves from idols" [1 John 5:21]). We create idols when we understand icons in an erroneous and exaggerated way. In the icon we have a place of God's presence for our prayer to Him, but if we excessively generalize and extend the idea of this presence, freeing it from all limitations, we identify the image with the Proto-image and transform the icon into a fetish, i.e., into a thing that is regarded as being a habitation for God and is thus identified with Him. This leads to superstition and idolatry of the sort the iconoclasts accused the icon venerators of (in certain cases not without foundation).[124] However high a value one places on the icon, its significance is nonetheless limited: i.e., it serves as a place for the meeting in prayer with God. Moreover, such a meeting through the intermediary of the icon is in no wise a necessary condition for prayer; it is only an auxiliary means without which it is still possible to pray. Such, in particular, was the nature of the whole of the Old Testament prayer. Therefore, though by their denial of icons they of course damage the true faith and the fullness of truth, contemporary icon deniers too are not deprived of prayer just because they do not pray before icons. To assert the contrary, to maintain that prayer is impossible without icons, would also be a kind of fetishism and idolatry. Man can address God and commune with Him directly in the spirit, for he is spirit, though an incarnate one, and this spiritual side of prayer constitutes in general a necessary condition for prayer — both in the presence of icons and apart from them.

Thus, the foundation of icon veneration is the *Image of God* that is revealed in creation — in the world and in man — and restored in Christ. Christ is true God and true Man, and the icon of Christ is the one image of God and of Man in the God-Man. That is the foundation of iconography. But the foundation of icon veneration is an efficacious power graciously

124. Such an exaggeration in the identification of image with Proto-image, widespread in that epoch, can be encountered even in Theodore the Studite, who in a letter to John Spapharius (*Works*, II, p. 233) fully approves John's use of an icon of the holy martyr Dimitrius as a baptismal font: "It is clear that the martyr through his image received the infant, since you believed that this was so . . . you have acquired such a godfather, as they say," etc.

communicated to the icon of Christ, which becomes a place of His ideal presence and, in this sense, a living image of Christ. Christ, having departed from the world in the Ascension, has retained a connection with the world and appears in it in a double manner: essentially, though mysteriously, in the Eucharist and ideally in His holy icon. The dogma of icon veneration must be understood in connection with the Eucharistic dogma in the sense that both attest to Christ's living connection with the world, as well as to His real presence in it, and this connection and presence are accomplished in a double manner: in His image and in the matter of His body — in the icon and in the Eucharist.

The possibility of icon creation consists in art whose power has been implanted together with the image of God in man: man is a creative being to whom is given the power to see the heavenly world and to embody in images that which he has seen. And every object of creative activity is an icon of Christ, understood in the widest sense as Christ's countenance[125] in the world, in the events of His human, pan-human life, of Christ in His humanity. The task of the iconographic art is above all and directly representational in character; it is the creation of images. But it cannot limit itself to this, just as art cannot limit itself to this, for its purpose is not only to proclaim to us about the ideal world, about the edenic state of the latter, but also to transform the world, to be projectively[126] active, theurgic. The Divine Eucharist, the transmutation of matter of the world into the body and blood of Christ, has not only a human but also a cosmic significance, and in the Eucharist is accomplished the transformation of the world in the corporeality of its matter on the path to its final transfiguration. In addition, in icon creation that is accompanied by sanctification, by the mysterious identification of the image with the Proto-image, Christ sketches in the world and in man His own image, and in the fullness of time it will shine forth in the world and in man. The Eucharist and the icon have the same meaning and power, insofar as here Christ, having defeated the world and expelled its prince, keeps imprinting His image in the world until it is imaged in all of creation. Thus the icon is not only a salvific fact of

125. "*Lik.*" See note on p. 159. — Trans.
126. See the following note. — Trans.

Divine economy (as Theodore the Studite defines it; see his *Works*, I, p. 125) but also a sketch of the plan of this economy in the world (a "project"[127]). Such is the eschatological meaning of the icon; the substance of this meaning is clear, but its content is difficult to discern. Therefore, those who deny the holy icon thereby diminish the power and effectiveness of the Divine Incarnation and oppose the latter. This is precisely what the holy fathers affirmed with respect to iconoclasm. That is the Church's general and fundamental view of the matter.

8. Different Types of Icons

The dogmatic controversy over icon veneration was concentrated, first of all, on the question of icons of Christ, in connection with which, however, attempts were made to resolve the question of other icons as well. In this sense the decree of the Seventh Ecumenical Council legitimizes not only icons of Christ but also icons of the Mother of God, of angels, and of all the saints. What are the dogmatic foundations for all of these icons? And first of all what are the dogmatic foundations for the icon of the Holy Trinity and in particular for the icon of God the Father, which is legitimized by church practice although it is not considered in the direct decree of the Seventh Ecumenical Council? Is it possible to have an icon of God the Father, Who is revealed only in the other hypostases while Himself remaining transcendent (the "Beginning") even in the interior of the Holy Trinity? It is evident that icons of such content cannot exist separately and independently. Even if the Father can be portrayed, it is only *in relation to* the Son, through the Son and in connection with Him, or alternatively on the icon of the Holy Trinity. If God is sometimes portrayed in the form of an elder, this is an anthropomorphic image of the one personal trihypostatic God (Elohim), and there are no grounds to see here precisely an icon of the Father (in general, pictures of this sort are not even icons but only church frescos).

This anthropomorphicity of the image of God the Creator (and this

127. Following Nikolai Fyodorov, the term "project" came to describe man's efforts to transform the world physically in accordance with God's plan. — Trans.

without any connection with the Divine Incarnation) clearly attests, in and of itself, that the image of God is sketched in man at his creation, or conversely that the human image is an attribute of God. The humanness of the Creator's image attests to the pre-eternal Humanity, or Sophia the Wisdom of God, the eternal Icon of God in God Himself, Who creates the world by means of Her, Wisdom. Therefore the Six Days of creation are, in essence, a sophianic icon. But this idea of the Divinity of the human image is also attested by the direct and indubitable image of God the Father together with the Son on the icon of the Holy Trinity: the Father is portrayed here in the form of an elder. What meaning can we find in this portrayal of the Father in the form of a man in spite of the fact that He was not in-humanized? The simplest explanation (though an obviously insufficient one) is that this is done by attraction, so to speak, to attest the resemblance of the Father and the Son, Who reveals the Father. But this consideration would not in any event justify this in-humanization of the Father on the icon, and if there was nothing more to it, one would have to avoid the icon of the Holy Trinity. But in our opinion there is something more here. This human image of the Father, as in the Six Days, attests that man is created as the living icon of God and that humanity is the direct image of God, as is attested also by the vision of the prophet Daniel (Dan. 7:9) prior to the Divine Incarnation as well as the vision of the prophet Ezekiel (Ezek. 1ff.). However, this Humanity which exists in the Holy Trinity is concretely revealed only in the Son, who already has the individual human image of Jesus, Son of David, Son of Abraham. The Father does not have such a personal image, except through the Son. And only in relation to this image is the first Person of the Holy Trinity portrayed, as the Father of the Son. Strictly speaking, what is portrayed is not the human person of the Father, which does not exist, but Humanity as the image of the Holy Trinity individually assumed by the Son. In this sense one can truly say that the icon of the Father is the portrayal of the Son in the Father, Whom the Son revealed to men. Therefore, even if one can in fact see iconographic "attraction" in the human image of the Father, this "attraction" represents not an external way out of the impasse but its internally justified resolution.

There is another type of icon of the Holy Trinity, i.e., with the portrayal of the theophany to Abraham in the form of three angels. To understand this portrayal it is necessary to remember that the image of the angels is a *human* image, and that the icon of the Holy Trinity in the form of three angels[128] is nevertheless, in spite of the inevitable presence of features that characterize angels, a humanlike portrayal of Divinity. In particular, here too there is a humanlike portrayal of God the Father, in the form of the central angel. It is worthy of note that, although the hypostasis of the Father which is transcendent to the world is portrayed in a human image, we find the hypostatic portrayal of the Holy Spirit in human form neither separately nor even on icons of the Holy Trinity. The only exception is Rublyov's icon, but in this icon the main accent lies not on the personal character of each of the three angels but on their trinitarian correlation: the three are portrayed in unity, not as three separate individuals, with the particular characteristics of the different hypostases being barely sketched. On the icon of the Holy Trinity the Holy Spirit on icons is portrayed only emblematically or allegorically in the form of a dove, or in the form of tongues of fire on the icon of the descent of the Holy Spirit. Meanwhile, the portrayability of the Holy Spirit would appear to be free of the main obstacle that prevents the portrayability of God the Father, namely His transcendence. By contrast, though the Holy Spirit is not inhumanized, He is sent into the world and makes His abode in human beings. How should one understand the fact that there is no icon of the Holy Spirit by Himself? Do we not have His indirect, mediated portrayal in general in the persons of the saints, spirit-bearing men, and first and foremost and in an exclusive sense, in the icon of Her Who is truly the Spirit-bearer after the Annunciation? In the icon of the Mother of God do we not have in a hidden manner an icon of the Third Hypostasis in human form? Nonetheless, no *direct* portrayal of the Third Hypostasis exists; the wisdom of the Church does not permit it: in this respect there is an analogy between the absence of icons of the Holy Spirit and the absence of a proper feast of the Holy Spirit. True, the Orthodox Church celebrates the "Day of the Holy Spirit"[129] the day after Holy Pentecost as the fulfillment of the lat-

---

128. For more detail about this, see my book *Jacob's Ladder*, the chapter on theophanies and angelophanies.

129. In the West this is known as Whit Monday or Pentecost Monday. — Trans.

ter.[130] Being represented symbolically as it were, the Holy Spirit remains in the shadow of the feast of the Pentecost, not even having His own service, this liturgical icon, so to speak. In this mystery of Divine guidance, one can see a similarity with the Old Testament prohibition against icon images. This prohibition signified not the inadmissibility of icons in general but only that the time had not yet come for the appearance of the human form in the God-Man. Does not this prohibition also signify that the revelation of the Holy Spirit is found not in His gifts but in His very hypostasis and that it belongs only to the future age?

Can the holy angels, the bodiless spirits, be portrayed on icons? Though at the Council this question was answered in the affirmative (evidently because the Old Testament permits their portrayal), no dogmatic justification was presented for this.[131] The portrayability of the holy angels is rooted not in their pseudo-corporeality (in general, corporeality is not proper to bodiless spirits) but in their cohumanity. These icons are not portrayals of their nonexistent bodies but symbolic images of their spiri-

---

130. Liturgically the Day of the Holy Spirit is totally analogous to the usual celebrations in memory of the main participants of the celebrated event the day after a feast. Thus, the day after Christmas one celebrates the "synaxis of the Mother of God"; the day after the feast of the Baptism one celebrates the "synaxis of John the Forerunner"; the day after the Annunciation one celebrates the "synaxis of the archangel Gabriel"; the day after the birth of the Theotokos one celebrates the memory of the holy and righteous Joachim and Anna; the day after the Feast of the Presentation of the Lord one celebrates the memory of Simeon the righteous and Anna the Prophetess; and *the day after Pentecost one celebrates the Day of the Holy Spirit*. It is clear that this liturgical juxtaposition diminishes even further the independent significance of this day.

131. In the fifth Act of the Seventh Ecumenical Council an extract from the book of John, bishop of Thessaloniki, was read where he says that the angels are portrayable because they have bodies that are "subtle, airlike and firelike . . . only the Divine essence is bodiless and unportrayable, whereas intelligent creatures are not fully bodiless and invisible the way the Divine essence is." Thus, angels too are "not bodiless" (p. 188) and they are therefore portrayable. This opinion that angels are corporeal, though it was confirmed by Patriarch Tarasios and was not rejected by the Council, remains in essence highly dubious and in any case is not relevant to the Council's decrees. Therefore it is only natural that, even after the Council, Patriarch Nicephoros was compelled to defend the portrayability of angels in an extensive discussion of their unportrayability and portrayability (*Works* II, pp. 110-19).

tual essence, as if a translation of the properties of this essence into the language of forms and colors. Thus, in their meaning, the icons of angels, as well as those of the Holy Trinity and of God the Father in particular, differ from icons of Christ and of the saints by the fact that in them there is no portrayal of the body as the vessel of the spirit but the spirit itself is portrayed in images of the corporeal world. The humanlike portrayals of angels attest to the fact that both angels and man are created in the same image of God; and being connected by this unity of the Proto-image, angels in their cohumanity are portrayed in a humanlike manner, as if borrowing their image from man himself in order to appear to man. The special attributes of angels — wings, circles of fire, etc. — also have a conventionally symbolic (and of course by no means a naturalistic) character and are grounded in Biblical images of the appearances of angels (the vision of the prophet Isaiah [Isa. 6], the vision in Ezekiel [Ezek. 1], the Revelation of John the Divine).

In general the content of icons can in no wise be exhausted by or limited to the "portrayability" of sensuously perceived bodies about which so much was said in the controversies over icon veneration. Such corporeal portrayability is by no means the sole source of the images; the latter could have a spiritually symbolic meaning and therefore another origin. And in this we find revealed once again but from another angle the weak side of the teaching, common to both the defenders and the opponents of icons, that the spirit is unportrayable in images of the human world. On the contrary, besides direct portrayability, the forms and images of this world also possess symbolic meaning. True, the necessary connecting link between the spiritual and corporeal worlds is nonetheless man, who possesses a "portrayable" body as well as a spirit whose image is the body. Therefore it is possible for him to find images for the symbolic representation of spiritual beings who are actually bodiless. Such are the holy angels, who are portrayed in corporeal images in the symbolic but *not* in the descriptive sense (it is this descriptive sense that is imparted to the images by those who attribute subtle, "gaseous" bodies to angels). Such in general is the symbolism of the spiritual world which is portrayed in images and forms of the corporeal world with its space (and its distinctions between "up" and "down," "right" and "left": e.g., "seated at the right hand of the Father"). This symbolism enters into the content of many icons alongside human images and, in general, images of objects of the visible world. Of this sort are many icons that can be defined as dogmatic. They are not mere allegories, though neither are they "descriptive" in character. They are distinguished by a symbolic realism featuring the intergrowth or concretion of image and idea.[132] Such, for example, are the icons of St. Sophia of the Yaroslavl and especially of the Novgorod types (a fiery angel on a throne with the Mother of God on one side and the Forerunner on the other, and the Savior and the noetic heaven above). This type of icon, first of all, is not a theological schema or allegory but a noetic vision, a revelation in artistic and mystical contemplation. Secondly, the fiery angel is therefore not an allegorical but a symbolic image of the pre-eternal Spiritual Humanity in Divinity which is disclosed in the creaturely world in man: in Christ as the God-Man, in the Mother of God and the Forerunner as realizing and representing the peak of humanity, and finally in the angelic world. And the whole composition is the icon of the Wisdom of God, noncreaturely and creaturely, of pre-eternal and created humanity in their unity and connectedness. Of course, it is easy to fall from these vertiginous heights of contemplation into abstract schematism. For symbolism that is insufficiently lived and sincere sometimes becomes, wholly or in part, an allegorism or schematism analogously to how realism of representation can become naturalism. Both allegorism and naturalism are phenomena of decadence in iconography; however, they are connected not with the essence of the icon but with the ineptitude of its creators. Here it is self-evident that holy naming, accomplished through icon sanctification, retains in all these icons the same significance as in the icons of Christ and of the saints.

The necessity of such dogmatic icons is sufficiently justified by their origin: their inspiration is engendered in visions of Divinity, in reflection on Divine things. And is it possible to extinguish the spirit and to nullify prophecy? Do we not find a response to this in Moses' words addressed to

---

132. As John of Damascus says (*Third Oration*, XXIV, p. 403), spiritual beings are "portrayable bodily but in such a way that the bodily image demonstrates a certain bodiless and mental contemplation."

Joshua the son of Nun, who said to the prophet: "My lord Moses, forbid them [from prophesying]"? Moses' answer was: "Enviest thou for my sake? would God that all the Lord's people were prophets, and that the Lord would send the Holy Spirit upon them!" (Num. 11:28-29).[133] Another question must also be resolved in connection with this: Can *new icons* with dogmatic content or *new types* of already existing icons arise even at the present time, or are the possibilities of the icon limited to and exhausted by the existing iconographic canon, which it is necessary to observe in the "Old Believer" manner? There is no doubt about the answer to this question: yes, *they can*. For God does not give the Spirit by measure and the Church is never deprived of the Spirit, the Church which is equal to herself in all the epochs of her existence. This does not mean, of course, that it is permissible to invent all sorts of icons without any connection to tradition, not taking into account or (which is especially common among us) simply not knowing the "originals." All movement in church life, as well as in art, is accomplished only under the condition of such a connection and on the basis of it.[134] Novelty in icons must therefore be spiritually compelled by religious contemplation and creatively justified by artistic vision. Therefore, this novelty can be a matter neither of rationalistic allegorism nor of iconographic "daubing," but must represent a union of religious illumination and artistic inspiration, and such a union is, of course, an extremely rare gift. But in the case of such a gift it is fully revealed that iconography is an art — a *religious art*. The service of Andrei Rublyov, who embodies for us the ideal image of the icon painter, as well as the service of all those who follow him on this path, is religious artistry as an express gift of God and a special service to the Church.

Alongside symbolic icons there also exist icons whose foundation is human portrayability and whose content is the representation of saints. The general foundation for the human icon, which was prohibited in the Old Testament but permitted in the New, is that the image of God was re-

133. The King James Version has been slightly modified to conform with the Russian version. — Trans.

134. Thus, in particular, intentional distortion responsibly carried out presupposes complete knowledge and mastery of normal form (both in iconography and in secular art) and is not just an inability to correctly represent form, not just a kind of artistic illiteracy.

stored in the man Christ, Who in His humanity manifested the true human image. And therefore all human images, insofar as they are not darkened by sin, are images of this Image: in all of them is imprinted the same Person; all the icons of saints are, in a certain sense, a multi-personal icon of Christ; "Christ is imaged" (Gal. 4:19)[135] in them. The saints are "gods," as St. John of Damascus indicates.[136] The saints are glorified by virtue of Christ's redemptive sacrifice and by union with Him. It is remarkable that on icons are portrayed and venerated not only New Testament saints but also Old Testament ones, whose portrayal was prohibited in the Old Testament. From the Jews even the place of Moses' burial was deliberately hidden (Deut. 34:6). The saints' human images shined also in the light of Christ's Resurrection and by the power of His in-humanization. And just as it is impossible to separate Christ from His humanity, so we, venerating in the saints the friends of God, also venerate their icons. The icon of a saint is not a photograph, nor in general a naturalistic image in which an instantaneous and external resemblance is sought. It is not even an artistic portrait, whose aim is still to offer a natural image, though an ideal one. This icon portrays a glorified, spirit-bearing saint not as he was on earth but in his glorified, heavenly aura (which, externally, is symbolized by the halo). But since this glorified, spirit-bearing flesh remains transcendent for us and for our vision, the image receives a typological and symbolic character, though it retains certain individual traits of resemblance. It is this stylized image that is fixed in the original, which expresses the type of the image of the saint established in church tradition, his hieroglyph. In this sense the portrait (or picture) of a saint and his icon differ with respect to purpose. The portrait seeks to express his natural individual aspect, whereas the icon seeks to express his supernatural glorified aspect. Here we have the same distinction as between a picture (religious or historical) of Christ and His icon. For full clarity it is necessary to add that icons of the saints portray of course not only their bodies (whose most character-

135. Translated from the Russian Bible. — Trans.

136. *First Oration*, XIX, p. 356. "Thus we portray Christ the King and Lord without depriving Him of His army; and the Lord's army is the saints" (XXI, p. 357). Cf. *Second Oration*, XV, p. 381; *Third Oration*, XXVI, p. 405: "I venerate the saints, slaves by nature, friends and sons by election, and heirs by divine grace."

istic features are usually indicated on the "original") but also their souls, or more precisely bodies animated with souls, for a body without and apart from a spirit living in it does not exist. In the epoch of the struggle for the icon both sides, both the iconoclasts and the icon venerators, converged in recognizing that the spirit is in general unportrayable, and that only the body is portrayable. This idea was applied (pro by one side, contra by the other) to the icon of Christ and thus to the icon of any saint. But just as previously we rejected this idea with reference to the icon of Christ, so now we reject it, on the same grounds, with reference to the icons of saints. It is necessary to overcome and eliminate the prejudice that the spirit is supposedly unportrayable, for the body is precisely the image of the spirit living in it — the body is the spirit's living icon not made by hands. Thus, for example, when we say "the icon of St. Sergius," we do not mean that this is only the icon of his soulless body; we mean, rather, that it is the icon of his integral human image, i.e., of his spirit living in the body. A soulless body is not a body, but a corpse.

Of essential importance for the icons of saints is their naming, through which the image receives its completion (as we indicated above). This naming, expressed externally in the inscription of the name on the icon, is sacramentally accomplished by the Church through the sanctification of the icon, which establishes a special gracious presence of the saint in his icon. For the sanctification of the icons of saints there is a special rite that expresses the dogmatic foundation for the veneration of these icons.

Here it is appropriate to say a few words about the distinction between the icon of a saint and his relics. Both the icon and the relics are places of the special gracious presence of the saint, but they are so in different senses. In the icon the saint is graciously present for the reception of prayer in his image by virtue of his connection and *ideal* identity with the proto-image. By contrast, in his relics the saint is present for the reception of prayer by virtue of a *real* connection of his spirit with his body. Here, strictly speaking, there is no image of the saint, because his remains can be completely deprived of the fullness of the bodily image (even a tiny particle of the holy relic is already equivalent to the whole relic); instead, what is present is the real matter of his body. The power of relics consists in the fact that the body of the saint, embraced by his spirit, retains a connection with the latter even after death, so that in its after-death image this body has the power of immortality and in the image of decomposition and absence of glory it already contains the seeds of future glory. Nevertheless, a relic is not an image or icon of the saint. In a certain sense, a relic is more than an icon, because there can be an indeterminate number of icons of a saint, whereas there is only one relic (although it can be fragmented into pieces). But a relic is also less than the icon, because it does not possess the ideal image of the saint.[137] There exists a certain analogy (though only within certain definite limits) between the relation of the icon of a saint to his relics and the relation of the icon of the Savior to the Holy Gifts (which, as we know, the iconoclasts erroneously took to be His unique icon). The Holy Gifts contain the body and blood of Christ in a hidden manner, i.e., without image (which of course is essential to the icon). Every particle of the Holy Gifts in this sacrament communicates to the communicant the partaking of the body and blood of Christ in the same way that every particle of a holy relic contains the entire relic. But of course remaining in full force is the difference that whereas the body of Christ is offered mystically at all times and on all altars, being limited neither by place nor by time, holy relics exist only in a particular place, cannot be multiplied, and sometimes cannot even be preserved.

A special place among icons belongs to the icon of the Mother of God. The general basis for Her portrayal on an icon is the same as that for the saints: Her icon portrays Christ's saved and redeemed humankind, which is revealed, glorified, and deified in Him. The decree of the Seventh Ecumenical Council did not put any emphasis on the icon of the Mother of God: it is named and enumerated only among and alongside the other icons, and the question of this icon did not receive any special emphasis in the Council's judgment (Acts of the Council, pp. 239-40). Nevertheless, the Church's practice of icon veneration does place a special emphasis on it. First of all, the icon of the Mother of God occupies the first place after the icon of Christ both in the number of its variants and in the particular intensity of its veneration. Here one cannot confine oneself to the same gen-

---

137. See my essay on relics (in ms.). [Translated by B. Jakim in *Relics and Miracles: Two Theological Essays* (Grand Rapids: Eerdmans, 2011). — Trans.]

eral considerations that can be adduced with respect to the icons of saints. The Mother of God belongs, of course, to the saintly humankind of Christ's Church, but She belongs to the Church not just as one of her members but as her Mother and Empress, "more honorable than the cherubim and more glorious beyond compare than the seraphim,"[138] higher than all creation and standing at the head of the latter. Furthermore, the humanity of the Mother of God is also that of Her Son from Whom She is inseparable from His birth. This inseparability is expressed in the dominant type of icon of the Mother of God: the portrayal of the Virgin Mary together with the Infant. About this type of icon of the Mother of God it is even difficult to say whether it is an icon of Christ (since His image too is present in it) or of the Mother of God, to whom the icon is directly dedicated. More correctly, what we have here is an icon of Divine Maternity or Divine in-humanization, in which the Word of God receives the Mother of God's human nature and the pre-eternal humanity is united with earthly human nature, Divine Sophia with creaturely Sophia.[139] In *this* sense — in the sense of the union of the Divine and creaturely natures — the icon of the Mother of God with the Infant belongs among the sophianic icons. On the other hand, the Virgin Mary is the holiest vessel of the Holy Spirit, the Spirit-bearer; and the icon of the Mother of God, especially *without* the Infant, is a human image of the Holy Spirit in the sense that, for the Holy Spirit, Her human person is totally transparent. She is not the incarnation of the Holy Spirit but His highest *appearance* in a human person. Finally, Her icon is thereby the icon of the entirety of saintly spirit-bearing humanity, the icon of the Church. This idea is expressed with particular clarity in the Sophia icon of the Kiev type, which depicts the temple of Wisdom with the Mother of God surrounded by the prophets and the apostles, i.e., the Church.

In connection with this image of sophianicity in the icon of the Mother of God there is another important variant of this type, namely Her cosmic

---

138. From an Orthodox hymn in honor of the Theotokos. — Trans.

139. Does this not constitute the hidden meaning of that Church custom according to which the "local" icons in the iconostasis always unite the image of the Savior (on the right) with that of the Mother of God (on the left)?

icon, in which the sophianicity of all creation is portrayed through and in the person of the Mother of God: these are icons of the Mother of God with cosmic attributes ("It is worthy," "the Burning Bush," "the Theotokos of the meadows," which hung in the cell of Starets Amvrosii,[140] "In Thee rejoices," etc.). But even with this sophianic, pan-human, and cosmic significance[141] of the portrayal of the Mother of God on the icon, it retains a personal character: this is an icon not only of the Empress of heaven and earth and all creation, but also of the Virgin Mary, Who has a definite personal character and Her personal destiny on earth (which is clearly manifested on icons of feasts of the Theotokos). How is it possible to portray this most holy sophianic Being who has Her own human personal character, since, of course, we have no pictures of Her made during Her lifetime, and no such pictures are even mentioned anywhere? In Her humanity the Mother of God is more accessible to portrayal than the God-Man. Her icon is naturally warmer in character and less conventionally hieroglyphic than that of the Savior. But, of course, Her person too cannot be conveyed by means of naturalistic representation. The icon of the Mother of God is a vision that is given to the icon painter's spiritual insight, but it is not given uniquely to any individual master; rather, it is given in the Church, in the Church tradition.[142] Having arisen mysteriously, these images live in the iconographic canon as certain guiding types in which the icon painter sees also his own vision, expressing it in his *own* execution of the established original. In the church iconography of the Mother of God there is absolutely no place for the portrayal of any *woman* in her natural image, however beautiful the latter might be. This is a sin of western iconography even in its best examples, which sometimes appear to portray something like the "beautiful lady."[143] Of course, in the beauty and purity of a maiden's or woman's face the iconographic artist can have glimpses of individual fea-

140. Starets Amvrosy (1812-1891) was a great elder of the Optina Monastery. — Trans.

141. For a dogmatic development of these ideas, see my book *The Burning Bush* (The Orthodox Doctrine of the Mother of God).

142. Tradition attributes the first icon of the Mother of God to the Evangelist Luke, who evidently drew a verbal icon of Her in his Gospel.

143. A mystical-erotic figure in the poetry of Alexander Blok. — Trans.

tures of the Heavenly Countenance which he seeks to express in the icon, but nevertheless these are glimpses *through* and *beyond* this earthly countenance. This impression can creatively enrich the artist, but this countenance itself must not appear to him in a naturalistic manner. Therefore, in the icon image of the Ever-Virgin and Mother of God one absolutely does not feel a feminine being, although this does not diminish the presence of the feminine principle in it. For though Her Ever-Virginity is united with the feminine principle, it lies beyond sex in the fleshly sense. Because of this, in the portrayal of the Mother of God there can be no place for sensuousness connected with naturalism, although there must also be no aridity connected with schematism. Icons of the Mother of God must be characterized by a special warmth and beauty: here the language of colors and forms must be especially supple, tender, and rich with nuances. In Her icons the world itself and all of humankind seek to express their beauty with all the richness of their palette. For beauty is a palpable manifestation of the Holy Spirit, which is precisely why the image of the Spirit-bearer is adorned with a special beauty. To this corresponds the diversity and multiformity of the icons of the Mother of God found in the Church, and this diversity and multiformity ceaselessly keep increasing owing to the creation of new types of icons of the Mother of God arising as a result of imperceptible changes of the original, some of which are intentional and some of which are purely accidental. But these icons, becoming "venerated" or being glorified as "miracle-working," lay the foundation for new types. Therefore in the iconography of the Mother of God, in the presence of the richest canon, there is especially noticeable a creative movement that ceaselessly, so to speak, enriches this iconography. And it is appropriate here, with reference to this particular case, to pose a question that we already answered above in a general form: Can there be *new* icons of the Mother of God? The answer here must be even more certain and self-evident than before: yes, *there can be.* But here the requirements of religious art remain unchanged: spiritual insight and artistic contemplation united without separation. It is natural that the icon of the Mother of God gives the most scope for the inspiration of religious artistic skill and mastery. Therefore this icon constitutes the most beloved domain of iconography.

Another question arises on the basis of the aforesaid: although a precise count is impossible here, the general impression cannot be denied that, in general, the "miracle-working" and "revealed" icons of the Mother of God are more numerous and widespread than all other icons, not excluding icons of the Savior. Of course, we cannot explain the will of God revealed here, but we must also not ignore the significance of this fact for us. The Lord appears to us first of all in the Divine Eucharist, which is, of course, the fundamental mode of His abiding with us and more important in this respect than His icon. Further, the Lord is revealed and appears to us in the Holy Gospel, which is His verbal icon, as well as in His Most Holy Name. Therefore His icon is only *one of the modes* of His appearance, a mode to which of course a unique significance should not be attributed and which should not even be regarded as equal to the Eucharist.[144] In the Holy Gifts we have the miracle-working presence of the Lord, and in a certain sense they can in fact be likened to miracle-working icons of the Savior: they are the mode of His descent into the world after the Ascension, a mode indicated by Him Himself. At the same time His Ascension, signifying His departure from the world and His transcendence in relation to the latter, sets a limit to this closeness of His to us in the icon. However, it is precisely in the sense of a special palpability of this closeness to us that an icon is called miracle-working (for in the strict sense the working of miracles is only an external and inconstant manifestation of this closeness). The palpability of Christ's presence in the world in His appearances is therefore distributed doubly: *realiter* in His Eucharistic presence and *idealiter* in the icon, and this separation and distinction is unavoidable. Of course, the Lord is present in His image in every sanctified icon, and this gracious presence of His in the image is what serves as the basis of icon veneration. But the mode and measure of this presence in the icon are nevertheless determined by His transcendence to the world, a transcendence that is not overcome by His ideal presence in His image. He becomes immanent to the world only in the Holy Gifts, in which He descends to earth while remaining in heaven.

---

144. According to a remarkable custom of the Orthodox people, icons are kissed by communicants only prior to communion, not after it (the only exception involves the altar cross, which the priest gives to the faithful to kiss at the end of the liturgy).

This is one side of the question, but there is another side: Why are miracle-working icons of the Mother of God so numerous? And what does this miracle-working character of theirs mean? It expresses a special presence and closeness of the Mother of God, as if She actually dwells in the icon. This does not change the ideal character of the icon and does not transform it into a fetish (in the sense indicated above), but rather imparts to it a special objectivity and power: Her icon becomes not only a place in general of gracious presence for prayer but also an *appearance* of the Mother of God, which is something greater than the former (as is related about the appearances of the Mother of God in the Lives of the Saints). This abundance of the miracle-working icons of the Mother of God is a sign of Her closeness to the world: She lives one life with the world and shares its sorrows. In St. Andrew's Pokrov vision of the Mother of God,[145] She weeps for the world, and in his vision of the heavenly paradise She is absent in the heavens, because for a time She has come down into the world. This closeness corresponds to maternal love, which inheres in the heart of every creature, and this closeness is felt with particular warmth in the veneration of Her icons.

However, the following perplexed question can arise here: Was the Mother of God, raised from the dead by Her Son, not taken up by Him into heaven; and did She not become, like Him, transcendent to the world? But this taking up of the Mother of God signifies not Her departure from the world ("in Thy dormition Thou has not deserted the world," the Church sings) but only Her glorification. Just as Her raising by the Lord is not Her self-resurrection, so the assumption of Her body to heaven is not an ascension, or if it is, it is such in a different sense from the Ascension of Christ. In His Ascension the Lord took Himself up, by the power of God, the power of the Holy Spirit, and He seated Himself at the right hand of the Father as one in the Holy Trinity. By contrast, the Mother of God, sitting at the right hand of the Son, is the glorified creation: She does not abide in the interior of Divinity. She is perfectly deified, communing with Divine life, so that in Her is pre-fulfilled the word: God will be *all in all*, but

---

145. Reference to the Protection of the Mother of God, celebrated on October 1 as one of the twelve great feasts of the Orthodox Church. — Trans.

She remains with the world and in the world: "All of creation rejoices in Thee who art full of grace."[146] Therefore, between the Mother of God and the world there is not only a connection but a direct ontological unity: there is no being closer to the world, no being more cosmic, just as there is no being closer to humanity, more human, than the Most Pure Mother of God. And She manifests this closeness in Her miracle-working icons. The miracle-working icons of saints should be understood in a similar sense. Saints too belong to the creaturely world, though they are now outside the limits of earthly existence; they too belong to humankind and are connected with it by ties of love, and, as friends of God, they intercede for man and manifest to their co-brothers their gracious presence in their venerated icons.

Of course, the boundary between miracle-working and non-miracle-working icons is not absolute but relative; it is not fundamental but only de facto. Every sanctified icon, i.e., every venerable image of a holy person named by the Church, is already an icon and, as such, it is miracle-working. This miracle-working character consists in the gracious presence of the proto-image in the icon, whether the icon is a revealed one or not. One can even say that every icon before which we pray ardently and sincerely, so that the closeness of the one portrayed in it becomes palpable for us, is already miracle-working for us, and the personal chapel of every devout person is full of such miracle-working icons. This can also be said regarding the temple icon for those praying in a given temple. But if this feeling unifies the whole national Church, and this over many centuries, and is intensified by miraculous signs from such an icon, then the whole nation glorifies it as miracle-working.

In the decree of the Seventh Ecumenical Council, as well as in the works of the holy fathers, another meaning of icons is repeatedly indicated, one that is related to narrative and remembrance. There is no doubt that, within certain limits, icons are also religious pictures, which speak by their content and are irreplaceable means for the clear teaching of the truths of the faith (which has a particular significance for lands with a low level of literacy). This is particularly applicable to representations of vari-

---

146. From a hymn to the Mother of God sung in the Liturgy of St. Basil. — Trans.

ous events from both Gospel history and Church history (icons of feasts, icons from the lives of the saints, etc.). It would of course be one-sided and erroneous to reduce to this the *whole* essence of the icon, ignoring its significance for prayer. But once one has in general admitted representational art into the Church, it is impossible to deny to such representational icons the right to exist. For iconography is based on the recognition that Divine being can be portrayed in images of the world. Thus, in addition to sanctification, representation in and of itself can be regarded as a significant element of icons when it serves as testimony about the spiritual world. One can say that, in this latter sense, representation, containing the image itself, is, for the being of the icon, *equivalent* to sanctification insofar as the latter includes naming. On this basis it is possible to have erroneous naming, or sanctification of a false image, and in general not every picture is sanctifiable. Furthermore, there is also a place in the Church for the independent existence of images of Divine life and portrayals of sacred events that are not intended for sanctification and prayer but are nevertheless prepared expressly for the Church, differing from pictures of a secular character, even those with a religious content. This is the wall art that adorns the interiors of churches, representing something like artistic sermons, teachings in colors and forms. Such wall art occupies an intermediate position between iconography (because it is not iconography) and mere religious pictures (because it is intended, if not for prayer, then at least to stimulate reflection on Divine things). In its content this wall art has a wider scope than iconography, because it can include not purely iconographic themes of Biblical or mystical character (the creation of the world, the Fall of man, the Deluge, the wandering of Israel in the wilderness, Christ and the sinning woman, Christ at Martha and Mary's, etc.), events from the history and everyday life of the Church (the ecumenical Councils, the baptism of Russia, etc.), and even religious-cultural and religious-historical themes (e.g., portrayals — though, to be sure, only in church vestibules — of pagan philosophers, "Christians before Christ," i.e., Socrates, Plato, Aristotle, Ptolemy, the Sibyls, etc.). Included here is special church ornamentation of symbolic character (grapevines, fruits, flowers, trees) that has its origin in the Old Testament temple: "And the cedar of the temple within was carved with the *likeness* of cucumbers and open flowers. . . . And he carved *thereon* [on the doors] cherubim and palm trees and open flowers: and covered them with gold fitted upon the carved work" (1 Kings 6:18, 35).[147] Ornamentation as part of church wall art has entered the tradition, but of course not as something fixed and absolute but as a collection of themes. Here we can include stylized pictures of monasteries, churches, and holy places.

The religious landscape painting that we find in some icons deserves a special examination, though on this theme we will limit ourselves to the most general and basic judgments (this aspect of iconography is still awaiting competent religio-artistic investigation). The first impression we get from icon landscape painting is that it has a conventional character and stylized aridity, as if all it is doing is paying its dues to the necessity of representing the required content of the surroundings, not more, with considerations of a decorative-compositional character having the guiding significance here. However, the icon landscape can also have a completely independent significance: it is a kind of icon of nature, an icon not of nature's natural aspect but of its spiritual, sophianic countenance. The character of this landscape painting is subordinate to the main theme of the icon: the landscape enters into the image, is its external continuation and emanation as it were, and in this sense it itself becomes spiritualized. In the icon landscape the dualism of nature and man and the bad dependence of nature on man that nature acquired as a consequence of his Fall (and about which it groans in pain, yearning for its deliverance) are eliminated, and the unity and mutual-penetration of the two are restored. This is not that lyricism of nature which can be expressed in a concentrated manner in a lyrical landscape, where man expresses his mood on a background of corresponding nature. We see this in works of art, and love and value the lyricism of these poems in forms and colors that remind us of Fet.[148] The icon landscape prefers to stay away from lyricism, since the latter is nonetheless in thrall to the subjectivity of "psychologism." It is onto-

147. The King James Version has been modified to conform with the Russian version. The italics are, of course, Bulgakov's. — Trans.

148. Afanasy Fet (1820-1892), a Russian poet known for his lyrical nature poetry. — Trans.

logical in the sense that it expresses the humanity of nature as well as the naturality of man. The mountain of the Transfiguration belongs to the portrayal of the Transfiguration not only as an external background but as an integral part of this mystical event, for it too is transfigured together with the Savior; likewise, the Jordan in icons of the Baptism is not only the place of baptism but also an image of the "Jordan" water of baptism, i.e., of the transfigured water of the future age. And one can say that the sanctification of such an icon, which represents not only a person but also nature, applies to the landscape as well, giving it the possibility of being an icon of the natural world of the future age. This character is particularly evident in icon images of the "cosmos" (in the descent of the Holy Spirit and other icons), of the earth, sun, moon, fire, water, etc. And insofar as the landscape is portrayed not on icons but in church wall art, it shares the general character of this wall art: though not sanctified, it is nevertheless a sacred image of nature, an icon of the world.

Now let us briefly touch upon the image of the *cross*. We have already seen that the portrayability of the cross was not disputed even by the iconoclasts,[149] and it was also confirmed by the decree of the Seventh Ecumenical Council in the capacity of the general foundation and example of icon veneration: "Holy and honorable icons should be offered [for veneration] in exactly the same way as the image of the Holy and Life-giving Cross" (Acts of the Council, p. 285). Furthermore, in Act 6 we find the following thought: "though no prayer is stipulated for its sanctification,[150] the image of the Life-giving Cross is judged by us to be worthy of veneration and serves for us as a sufficient means to attain sanctification" (Acts of the Council, p. 235). One can distinguish the cross as the icon of the crucifixion from the cross as the sign of the cross. In the first case the cross is not distinguished from the icon, and in this sense (though only in this sense) can one say together with Patriarch Nicephoros that "the cross exists because of the icon and not conversely that the icon exists because of the im-

---

149. Constantine Copronim: "We venerate the image of the cross for the sake of the One crucified on it" (Patriarch Nicephoros, *Works*, II, p. 173).

150. This attitude of the Seventh Ecumenical Council toward the sanctification of icons was examined above. Let us add that the Church has special rites of sanctification for altar crosses, neck crosses, and those erected on churches.

age of the cross."[151] The cross differs from other icons by the fact that it is not only the icon of Christ's crucifixion, not only the symbol of His Passion, but also something that has independent significance in that it "bears the image of the Holy Trinity, is an emblem of the Latter."[152] The cross, being the image of sacrificial self-renouncing love in the Holy Trinity, is also the sign of God's love for the world, of the Passion (the Crucifixion). The cross as an icon is either the icon of Christ's Passion (the Crucifixion) or a metaphysical icon, the icon of "the unfathomable and divine power of the Holy and Life-giving Cross."

Without going deep into the theology of the cross, let us note a fundamental characteristic that truly distinguishes the cross from other icons and gives it immediate power. As an icon the cross is not yet venerated prior to sanctification, though it is honored. But the cross is also the sign of the cross, which we make in the air, over ourselves and over others, and this sign of the cross, united with the Name of God pronounced or even only implied, has immediate sanctifying power. Such is the theology, first of all, of bishops and priests, and then offered to all Christians (for example, a mother baptizing her infant). The sign of the cross is a kind of thought-icon, possessing and providing immediate sanctification. And this power of the cross as a sign is religiously self-evident. It constitutes the reason why the veneration of the cross is preserved even among iconoclasts, ancient and modern; for example, even among extreme Protestants who have expelled all icons, the cross remains on their churches, inside their churches, and sometimes even in the external form of the church building. The same sign of the cross is contained in the structural form of our bodies, which is yet another indication of the image of God in

151. *Works*, II, p. 178. But it is not possible for us to agree, at least in such a general form, that "an icon representing for us Christ Himself is more worthy of veneration than the cross, which shows the mode of His Passion" (p. 176). It is difficult to compare the degrees of veneration that must be offered to the icon and the cross, though it must be said that the latter is not just a symbol of the Passion.

152. "This sign of the cross is erected in glorification of Thee, God and Father, and Thy consubstantial Son, and Thy co-natural Spirit, and in memory of His most glorious victory over the devil of death and hell and in memory of our deliverance" (from the Rite of Blessing of a Newly Erected Cross). Cf. my essay "Chapters on Trinitarity," in *Pravoslavnaya Mysl'*.

man. And the restoration of the image of God in the fallen Adam was accomplished by the new Adam through the death on the cross, through the appearance of the cross in the Man who was also God. Therefore the image of the cross is not only an object of veneration but also an instrument of sanctification: during the blessing of water, the Holy Cross is immersed in it by making the sign of the cross, and the water is blessed by the priest making the sign of the cross over it; and in general all sacramental acts are performed by making the sign of the cross (the blessing of the Holy Gifts, anointing with holy myrrh and oil, tonsure and the laying on of hands, etc.). In the cross as sign we have a direct unity of symbol and power, its inscription with the name of the Holy Trinity already containing its naming and sanctification. In this sense the cross is the proto-image of the icon, or the seed from which the icon develops. Together with that, it contains an indissoluble unity of external and internal, of power and image; it is a direct symbol of the Divine, for in it the supracreaturely and creaturely principles are united and intergrown. And in this inseparability of these two principles the cross is an image of Sophia, the Wisdom of God, noncreaturely and creaturely, heavenly and earthly; it is an image of the Humanity of the first and of the second Adam. The Sophia of the cross (to which corresponds the Yarsolavl type of Sophia icon) is also the Church, which is one, but heavenly and earthly; and therefore it is natural that the cross adorns the top of the Church, and that every member of the faithful bears the cross over his breast and in his heart. The cross is the sacred hieroglyph of the Divine Sophia-Church, in which the image of the Holy Trinity is imprinted; and it is the sign of our salvation. Therefore the cross truly is the image of all iconicity — it is the *icon of the icon*.

* * *

Iconoclasts like to quote the words of Gregory the Theologian: "It is wrong to confine faith in colors, and not in one's heart, because that which is confined in colors is easily erased and colors are easy to wash away: as for me, I love depth."[153] And it is correct to say that an icon vener-

---

153. *Works*, II, p. 248.

ation that is only external in character is capable of leading to superstition and to an imperceptible idolatry. It is not icon veneration that constitutes the central nerve of a man's personal religion, but the worship of God in spirit and in truth. In this sense icon veneration belongs not to the center but to the periphery of the worship of God: "faith is contained not in colors but in the heart." However, it is impossible to diminish the significance of the periphery (which is inseparably connected with the center) without crippling, impoverishing, and distorting the worship of God itself, without transforming this worship from something spiritual into something abstract. Man himself is an image of the Image, and he is characterized by imagedness of experience. In this sense, he is an imaging being (*zōon eikonikon*), who not only thinks in images and receives images, but also creates images. This creation is art, whose path is contemplation while its efficacious power is beauty. Art is both knowledge and adornment with beauty; it is beauty permeated with thought. It is an appearance of Sophia, a revelation of Her. And it is not confined to creaturely images; it penetrates also into the Divine world, which, though separated from the creaturely world that was created out of nothing, is also inseparable from the creaturely world in its Divine foundation. The world is full of Divine images, and Divine being too is characterized by images and is therefore portrayable in art. This is the foundation of both iconography and icon veneration. In the struggle for the icon it was a question not of christological dogma and not of the truth of the Incarnation (for even docetism, which nonetheless recognized a certain mode of Christ's appearance, could allow the portrayal of this appearance) but of the co-imagedness of man to God, of the revelation of the Image of God in the image of man. In other words, the icon brings us news not of the opposition but of the union of the divine and creaturely worlds. The icon bears witness about the *sophianicity* of being. Sophia is the Icon of God in God Himself, and every one of our icons is an icon of the Icon. Therefore the dogma of icon veneration is essentially sophiological in character.

1930

Paris, the St. Sergius Theological Institute

The Name of God

Let it be blessed and glorified for ages of ages!

The purpose of the entire preceding discussion[1] was to allow us to achieve a correct and clear formulation of a great and terrible question that has thrust itself with irresistible force into the forefront of Orthodox theologizing: the question of the Name of God, of Its holy mystery. This question has two parts: on the one hand the Name of God is a name that is characterized by all the general features of a name, while on the other hand it possesses certain unique and exclusive features connected with its theophoricity.[2]

Every judgment is a naming, and every judgment is (or, more precisely, potentially is) a name, can become a name. Every predicate that we attribute to Divinity is also a naming of God: Providence, Creator, Good, Eternal, Blessed, Holy, and so on. Pseudo-Dionysius' doctrine of the Divine Names refers precisely to namings. The ineffable, mysterious, unknowable, transcendent essence of God reveals Itself to man in Its properties, which are predicates to the Divine Essence, and as predicates they, becoming in the capacity of subject *pars pro toto* so to speak, become

---

1. The first five chapters of *The Philosophy of the Name.* — Trans.
2. Theophoricity signifies God-bearingness. — Trans.

This essay is the sixth and final chapter of Bulgakov's *The Philosophy of the Name.* — Trans.

Names of God — in the plural. The plural is not accidental here but flows from the essence of the matter. Every subject can have an indeterminate plural number of predicates, or predicative names, and Divinity does not constitute an exception here among the total number of subjects. If God revealed Himself to men "at sundry times and in divers manners"[3] both in images and in a more direct way, these numerous revelations are also Names of God, and the meaning and significance of each of them can be disclosed more fully and deeply (which is what Pseudo-Dionysius does in his treatise). The general character of the predicateness, or attributiveness, does not change here: the noun, the subject, is in general not equal to its predicates; it is revealed in but not exhausted by them; in its ontological nucleus it remains transcendent in relation to them. The noun is something transcendent-immanent, which makes predicateness possible in relation to it as its revelation about itself, its immanent disclosure. Similarly, the subject of all subjects, the subject *kat' exochen*,[4] the basis of all predicateness, the subject of all predicates, Divinity, is revealed as transcendent-immanent; every revelation of God, every theophany, is a new predicate, a new name for the ineffable and unnameable. God reveals Himself to man and in man, and man names God, giving Him names by analogy with how he names those who are like him. Of course, it is God who names Himself in man and through man by His revelation; however, this is accomplished through religious experience, mystical contemplation, philosophical speculation, scientific insight, moral exploit — in short, through human creativeness and life. And it can appear (as it appeared to Feuerbach and to many before him and after him) that man creates God in his own image, as an objective projection of himself. This illusion is possible precisely because the naming of God is accomplished in man and through man; it is his act, an awakening of his theophoric and theophanic potential, a realization of the image of God contained in him, a realization of his primordial divine-humanity.

Strictly speaking, in this too — in its self-revelation through another, in its predicateness — the subject, Divinity, does not differ from any other

---

3. Hebrews 1:1. — Trans.
4. The subject par excellence. — Trans.

subject to which a predicate is attached. For this subject compels the one pronouncing the judgment to speak about it; it speaks in us, in anyone who judges or speaks; it is the revelation of a thing in us and through us. Ontologically, predicateness is based precisely on this possibility of finding all in all, in universality, in global connectedness. But at the same time no subject is exhausted by the given predicate, because, potentially, everything, the whole world, is a predicate for it. Predicates are the names of things, arising in acts of revelation of a thing about itself, in acts of judgment and naming.

The difference between Divinity and the world with its things lies not in this element of transcendence-immanence of every subject in relation to its predicates, but in a metaphysical hierarchy. Divinity's transcendence and the transcendence of a thing in relation to its predicates are of a wholly different order: Divinity is transcendent in relation to the world itself; It is supramundane. Divinity exists in Itself and for Itself; It is absolutely self-sufficient, and Its revelation in the world, expressed in world-creation, is the act of God's unconditional love and condescension, the act of His entering into the creaturely world, of Divine depletion. Thus, what we have here is the absolute revelation in and through the cosmos of the Principle which transcends the cosmos; here the transcendence is not intramundane, not cosmic, expressing the relation of the substance to the attributes, of the subject to the predicates; instead, it is supramundane. What we have here is the relation of "negative" (apophatic) and positive theology: the supramundane Divinity, the Absolute, becomes God for the world and is revealed in the latter. However, this distinction is situated beyond the limits of the relation of predicateness lying at the basis of naming. That God is the Absolute, not subject to any definitions; that He is the absolute NOT, negating all naming — this lies beyond the limits of sentence-judgments, which know only the relation of subject and predicate. But when the Absolute becomes God, It is transcendent-immanent, subject-object, a bearer of predicative connection.

The revelation of God in the world is an act of God, a manifestation of Divine energy: not the essential Divinity, transcendent to the world, but Its energy is what we call God. And if the acts of God in the world and, in particular, in man are revealed (as the wisdom of Pseudo-Dionysius expresses it) as Divine Names, these Names are manifestations of God's energy, which speaks itself, which names itself in man through naming. If, in general, it is not man who names things but they speak themselves through man, and this constitutes the ontologism of the word, then of course *a fortiori* it must be recognized that God, in revealing Himself in the world through man, bears witness about Himself in man's consciousness, names Himself, even if it is with man's lips: the naming is an act of God in man; it is man's answer to this act, a manifestation of Divine energy. This manifestation is both different from this energy and inseparable from it. It is different from this energy because it is actualized in man and by human means. It is inseparably linked with this energy because, according to the general nature of the word, the Divine energy itself speaks about itself in man, is revealed in the word, and the word, the naming of God, turns out to be the human incarnation of this energy as it were. "And the Word was made flesh" receives here an expanded interpretation: the Incarnation of the Word is accomplished not only in the Divine Incarnation of the Lord Jesus Christ but also by the namings that are effected by man in answer to God's act. For this reason alone the Names of God cannot be regarded as purely human creations, as names invented by man. To suppose this to be the case signifies not only a misunderstanding of the nature of the name but also the greatest of blasphemies. And characteristic to the highest degree is the helplessness with which the onomaclasts[5] try to make their psychological understanding of the nature of the word and name agree with that reverence for the Name of God to which they are compelled by their orthodox sense of ecclesial reality or at the very least by external correctness. They are trapped in a confusion between two affirmations: (1) the Name of God, like all names, is given by man and is therefore reducible to letters and sounds, but (2) at the same time It is holy and should be treated with reverence; however, they make not the slightest attempt to clarify the motives behind such reverence or the character of this holiness.

The question of the Divine Names had already been implicitly examined (in connection with other questions) and indirectly resolved by the

---

5. The opponents of Imiaslavie. See the Appendix to the Translator's Introduction.
— Trans.

universal Church at the Seventh Ecumenical Council. The problem of the icon, at least in connection with the portrayal of God, is analogous in many ways to the problem we are examining here. The main difficulty of the question of icons is that the meaning of icon veneration can fluctuate between two equally false and inadmissible extremes: at one extreme we have the understanding of the icon as consisting of purely psychological signs, of human images, to which Divine veneration is nonetheless proffered, resulting in the sin of idolatry, which is what the iconoclasts accused the orthodox of; at the other extreme we have the total divinization of icons, obliterating all differences between the icon and Divinity itself, and this results in the same idolatry, but now aggravated by the denial of the dogma of the inseparability and inconfusibility of the two natures in Christ, for here the Divine swallows up the creaturely and human. The objective foundation for resolving the question of icon veneration could only be the same as that for resolving the question of the nature of the Name of God: the doctrine of the Divine energy and the Incarnation of the Word, which doctrine has an objective, ontological basis in the image and likeness of God in man. The image and likeness is the real foundation of all iconicity realized by man, whether by word or in some other way, i.e., by paints, by a sculptor's chisel, etc. The fact that the image of God is the image of man and thus of the whole world (for the world is man; the macrocosm is the microcosm) is what, in principle, makes possible the icon as originating in theophany, divine revelation: God cannot reveal Himself to stone and in stone but He can reveal Himself to man and in man, and through man (and therefore in stone as well). The Divine energy acting in man unites itself with human energy, becomes incarnate in the latter, resulting in the inseparable and inconfusible union of Divine power and human activity, where the latter is the bearer of Divine power as it were. Therefore the icon is biune and Divine-human in its special sense: it cannot be confused or identified with that which is portrayed, but neither can it be separated from that which is portrayed — it is an antinomy made incarnate, like all unions of the Divine and the creaturely.

It is characteristic and inevitable that in the question of the icon the central significance should have resided in the question of names, and the whole controversy was, implicitly, a controversy over names and their significance, but this was something the disputants did not realize. In fact, in what is the Divine energy in an icon manifested with certainty? In the image? But the image has only an auxiliary character; it cannot be a question of any portrait-type resemblance (which is even impossible with respect to the unportrayable Divinity of the First Hypostasis and the Third Hypostasis, and in essence it is also impossible — though with a different kind of impossibility — with respect to the Savior and the Mother of God). Here the only thing that is necessary is that the requirements (often conventional) of the canon, of the iconographic original, be observed; many pictures have failed to become icons, bearers of Divine power, instead remaining only human psychological documents. The iconicity in the icon is formed by its inscription, by the name given to it, as the focus of the Incarnation of the Word, of Divine revelation. The whole icon is a name that has grown, that is clothed not only in the sounds of the word but also in different auxiliary resources, in colors, forms, images: the picture in the icon is a hieroglyph of the name, which therefore must be stylized in a determinate manner on the basis of the original, and it acquires the significance of a hieroglyphic ABC-book of sacred names. And the requirements of iconography become understandable if one takes into account this hieroglyphic character, this possible extinction of the personal and psychological, this premeditated objectification and schematization. Without names, without the inscriptions and the hieroglyphic character, icons would be totally impossible. This is exactly what is stated in the decree of the Seventh Ecumenical Council: "An icon is like its proto-image not according to essence but only according to name [*kata to onoma*] and according to the position of the portrayed members" (i.e., according to hieroglyphicity, which for its purposes can employ not only schematic portrayal but also intentionally allegorical symbolism: fish, lamb, shepherd, etc.). From this definition there flows not only the filling of the icon with Divine power but also its separateness from this power, its biunity: "The visible icon communes with its proto-image only according to name, not according to essence (*kata to onoma . . . ou kata ousian*)." "The true mind does not recognize anything in the icon except its communion according to name, not according to essence, with the one portrayed on it" (Mansi, III, 241, 244, 258). Therefore, even at that time the iconoclasts were also onomaclasts *(onomatomachoi)*, as Patriarch Nicephoros called them (Mansi, III, 178). Of course, the precision and clarity of these formulas leave nothing to be desired, the central significance of the name in the icon being distinctly highlighted in them. This question is also posed in Theodore the Studite's theologizing about icon veneration.[6]

The aforesaid has referred only to the icons of the Savior, God the Father, the Holy Spirit, and the Holy Trinity. But it is clear that, according to the meaning of the decrees of the Seventh Ecumenical Council, the nature of other holy icons as well — first of the Mother of God and then of the various saints — should be understood in a similar way. The iconography of the Mother of God, which has evolved historically, is characterized by a multiplicity of types or originals, corresponding to the large number of Her icons: the various schemata, which is what these originals are, corre-

---

6. Cf. N. Gross, *St. Theodore the Studite, His Era, Life, and Works* (Kiev, 1907), p. 170: "In the decrees of the iconoclastic council of 753 we find judgments that are astonishingly parallel to our present-day onomaclastic arguments. Here is an example: an icon painter has made an icon and called it Christ, and the name Christ is the name of God and of man. So it follows that the icon is an icon of both God and man and consequently the painter has represented both together the way his weak mind has imagined it: he has portrayed the unportrayable Divinity by the representation of created flesh, or he has fused the inconfusible union and committed the dishonorable error of confusion. In relation to Divinity he has thus committed two blasphemies: portrayability and confusion *(perigraphē te kai sugchusis)*. The same blasphemies are committed by those who venerate icons" (Mansi, 13, 252). We find the following dialogue in the Studite's *First Refutation of the Iconoclasts*: "**Heretic**: 'Should one venerate the inscription or only the image whose name is given in the inscription? And in any case, shouldn't one just venerate one of them, and not both? But which should one venerate?' **Orthodox believer**: 'This question is analogous to asking whether one should venerate the Gospel or the inscription written on it, an image of the cross or that which is written on it. With respect to people, I would add: should one venerate a certain man or his name, for example Peter and Paul? And this can be said about many particular objects of the same kind.... What visible thing is deprived of a name? And how can one separate that which is called [by a certain name] from its proper name in such a way that we venerate one but not the other? These things presuppose one another: a name is the name of the thing that is called by it and a certain natural image as it were of the object that bears it. In them the unity of veneration is without separation'" (*Works of Theodore the Studite* [St. Petersburg, 1907], vol. 1, p. 129). [This note has been shortened. — Trans.]

spond to different themes or events in the portrayal of the Mother of God (as is the case for the Savior too). However, what makes the icon an icon here is not the artistic quality of the drawing or the portrait resemblance (which is clearly something that is not possible) but the name that is applied externally in the form of an inscription. The name establishes the unity of the icon with the One portrayed; it invokes Her power. The name is an essence, or energy, that pours forth onto the icon. Therefore, in the portrayal too, in the drawing for the icon (of course, not for a mere picture), of significance is the schematism of the original, so that the whole icon consists, in essence, of a name, of an inscription — hieroglyphic and literal. At least precisely this is essential; all the rest, i.e., the artistry, has only an auxiliary and secondary significance for the icon — it is the human (and sometimes the all too human) in the divine. As an icon the Sistine Madonna[7] would not differ in any way from the most ordinary work of any Vladimir[8] dauber of icons: the effect produced by its artistic worth, acting upon the human soul, elevating and warming the soul with its artistic qualities, would be exactly similar to that produced, say, by good singing or a church organ, though the thing that would have decisive significance here is not *how* it is played but *what* is played. Meanwhile, of course, the power of grace can be transfigurative: it can transform the image itself, not in the artistic sense but with respect to the spiritual countenances that, generally speaking, iconography seeks to portray, in contrast to ordinary painting. (In the majority of cases, the paintings of the Renaissance, with all their artistic qualities, are totally unworthy of being icons.) To find an artistic equilibrium in the icon, to preserve the iconographic style without betraying the laws of art, is one of the most difficult tasks of icon painting, and this task can be accomplished only through a happy union of art and reverence.

The same thing can be said about icons of saints whose hieroglyphs are given by the "original": of decisive significance here is the naming, lit-

---

7. A famous painting by Raphael considered to be of great religious worth by Bulgakov, who had an intense mystical experience while viewing it. — Trans.

8. Probably a reference to the many reproductions of the icon of the Vladimir Mother of God. — Trans.

eral and symbolic; moreover, there can be different hieroglyphs depending on different aspects of the life of the one portrayed. This hieroglyphic character gives a greater scope to painting, to the element of the picture in general, which receives greater play here since it portrays men who lived and acted in a specific historical context. However, here too, the naturalistic element in psychology and history, no matter how artistically it might be expressed, can turn out to be superfluous and even alien in relation to the iconicity insofar as this element draws undue attention to itself and contradicts the hieroglyphic character of the image, making it a mere picture. The iconographic hieroglyph gives, though only schematically, an image of spiritual completeness rather than an image of becoming, of incompleteness, which historical paintings inevitably convey. Therefore, from the point of view of historical naturalism, the iconographic treatment of the subject is characterized by conventionality, stylization, even falsity, and vice versa. The judgments of Theodore the Studite about icons put special emphasis on the question of the Holy Cross, which is examined in the spirit of the general teaching about icons; i.e., here too, naming has decisive significance: "The cross onto which Christ was raised is called this also because of the significance of the name [*te oemasia tēs prosēgorias*], as well as because of the nature of the life-giving wood. Its image [*to ē ktupoma autou*] is called the cross only because of the significance of the naming, not because of the nature of the life-giving wood, since the image of the cross can be made of different materials. But nevertheless it participates in the name of the proto-image and therefore in the reverence and 'veneration' offered to this name" (Migne, 99, 361, A). Here he evidently has in mind not the image itself of the cross but the crucifix, which came to be indissolubly fused for Christians with the symbol of the cross. Sufficient and essential for the latter would have been not the literal inscription but the hieroglyphic one, i.e., the form itself of the cross embodied in one material or another. The cross is usually depicted in this way where it has an independent significance: on churches, on walls, when making the sign of the cross, when blessing, the sign alone is sufficient; by contrast, the crucifix, besides the appropriate image, also requires an inscription, i.e., it fully merges with the icon.

Thus, if the Name of God is, in a certain sense, the verbal icon of Divinity, then, conversely, the true icon of Divinity is His Name. And there are as many such icons as there are names, and there are as many names as there are namings. In the Old Testament we have a whole series of such names of the Lord obtained from namings: Elohim, Sabaoth, Adonai, Holy, Blessed, All-High, Creator, Good. Each of these names can be made the predicate to the subject — Divinity — and in actual fact each of them was such a predicate; each of them is an imprint of the Name of God in the word, like every icon.

In the problematic of icon veneration there arose not only the question of the meaning of all veneration but also the question of its limits, i.e., of the distinction between icon and non-icon: something can be a non-icon simply because it lacks iconic elements (but in the absolute sense this is impossible; and man — and through him the whole world — bears the image of Divinity; he is a natural icon, a divine symbol, a hieroglyph). In a particular sense, it can encompass chosen persons and even nations. Thus, Israel is repeatedly referred to as bearing the Name of God on its brow, meaning that it is a specially chosen icon of Him. Non-icons can also arise because what we have is more than an icon. What can be more than an icon? That in which is overcome the dualism of the icon, its human and hieroglyphic character, where we have the all-real and most real presence of Divinity. Such are the Holy Gifts of the Eucharist, which are not an icon, but more than an icon, for here we have the real presence of the One portrayed on icons: the Lord Jesus Himself in the form of bread and wine, with His Divine Body and Blood. In the icon we do not have such a swallowing up of the natural by the divine, such a transubstantiation; the icon's nature is heterogeneous in relation to such holiness and it always remains so. It is in this sense that the orthodox refuted the iconoclasts' teaching that the Eucharistic bread and wine is the true icon: the orthodox clarified that what we have here is not an icon but the true Body and Blood of Christ (Mansi, I, 260). But we have a non-icon not only in the unique and exceptional case of the Holy Gifts but also in the case of sanctified and transubstantiated matter: holy water, holy myrrh, holy bread. A pouring forth of the gifts of the Holy Spirit takes place here that we do not find in the case of the sanctification of holy icons; the substance of matter is sanctified here. Not name, not image, not symbolic penetration, but flesh itself, or matter, becomes heterogeneous with respect to itself; it becomes something that belongs to another world, whereas icons belong to our world, or rather they are situated at the intersection of the two worlds. The matter of a holy icon remains identical to itself: the board on which the icon is painted remains a board; the paints remain paints. Their use in the icon imparts to them a special honor or holiness that demands reverence toward them, but this is the result of the image they provide a place for. This image is above them and through them but not in them: it is a thin, barely perceptible layer on them that can be separated from them, although it sanctifies them too. Therefore, among other things, there is a palpable distinction in the venerableness of different icons, and of course there cannot be any analogy here with the holiness of the Holy Gifts or even with the holiness of holy water, etc., in different temples. The Holy Gifts are always equal to themselves and unchanging, so that the very idea of any distinctions between them would be dishonorable. By contrast, it is clear to everyone that icons differ in their efficacious power, having different intensities so to speak, which is expressed in the veneration of icons that are venerable or miracle-working, in the composing of special services for them, and so on. Here one can point to an analogy with the living icon, man, and to the degree of saintliness of different saints: star differs from star in glory. And if we regard the icon as only a place of the presence of God's power, and not this power itself, then we can naturally understand the possibility that icons differ, in principle, not only with respect to their venerableness (which is a subjective consequent) but even with respect to their efficaciousness or holiness (which is an objective ground: even though all icons are holy and, of course, potentially miracle-working, by God's will this character of icons is effectively manifested only in certain definite preindicated cases).

Our path has deviated from the question of the Name of God in the direction of the question of the meaning of icon veneration, but this is not by chance, for it has turned out that, in essence, these two questions are actually the same question. For a holy icon is not just a picture, a human artifact, a photograph; it is also a bearer of God's power and a holy hieroglyph of the Name of God; and the Name itself, the Name of God, is not just a means of designation chosen on the basis of considerations of convenience, not just an empty "symbol" (as they say sometimes, thereby distorting and denigrating the idea of symbols); it is also a Divine icon in word, a holy symbol whose essence consists in its having two natures. The Name of God is not only a means for designating or invoking Divinity but also a verbal icon, and that is why it is holy.

Thus, the Names of God are verbal icons of Divinity; they are an incarnation of Divine energies; they are theophanies, bearing the imprint of Divine revelation. Divine energy and the human power of speech are united here without separation and without confusion, as in the icon: man speaks and names, but that which he names is given and revealed to him. It is this human side of naming that gives skeptical onomaclasm a pretext to regard the Name of God as a human invention, something like an algebraic sign (and in this sense a "symbol"). But in order to be consistent in their point of view, the onomaclasts should take it to the extreme and assert that the content of a word-name is wholly a human affair, an act of human knowledge and totally immanent to the latter. This would signify that God is entirely immanent to the world and man, i.e., that the world and man are god; there would be no difference from Buddhism and contemporary monism, with their hostile attitude toward Christianity's belief in a transcendent Divinity revealed to man. For such a worldview the Name of God expresses concepts and judgments similar to those expressed by any other name, there being no difference here except in content between this Name and other word-names.

One can go even further in this monism and take the point of view of skepticism or even outright atheism. What can the Name of God mean for an atheist? First of all, it clearly *cannot* mean revelation with its own objective content, for no reality corresponding to the Name of God exists for an atheist. For him the Name of God means a certain abstract concept serving to express a certain "transcendental illusion," for which he may or may not have his own theoretical explanations. Here, in any case, the meaning of the Name of God is wholly tied to the subjective human sphere; it is enclosed in and generated by this sphere. If the atheist has a favorable view of this illusion, he interprets it ontologically as an expression of the higher hidden human essence, of Divinity in man, in the spirit of the religion of human Divinity developed by Feuerbach and Comte. If he has an unfavorable view of it, this name for him is nothing more than a phantom, a hallucination, a reverie, a "superstition." In both cases the Name of God is regarded as impotent. Objectively what we have here is lack of religious feeling, a blindness that for one reason or another is incapable of perceiving light. Here, although the atheist's lexicon includes a word for designating Divinity, it does not, strictly speaking, contain the Name of God, which for him (as for the onomaclasts) is a mere sound, a religious emptiness, an acoustic husk without a seed. However, it should be noted that this kind of emptiness exists only in the case of religious equilibrium, i.e., in the case of total blindness, indifference, and stupor. Such a state is so unnatural to human beings that it is for them something wholly exceptional. Much more often does the mask of indifference conceal hostile blasphemy and antagonism toward God, and the Name of God is abused and blasphemed the same way an icon is blasphemed when it is broken into pieces, not in the capacity of a mere board but precisely as an icon. In this case it is no longer possible to speak of emptiness, stupor, and absence of feeling; what we have instead is evil will, malicious blasphemy combined with disbelief. However contradictory such a state might seem, psychologically it is quite a common one. Theomachic blasphemy is not atheism, but antitheism, antagonism toward God; and the Name of God, even the blasphemed Name of God, consumes the blasphemers like a fire. For demons, who, since they belong to the spiritual world, do not have bodies and relative blindness to protect them, the Name of God, despite all their hatred of It, acts like a flame they cannot approach.

Let us take another case of immanentism related to the usage of the Name of God. This is not its religious but its *philosophical* usage, where one has in view the *idea* of God: this is the usage preferred by the philosophical mind however devout it might be, and we find examples of it in Aristotle, Spinoza, and Hegel. For the philosophical reason all problems are immanent to thought, and it encounters God only as an object of thought on the field of thought. Strictly speaking, here one can speak only of the kind of revelation in the immanent which is represented by every noun or subject, and the idea of God, though it differs in content from other ideas, does not differ from them qualitatively. If the Name of God is also an icon of Divinity, it is such only as a natural icon, in the sense that the image of God exists in man and in the world, and this image is known by philosophizing thought, which, however, has inevitable limitations and is characterized by psychologism. However, even the philosophizing reason, attaining at certain heights knowledge of Divinity, begins to apprehend the Latter not only as its own idea or as a problem of thought but as a living and active essence, and for it the Name of God increasingly becomes a Divine power not just subjectively but also objectively. The philosophizing reason is filled with reverence for this Name, which becomes for it an icon not made by hands, though a natural one. One should not forget the correlation that naturally and inevitably exists between philosophy and religion, where the first is only a derivative "superstructure" built on top of the second and differs from it not so much by its object as by its special manner of examining or relating things.

The next question that arises on this path exposes one to great temptation; it is the question of Names of God not in philosophy and not in atheism but in religions — but the religions we have in mind are not the "revealed" ones but the pagan ones. What do these religions signify? A philosophical idea? Clearly not, because they arise in religion and have a significance related to Divine service, to cult. Do they signify nothing, a mere illusion? This is also clearly not the case, because that would contradict everything we know about them: it first of all would contradict the fact that many of the names of the pagan gods clearly retain traces of their naturalistic origin and significance, and secondly it would in general be a religious absurdity that would also make meaningless the specific Biblical understanding of gods which by no means regards them as a mere illusion or their names as empty sounds: "make no mention of the name of other gods, neither let it be heard out of thy mouth" (Exod. 23:13). "And it shall come to pass in that day, saith the Lord of hosts, that I will cut off the names of the idols out of the land, and they shall no more be remembered" (Zech. 13:2). In this Biblical understanding there is as little basis for considering the names of the gods to be a mere illusion as there is for considering the sacrifices offered to idols and the idols themselves to be an empty place. Furthermore, we must take into account the fact that in paganism, in the so-called natural religions, among which there are enormous distinctions and nuances, we are dealing precisely with a religious, prayerful, incantatory usage of the Name of God or of the names of the gods. Sacrifices are carried out in their names, and the sacred hymns are full of these names. Our response to this fact will fundamentally be determined by what we think of pagan religion, of the objective character of its revelation and of the pagan gods (see the appropriate chapter in my *Unfading Light*). That the pagan gods are not an empty place, and that therefore their names have a certain power, is sufficiently attested by that "jealousy" which God, the jealous God, shows in relation to the constant deviations of the Jews toward idolatry. The existence of the nonrevealed religions alongside the revealed one is a providential riddle that remains unsolved even at the present time. But it would be madness and blindness to deny the realism of religion outside of Christianity, and if the falling away into paganism from Christianity is a worship of demons, then an initial abiding in paganism, especially when Christianity is unknown, can represent a natural piety and even a "natural" revelation — of Divine powers, of the sophianicity of the cosmos. For that reason we cannot assert that Zeus, Athena, Apollo, Isis, et al. were mere illusions and fantastic beings, and such an assertion would be even less valid with regard to the elevated veneration of deities in Hinduism (the Vedanta), with regard to Islam (though in relation to Christianity it contains certain anti-Christian and Christomachic elements), or in general with regard to any concrete religion. The names of the gods here are real powers of the revelation of these gods: in each particular case this reality and this revelation can differ in quality — ranging from genuine demonism to elemental naturalism, from orgiastic ecstasy to Socrates' elevated Divine-inspiration. The prophet speaks about this with calm laconic realism: "all people will walk every one in the name of his god, and we will walk in the name of the Lord our God for ever and ever" (Mic. 4:5). The ways of God are unfathomable. One thing does seem certain to us: an onomaclastically skeptical attitude is inapplicable even to the names of the pagan gods.

In agreement with all the preceding clarifications, we must say that such a skeptical attitude is blasphemous and meaningless when applied to the Name of God in revealed religion, in the Old and New Testaments. For if the true God really reveals Himself to men and these revelations are imprinted in the Names of God, how can one admit the blasphemous thought that the Name of God is nothing more than a human invention?

In that case the onomaclasts, in order to be consistent, should return to iconoclasm and, like the Protestants, see in icons nothing more than human illustrations to sacred events. To pray to these illustrations is a form of idolatry for them. But, truly, the Name of God is not only a cognitive, theoretical judgment, but also a means of invoking God in prayer; this Name is a ladder uniting heaven and earth: man addresses God, calls Him, and God hears His Name in these calls. Herein lie the power, holiness, mystery, and tremulous awe of the Name of God, for when we invoke It, we find ourselves before the presence of Divinity, we already have God in His very Name, we create His acoustic icon. If God were remote and alienated from us, if He were "transcendent" and cold like the abstract deity of the deists, then our word that names Him would be theoretical, inefficacious, abstract; it would resemble our abstractions that end with -ity (unity, quality, multiplicity, etc.). And if Divinity were our caprice and illusion, its name would be powerless. But in the Name of God the Lord Himself names Himself in us and through us; in this Name there resound for us the thunders and flash the lightnings of Sinai; there is present the energy of God which (according to the judgment of the Constantinople Council on the occasion of the Palamite disputes) is inseparable from (though not identified with) Divinity Itself. Our sinful indifference, our absentmindedness, our blindness prevent us from becoming fully conscious of the entire majesty of the Name of God: when we utter it, it is as if we are participating in God's power. Onomaclasm is an unconscious, unexamined human-Divinity,[9] or godlessness.

Let us return to the question of the Holy Name of God. In speaking about it to this point, we had in mind only the Divine Names (in the sense of Pseudo-Dionysius), i.e., namings that embody the revelations or properties of Divinity: predicates that were transformed into subjects, became nouns, acquired the substantiality, i.e., the Divine power, necessarily belonging to every Name of God. In *this* sense the *Name of God* is a general category embracing many names, each of which, however, is, in its own place, the Name. The *Name* is the foundation, the ontological place, so to

---

9. A condition (opposite to Divine-humanity) where man tries to set himself up in God's place. — Trans.

speak, for different namings of predicative origin. However, alongside these namings-predicates and the predicative names derived therefrom, conceivable perhaps is the "proper" Name of God, which, like any proper name, is not predicative or does not have such a significance (as was clarified above). It is no longer a crystal of naming but a name as a subject, as a substance for all other namings. It would be brazen to ask what the character of this Name is, whether it is unique. Even when, evidently as a result of misunderstanding, ignorance, or illegitimate curiosity, pious men found worthy of theophanies asked about this Name, they received the answer: "Why do you ask about my Name? It is miraculous." That is the answer received by the forefather of Israel, Jacob who wrestled God, when he asked the One he wrestled about His Name (Gen. 32:27-29). The same answer was received by Manoah from the Angel of God who foretold future events (Judg. 13:17-18). The Divine Name was not told to them. The Name of God, in the proper sense of the word, not as a revelation about God but as a direct power of God, an energy of God emanating from His substantial being, is not something that is present within man: he can find It neither in his thought nor in his life, for It transcends them. Every Name of God, received as a result of Divinity's revelation about Itself, is anthropomorphic in the sense that man in or through himself, as macrocosm or microcosm, knows God's being. Therefore, such names always have a human meaning and significance; they are a projection of the human onto the Divine or, conversely, of the Divine onto the human. This is a legitimate and inevitable anthropomorphism, for man has the image and likeness of God, and the Divine is revealed to him through the human.

That is why all the Names of God written not in capital but in small letters are also human names, are applicable also to man; such, for example, are Lord, Sabaoth, Adonai, Creator, Providence, Father: all of them have a human significance too and they become Divine Names only when they are referred to Divinity as the subject; they are made such by the agglutinating copula. By contrast, a proper name — even if it has a verbal, human origin — cannot be the predicate of anything, but only a subject. And just as man's proper name is his non-pronominal I, so the Name of God is God's **I**, terrible and miraculous. It is perfectly clear that *such* a name, the proper Name of God, or at the very least one of the innumerable veils covering this terrible NAME, can be communicated to man only by revelation; moreover this would have to be a revelation in the proper sense of the word, a communication of the transcendent in the immanent. The bridge through which the transcendent can be revealed without destroying the immanent, without tearing it into shreds, is the word-name, the logos in man. The acoustic mask of the word in this case veils the sun and protects man from being blinded and burned: just as we can look at the sun only through dark glasses, in the same way the NAME of God is hidden from us while being revealed in our human word, in the acoustic word, which turns out to be a certain absolute Icon of the unencompassable unbearable transcendent Name, of the very being of God, of God's **I**.

Here we have to return to a differentiation in the word that is already familiar to us — to the phoneme, morpheme, and syneme.[10] The phoneme corresponds to the paints and board in the icon; the morpheme corresponds to the hieroglyph of the icon's "original," giving the schema of the image; the syneme is the name itself, the power of the image. With respect to the syneme there is another distinction, a twofold one: the distinction between (1) the direct sense of the word as a human word — that which corresponds to the "internal form of the word" (e.g., Jehovah, the "Existent": this is an adjectival form from the verb "to be" and has a corresponding meaning); and (2) the sense of a transfigured, transubstantiated word which has become the Name of God. The difference between the Names of God and the Name of God as such is that, in the Names dwells their independent verbal predicative sense, whereas in the Name this sense is wholly absorbed into the Name, exists only as the Name. In both cases God's grace and power are present, which is why the Name of God is always and everywhere holy and worthy of veneration. But in the first case we have only the gracious sanctification of the element, i.e., of the word; we have, so to speak, the holy word, analogously to how we have holy water, holy blessed bread (the prosphoron or the antidoron[11]), and even holy myrrh; though here the grace of the Holy Spirit descends, nevertheless the

---

10. For Bulgakov the "syneme" is the element of verbal meaning, as opposed to the phoneme, which is the element of verbal sound. — Trans.

11. Types of holy bread distributed during the Orthodox liturgy. — Trans.

element retains its proper nature: it remains holy *water,* holy *bread,* etc. It, this element, is the natural vessel for the reception of the grace of the Holy Spirit, and — what is more — it receives this grace precisely in its substance, as do water, bread, etc. In the second case, where we have the proper Name of God, God's **I**, as it were, in this case the proper nature of the word, its "internal form" or significance, disappears as it were. Jehovah is the Name of God not at all because it means "existent," for the attribute of existence does not yet express God's being in any exclusive sense; rather, it stands here alongside other attributes, or Names. This word makes the Name of God the exclusive presence of God's power in it. One could suppose — of course, purely theoretically — that for the Name of God one of the other Names of Divinity could have been chosen: Elohim, Sabaoth, Creator, Father, etc. (we understand how impossible such a supposition is in the face of the accomplished revelation about His Name that God has given to men, but we are employing this supposition as an auxiliary hypothesis to illustrate our thought); however, once the revelation was accomplished and the Lord declared "I am Jehovah," the independent meaning of the word "existent" dissolved completely and became only a verbal form for receiving the Name of God, for receiving that which, being a word for human reception, is the Super-word for human language. One can say that the word "Existent" no longer has the proper sense it had at the moment when it was chosen for the Name. After this, it becomes a transparent glass that transmits but does not reflect rays of light. If we return to our comparison, we have to say that the proper element of the word was not preserved here the way their proper element is preserved in holy water or holy bread; rather, it was transubstantiated similarly to the way bread and wine are transubstantiated fully and to the end *under the form* of bread and wine. That which had its own elemental character and nature now becomes only "under the form"; it stops being itself, it is transubstantiated to the end. However (to continue this analogy), to go from the bread and wine to the accomplishment of the sacrament it is necessary to have definite, very strictly fixed qualities, which are preserved even when the bread and wine become only their own appearance. So, the word too which served as the matter for the Name of God retains its verbal nature and its meaning. But just as an immeasurable distance exists between these definite and pre-specified qualities of the bread and wine and the Body and Blood of Christ, and this chasm can be overcome only by the miracle of God's grace, so between the meaning of the word "existent" in and of itself (which has long existed and continues to exist in the human lexicon as one of the countless number of words that have their definite proper meaning) and the Name of God *Jehovah,* there lies a chasm that can be overcome only by God's will, unfathomable for us and having the power of absolute revelation. We understand the full audacity of making analogies and comparisons with something so holy as Christ's terrible Mysteries, but it seems to us that we are compelled to do so by the essence of the matter. Since in the sacrament we are always dealing with an absolutely irreducible concrete element, we can speak only of analogies, of explanations based on likening or comparing one miracle of gracious transubstantiation to another.

And in the Name of God we have such a unique *sacrament of the word,* not reducible to anything else; we have its transubstantiation by virtue of which the word chosen to become the Name becomes the verbal throne of the Name of God. It becomes more than an icon: it becomes the temple, the altar, the ark, the Holy of Holies, the place of the presence of God and of the meeting with God. And the Lord commanded that a tabernacle, a "sanctuary," be made "that I may dwell among them" (Exod. 25:8). "And there I will meet with thee, and I will commune with thee from above the mercy seat, from between the two cherubim which are upon the ark of the testimony, of all things which I will give thee in commandment unto the children of Israel" (25:22). This sanctuary, tabernacle, and, later, the temple are made in order that the Name of God dwell in them (about which below). Any stumbling block that might be represented by the idea of the word-icon and by the transubstantiation of the word in the Name of God disappears when we stop regarding the word as a kind of human fabrication, and even one that does not have a natural (let me say: material) character. On the contrary, one must understand and feel that the human word is an element, natural and peculiar, which is accessible to illumination, regeneration, transubstantiation, transfiguration, like all other natural elements, like all other human power and energy.

The word is a symbol, but it is a symbol not in the nihilistic sense of a sign invented by man (as onomaclasts and iconoclasts always understand it) but in the sense of the union of two natures, and therefore in the sense of power and depth. The word is not the only thing that is a symbol; the forces of nature and the natural elements, having become vessels of a different content, of different powers, can also be symbols. It is in this sense (and not in the sense of some allegory) that liturgy is symbolic, that the sacraments are symbolic. And it is in this sense of the co-presence of different natures (the only sense that is worthy of the idea of the symbol) that the inseparable and inconfusible union of God and man in Jesus Christ is the holiest of the symbols, and then the Holy Name of God is the holiest verbal symbol. It is precisely by taking as one's starting point the idea of the symbol and of the symbolic nature of the word that one can understand the symbolic meaning of the Name of God and the real presence in this Name of the Power of God.

This form, this Name uttered in human language, this incarnation of the Name, the verbal Divine-incarnation in the precise sense of the word, could appear only as the result of a special act of God's will, of God's love for man and His condescension, of His voluntary kenosis. Corresponding to the two Testaments, there were two revelations of the Name of God: the Old Testament *Jehovah* was revealed to Moses and the New Testament *Jesus* was revealed to the Virgin Mary, and in Her to all of humankind: these were the two images of the Name of God not made by hands. Let us recall the description of this unique and stupendous event in the Old Testament: "And Moses said unto God, Behold, when I come unto the children of Israel, and shall say unto them, The God of your fathers hath sent me unto you; and they shall say to me, What is his Name? What shall I say unto them? And God said unto Moses, I AM THAT I AM [the Existent]: and he said, Thus shalt thou say unto the children of Israel, I AM [Jehovah, the Existent] hath sent me unto you" (Exod. 3:13-14). "And I appeared unto Abraham, unto Isaac, and unto Jacob, by the Name of God Almighty, but by my Name JEHOVAH was I not known to them" (Exod. 6:3). God communicates as a new revelation His Name, which then is guarded like a terrible Mystery, Holiness, and Power, being known to the high priest alone, who, according to tradition, would utter it on the feast of purification when entering the Holy of Holies to sprinkle sacrificial blood.

For every reverent or even merely attentive and conscientious reader of the Old Testament it must be clear that the expression "Name of God" possesses a completely special and independent significance here. To say that it is only a means of expressing the idea "God" is to say nothing, while manifesting a frivolous and blasphemous attitude toward the Biblical text to the point of an outright distortion of the latter. For even if the verbal equality "the Name of God = God" were true, there would still be the question of the meaning and origin *precisely of such* a descriptive expression. But, of course, this summary characterization is untrue; it can be explained from the desire to look closely into the Biblical text, where different cases and nuances in the usage of the Name of God are completely evident. The first thing that strikes the eyes is cases where the expression "Name of God" can in no wise be interpreted just as a synonym, as a descriptive expression replacing "God," but signifies a special mode of God's presence, of the power of His Name in His Name.

The Name of God is united with and likened to the concept of God's Glory, which even lovers of simplified synonymology cannot refer just to descriptive expressions (Exod. 25:7, 10; Num. 25:19; 1 Kings 13:10-11; Exod. 35:2, 40:5; Sir. 45:3). "And he [Moses] said, I beseech Thee, shew me Thy glory. And He said [the Lord to Moses], I will make all My glory pass before thee, and I will proclaim the Name of Jehovah before thee; and will be gracious to whom I will be gracious, and will shew mercy on whom I will shew mercy" (Exod. 33:18-19). "And the Lord descended in the cloud, and stood with him there, and proclaimed the Name Jehovah" (34:5).[12] Here the appearance of God's Glory and the uttering of the Name of God are juxtaposed as two sides of the theophany, as theophanic energies. This enables us to understand the meaning possessed by the commandment that not only prohibits a nonreverent attitude toward Divinity that is actualized through the word but also expressly protects the holiness of the Name of God, just as the holiness of God's Glory which appeared in the tabernacle of the congregation was expressly protected (as is attested by the story of the "protestant" uprising of Korah, Dathan, and Abiram in Numbers 16).

12. In citing Exodus 33:18-19 and 34:5, I have modified the King James Version to conform with the Russian translation used by Bulgakov. — Trans.

"Thou shalt not take the Name of the Lord thy God in vain; for the Lord will not hold him guiltless that taketh His Name in vain" (Exod. 20:7; with parallels in Lev. 19:12, with a different nuance and a narrower content;[13] Deut. 5:11, which is identical to Exodus; and Prov. 30:9). If we direct our attention to the general context and content of the Decalogue, the specific content of the Third Commandment will become even clearer: after the proclamation of faith in the one true God and the prohibition against idolatry there is established the veneration of the Holy Name, which had just been solemnly revealed and proclaimed on Sinai; and this is followed, in the Fourth Commandment, by the establishment of the holy Sabbath day. We can also refer thereto, for example, the prophet Isaiah's juxtaposition: "For My Name's sake will I defer Mine anger, and for My Glory will I refrain for thee, that I cut thee not off" (48:9).[14]

The expression "Name of God" has a wholly special meaning in connection with the temple and with cult in general. Here there cannot be any question of *pars pro toto*, of directly using this expression instead of "God." No, here the Name of God is taken directly as a real living force, as a Divine energy that abides in the center of the life of the temple. The temple is the dwelling place of the Name of God, and it was built for the Name of God. If we recall what is known about the great reverence felt by the Old Testament Jewry for the sacred tetragrammaton and about the place occupied by the tetragrammaton in the Divine service, about the fact that it represented the heart of the service (since it was proclaimed by the high priest at the most solemn and mysterious moment of the life of the service — dur-

---

13. "And ye shall not swear by My Name falsely, neither shalt thou profane the Name of Thy God" (Lev. 19:12). In paganism too there was sometimes a tendency to avoid saying the names of the gods, here too out of veneration toward them. Thus, for example, in Rome, "the true names of the gods were considered taboo because to disclose these names would be to 'summon' these gods into existence. That is why we are chiefly acquainted with epithets that replace the divine names. Even the city of Rome had a secret name that was used only in cases of the most solemn apostrophes to it. The mystery of this name was guarded so closely that it is now not known to us" (Solomon Reinam, *Orpheus: A Universal History of Religions,* p. 121).

14. The King James Version has been modified to conform with the Russian translation used by Bulgakov. — Trans.

ing the sprinkling of the Holy of Holies with sacrificial blood), we will understand that for the Jews with their religious realism there was never any possibility of conceiving the temple as anything other than the dwelling place of the Name of God, as is attested by the sacred chronicles. As early as Deuteronomy we find Moses' testament: "Then [after they make their dwelling in the promised land] there shall be a place which the Lord your God shall choose to cause His Name to dwell there; thither shall ye bring all that I command you" (Deut. 12:11). The first book of Kings tells about the building of the temple by Solomon. First, before it was built, "the people sacrificed in high places, because there was no house built unto the Name of the Lord, until those days" (3:2). Although David still thought in those terms, it was proclaimed to him through the prophet Nathan that Solomon "shall build an house for My Name" (2 Sam. 7:13); or simply: "He shall build Me an house" (1 Chron. 17:12). The time comes for building it, and Solomon sent to Hiram, king of Tyre, to say: "Thou knowest how that David my father could not build an house unto the Name of the Lord his God for the wars which were about him on every side, until the Lord put them under the soles of his feet. But now the Lord my God hath given me rest on every side, so that there is neither adversary nor evil occurrent. And, behold, I purpose to build an house unto the Name of the Lord my God, as the Lord spake unto David my father, saying, Thy son, whom I will set upon thy throne in thy room, he shall build an house unto My Name" (1 Kings 5:3-5). We find a parallel in the first book of Chronicles, where David himself speaks about building the temple in exactly the same terms as Solomon: "Then he [David] called for Solomon his son, and charged him to build an house for the Lord God of Israel. And David said to Solomon, My son, as for me, it was in my mind to build an house unto the Name of the Lord my God: But the word of the Lord came to me, saying, Thou hast shed blood abundantly, and hast made great wars: thou shalt not build an house unto My Name" (12:6-8). "He [Solomon] shall build an house for My Name. . . . Now, my son, the Lord be with thee; and prosper thou, and build the house of the Lord thy God, as He hath said of thee" (12:10-11). David uses the same expressions when he speaks about this before the gathering of the elders: "But God said unto me, Thou shalt not build an house for My Name, because thou hast been a man of war, and hast shed blood" (28:3). "Solomon thy son, he shall build My house and My courts" (28:6). And then there is this parallel to the story about the sending to Hiram: "Behold, I build an house to the Name of the Lord my God, to dedicate it to Him, and to burn before Him sweet incense" (2 Chron. 2:4), etc. Then the liturgical, or cultic, purpose of this house is defined more precisely: "And the house which I build is great: for great is our God above all gods. But who is able to build Him an house, seeing the heaven and heaven of heavens cannot contain Him? Who am I then, that I should build Him an house, save only to burn sacrifice before Him?" (2:5-6).

Let us now consider the description of the sanctification of the temple. When the priests brought in the ark of the covenant, the Glory of the Lord in the form of a cloud filled the temple: "Then spake Solomon, The Lord said that He would dwell in thick darkness. I have surely built Thee an house to dwell in, a settled place for Thee to abide in for ever" (1 Kings 8:12-13). This is followed by the story of the building of the temple: God said: "Since the day that I brought forth My people Israel out of Egypt, I chose no city out of all the tribes of Israel to build an house, that My Name might be therein [but I chose Jerusalem that My Name might dwell in it]. . . . And it was in the heart of David my father to build an house for the Name of the Lord God of Israel. And the Lord said unto David my father, Whereas it was in thine heart to build an house unto My Name, thou didst well that it was in thine heart. Nevertheless thou shalt not build the house; but thy son . . . shall build the house unto My Name. And the Lord hath performed His word that He spake, and I . . . have built an house for the Name of the Lord God of Israel" (8:16-20).[15] In Solomon's prayer before all

---

15. There is a parallel in 2 Chronicles 6:5-10: "Since the day that I brought forth My people out of the land of Egypt I chose no city among all the tribes of Israel to build an house in, that My Name might be there. . . . But I have chosen Jerusalem, that My Name might be there. . . . Now it was in the heart of David my father to build an house for the name of the Lord God of Israel. But the Lord said to David my father, Forasmuch as it was in thine heart to build an house for My Name, thou didst well in that it was in thine heart: Notwithstanding thou shalt not build the house; but thy son which shall come forth out of thy loins, he shall build the house for My Name. The Lord therefore hath performed His word that He hath spoken: . . . I . . . have built the house for the name of the Lord God of Israel."

the people we also read: "That Thine eyes may be open toward this house night and day, even toward the place of which Thou hast said, My Name shall be there" (8:29); with the parallel: "upon the place whereof Thou hast said that Thou wouldest put Thy Name there" (2 Chron. 6:20); and then he beseeches God to listen to those who come to pray there "to confess Thy Name" (6:24, 26; cf. 6:33, 35). "Moreover concerning a stranger, that is not of Thy people Israel, but cometh out of a far country for Thy Name's sake (for they shall hear of Thy great Name, and of Thy strong hand, and of Thy stretched out arm); when he shall come and pray toward this house; Hear Thou in heaven Thy dwelling place, and do according to all that the stranger calleth to Thee for: that all people of the earth may know Thy Name . . . that they may know that this house, which I have builded, is called by Thy Name" (1 Kings 8:41-43).[16] And later in the same prayer: "and toward the house that I have built for Thy Name" (8:44, cf. 8:48). After the sanctification of the temple there took place God's (second) appearance to Solomon. God said to him: "I have heard thy prayer and thy supplication, that thou hast made before Me: I have hallowed this house, which thou hast built, to put My Name there for ever; and Mine eyes and Mine heart shall be there perpetually" (1 Kings 9:3; cf. 2 Chron. 8:16). Also: "this house, which I have hallowed for My Name" (1 Kings 9:7; cf. 2 Chron. 7:20). Also compare: "And he [Manasseh] built altars in the house of the Lord, of which the Lord said, In Jerusalem will I put My Name" (2 Kings 21:4); cf. "in Jerusalem . . . will I put My Name for ever" (21:7).

Thus, the temple is the dwelling place of the Name of God, the place where this Name is "put forever." Other writers sometimes define the temple as the place that is called by the Name of God. Thus, in Isaiah we have: ". . . to the place of the Name of the Lord of hosts, the mount Zion" (17:7). Also, in Jeremiah we have: "And come and stand before Me in this house,

16. There is a parallel in 2 Chronicles 6:32-33: "Moreover concerning the stranger, which is not of Thy people Israel, but is come from a far country for Thy great Name's sake, and Thy mighty hand, and Thy stretched out arm; if they come and pray in this house; then hear Thou from the heavens, even from Thy dwelling place, and do according to all that the stranger calleth to Thee for; that all people of the earth may know Thy name, and fear Thee, as doth Thy people Israel, and may know that this house which I have built is called by Thy Name."

which is called by My Name, and say, We are delivered to do all these abominations? Is this house, which is called by My Name, become a den of robbers in your eyes? . . . But go ye now unto My place which was in Shiloh, where I set My Name at the first, and see what I did to it for the wickedness of my people Israel. . . . Therefore will I do unto this house, which is called by My Name" (7:10-12, 14).[17]

The texts we have presented attest sufficiently that the expression "Name of God" in connection with the temple is not at all just a replacement for or a synonym of the word "God"; rather, they attest that it has a completely independent meaning and that to negate this meaning is to do violence to the text. What we have here is the express dwelling of the Name of God in the temple, along with the Glory of God, as a power of God, as an energy of God. That there was nothing strange or contradictory in this for the Jewish religious consciousness is already clear from the central significance in the cult that belonged to the solemn proclaiming of the Name of God. This Name was not only proclaimed but also existed as a living energy outside this proclaiming, Its special dwelling place being the temple as the center of the Divine service. (If the voice of skeptical rationalism will say that there cannot be a special dwelling place for the Name of God, since It, as an ideal form, is not associated with any particular place, then one must point out that exactly the same argument is applicable to the temple as the place of the express dwelling of Divinity, God's house, for Divinity is not associated with any particular place. If God's condescension to man that is expressed in theophanies and Divine revelations includes a corresponding anthropomorphism, or anthropologism,

---

17. One can note the following parallels: "But they set their abominations in the house, which is called by My Name, to defile it" (Jer. 32:34); ". . . ye had made a covenant before Me in the house which is called by My Name: But ye turned and polluted My Name" (34:15-16). This idea is expressed with less definiteness by the prophet Ezekiel, when he describes the temple of Jerusalem. After the Glory of God enters the temple, a voice is heard from there: "Son of man, the place of My throne, and the place of the soles of My feet, where I will dwell in the midst of the children of Israel for ever, and My holy Name, shall the house of Israel no more defile. . . . In their setting of their threshold by My thresholds, and their post by My posts, and the wall between Me and them, they have even defiled My holy Name by their abominations . . ." (Ezek. 43:7-8).

and there are no obstacles to regarding the temple as God's house, there are also no obstacles to regarding it as the dwelling place of the Name of God.) The express connection of the temple with the Name of God, a connection that for onomaclasm must appear to be some sort of incomprehensible caprice of language, in fact follows directly from the connection of cultic sacrament and divine service with the Name of God, which is precisely the ladder that raises one from earth to heaven. And therefore one must regard as absolutely reliable and authentic the sacred text's testimony that the Name of God dwelled in the temple.

The understanding of the Name of God as power or energy is also found in a number of texts in which the calling by the Name of God or the presence of this Name is both the sign and the basis of a special chosenness and bestowal of grace. In this sense, God's chosen nation is said to be called by this Name: "And they shall put My Name upon the children of Israel; and I [the Lord] will bless them" (Num. 6:27). "And all people of the earth shall see that thou art called by the Name of the Lord; and they shall be afraid of thee" (Deut. 28:10). "My people, which are called by My Name, shall humble themselves" (2 Chron. 7:14). "Even every one that is called by My Name: for I have created him for My glory, I have formed him; yea, I have made him" (Isa. 43:7). "We are Thine: Thou never barest rule over them; they were not called by Thy Name" (Isa. 63:19). "I am sought of them that asked not for Me; I am found of them that sought Me not: I said, Behold Me, behold Me, unto a nation that was not called by My Name" (Isa. 64:1). "Thou, O Lord, art in the midst of us, and we are called by Thy Name" (Jer. 14:9) "Behold . . . the city which is called by Thy Name . . . defer not, for Thine own sake, O my God: for Thy city and Thy people are called by Thy Name" (Dan. 9:18-19). "Israel and his posterity is called by Thy Name" (Bar. 2:15; cf. 2:26). ". . . and so shall Thy Name nowhere be found but in Israel" (4 Ezra 3:34). Also, from New Testament texts: "and I will write upon him the Name of My God, and the name of the city of My God, which is new Jerusalem, which cometh down out of heaven from My God: and I will write upon him My new Name" (Rev. 3:12). "A Lamb stood on the Mount Sion, and with him an hundred forty and four thousand, having His Father's Name written in their foreheads" (14:1).

In a similar sense, in a number of other texts the expression "Name of

God" is used to mean the power of God: "in all places where I record My Name I will come unto thee, and I will bless thee" (Exod. 20:24). "I send an Angel before thee . . . he will not pardon your transgressions: for My Name is in him" (23:20-21). "Behold, the Name of the Lord cometh from far, burning with his anger" (Isa. 30:27). "So will I make My Holy Name known in the midst of My people Israel; and I will not let them pollute My Holy Name any more: and the heathen shall know that I am the Lord, the Holy One in Israel" (Ezek. 39:7); "and will be jealous for My Holy Name" (39:25); "and My Holy Name, shall the house of Israel no more defile" (43:7). "For from the rising of the sun even unto the going down of the same My Name shall be great among the Gentiles; and in every place incense shall be offered unto My Name, and a pure offering: for My Name shall be great among the heathen, saith the Lord of hosts. . . . My Name is dreadful among the heathen" (Mal. 1:11, 14).

There are numerous cases when the expression "Name of God" is used in the direct and proper sense, sometimes directly having in view the Divine names and sometimes clearly designating God Himself and thus being a descriptive expression. It is certain that under this case, which the onomaclasts regard as typical, one cannot by any means subsume all such expressions, even apart from the above-mentioned categories, but here, in and of itself, this usage demands and presupposes an explanation: Why in fact does the genius of language (in this case, of Hebrew), and, moreover, through such a divinely inspired writer, permit such a replacement? Why does precisely the *Name* turn out to be such a substitute? A sufficient answer to these questions can be found in all our above discussions; here the only thing we can add is that precisely this frequent usage, where God is replaced by His Name, does not by any means support onomaclasm, but just the opposite. And therefore our final opinion concerning these texts is, essentially, that even where the "Name" is clearly only a synonym, this expression introduces a real nuance into the very meaning and attests to the touching of the Name of God, of God in His Name, through the photosphere of the Divine Name. In other words, it is in this way that God most easily and naturally addresses Himself to those who worship Him and becomes accessible to them through His Holy Name. Thus, the expression that interests us is so widespread in the Biblical language for entirely real and ontological reasons and not just rhetorical ones. The Biblical usage with this juxtaposition of the expressions "God" and "Name of God" expresses the correlation between the transcendent, unfathomable, and unnameable Essence of God, of God in and for Himself, and the God of religion and cult, who, in practical terms, is represented precisely by the Name of God. Therefore, in essence this expression signifies nothing other than God worshiped by man.

The Divine Names, including the sacred tetragrammaton, are only symbolic projections of the transcendent and immanent; they are only touchings of Divinity, illuminating the darkness with flashes of lightning, blinding rays of the sun that do not permit us to gaze at it. This is a schematic imprint of the Divine in the human, where, simultaneously with the approach and revelation of the Divine, one feels with new intensity the absolute chasm that separates the Creator from the creature. It is for this reason there are so many Divine Names in the Old Testament, and if there is the preeminent Name, as if the proper Name of God, this is by virtue of God's unfathomable will. The Divine Names are modes of the revelation of God, theophoric theophanies, modes of Divine condescension. In a certain sense it is *man* who names God, feeling upon himself His revelations and responding to them with the name-creating faculty of his spirit. Man names God, and this is true even when God directly proclaims His Name as Jehovah, for it is said not that this is the Name of the Lord Himself but that it is only a revelation of It to man: "And I appeared unto Abraham, unto Isaac, and unto Jacob, by the Name of God Almighty, but by My Name JEHOVAH was I not known to them" (Exod. 6:3). The Name of God exists for man and in man; it is an echo in him of the Divine. And nowhere is this boundary that separates man from God felt so clearly and acutely as in the Old Testament, in virtue of the purity and clarity of the consciousness of God in this Testament, as a result of the intensity of the transcendentism of this consciousness. Paganism, thanks to its confused nature and lack of rigor, fuses God with the creaturely world and with man to a very significant degree: here, anthropomorphism inevitably becomes a defining characteristic, and the Divine Names merge with human ones, just as Divine Incarnation or human divinization is received rather easily. The most convincing examples of this can, of course, be found in ancient Greek religion. But this religion contained as many true presentiments and previsions as falsehoods and errors; and in any case these well-trodden little pathways of religious psychologism must now be forsaken forever.

The ladder from heaven to earth was erected through the Incarnation from the Most Pure Virgin of the Son of God: Jacob's dream became a reality: "Hereafter ye shall see heaven open, and the angels of God ascending and descending upon the Son of Man" (John 1:51). The Lord Jesus Christ is perfect Man and true God: in Him were united without separation and without confusion two natures and two wills, with one hypostasis. And the oneness of the hypostasis signifies, among other things, the oneness of the Name in which is expressed the individual being, the personhood, i.e., precisely the hypostaticity. According to the meaning of the fundamental dogmatic definitions, the Name of the Lord Jesus Christ belongs to both natures; It is the Name of God and of Man in their unity. Thus, here this Name has a completely different meaning than the Old Testament Names of God: in the Old Testament they were for man but did not belong to man; they had their foundation in God but did not belong to God — they were only given to Him by man in response to His revelation. Now the Name must belong to the very being of both God and Man who are united in the God-Man. The Name of the God-Man is the Name of God for man in a completely special and *new* sense, for It is the Name of the Man too, penetrating into the very depths of His being and forming His core; and at the same time this Name is also the Name of God who has made Himself incarnate in man. Thus, what we have here is not only a revelation of God to man, imprinting the Name of God in man or through man; what we have here is not a symbolic exchange of communications, not a "question-and-answer session" between the transcendent and the immanent, but their perfect unity, their interpenetration. How is this possible? This is the unfathomable mystery of the Divine Incarnation, which is also the unfathomable mystery of the Name of the God-Man, of the oneness of the hypostasis and the oneness of the Name with two natures and two wills, united without separation and without confusion. This is a mystery for the mind in the sense that it finds itself confronting a certain primary fact that cannot be analyzed further, a fact that must be accepted as such in all the unfathomability of its factual content. But this mystery of the Divine Incarnation also includes (and this is something that heretofore has not been sufficiently disclosed and felt in the dogmatic consciousness) the *oneness* of the Divine and human *Name,* of the Divine-human Name, of this living and true ladder between heaven and earth. The Incarnation of God is, and must necessarily also be, the Incarnation of the Name — the deification of the human name and the humanization of the Divine Name. And the sacred, terrible, transcendent Name Jehovah, the Old Testament revelation, became truly "old" testamental when the Only Begotten Son, existent in the bosom of the Father, "revealed" God (John 1:18) and to those who received Him gave "power to become the sons of God, even to them that believe on His Name" (1:12). "God, who at sundry times and in divers manners spake in time past unto the fathers by the prophets, hath in these last days spoken unto us by His Son, whom He hath appointed heir of all things, by whom also He made the worlds; who being the brightness of His glory, and the express image of His person, and upholding all things by the word of His power, when He had by Himself purged our sins, sat down on the right hand of the Majesty on high; being made so much better than the angels, as He hath by inheritance obtained a more excellent Name than they" (Heb. 1:1-4). This "Name . . . is above every name: That at the Name of Jesus every knee should bow, of things in heaven, and things in earth, and things under the earth" (Phil. 2:9-10).

The Name of the God-Man, this Name that is connected with the oneness of His hypostasis, clearly cannot have just a temporary, episodic significance, a significance just for His earthly existence. (Contrary to what the onomaclasts think, it cannot be just an ordinary name, given to him because there is a practical need for everyone to be called by some name.) On the contrary, this Divine Name comes into this earthly life and accompanies its Possessor, but it also goes beyond this life, into the supratemporal, into eternity. He is called by the name *Jesus* not by man but by the Angel sent by God, i.e., by God Himself (for, of course, the heavenly messenger pronounced this Name not by his own caprice but carrying out the will of God). The Annunciation (and this must be underscored with great force!) was the Annunciation not only of the conception of the Divine Infant and of the imminent Divine Incarnation but also of His Name, as the Divine Incarnation that was already being accomplished. The Annunciation announced also the Name Jesus (and these glad tidings were repeated by the angel to Joseph in his dream). Thus, the Name Jesus *preceded* His conception and birth from the Virgin; it was born *before* its Possessor; or more precisely, as Divine, as Divine-human, it was not born at all, but pre-eternally *is in God* and therefore appears in an earthly incarnation only in the fullness of time. For the Lord is in-humanized, becomes incarnate in His Name; His Name becomes incarnate, and around this nucleus of the personhood a crystallization, a solidification, coverings are formed. This Name accompanies Him in earthly life and in death, on the cross, on which it is inscribed indelibly forever. "And the writing was, JESUS OF NAZARETH THE KING OF THE JEWS" (John 19:19). "And a superscription also was written over Him in letters of Greek, and Latin, and Hebrew, THIS IS THE KING OF THE JEWS" (Luke 23:38; cf. Mark 15:26). "THIS IS JESUS THE KING OF THE JEWS" (Matt. 27:37). And if "the unfathomable Divine power" of the Holy Cross will appear as the sign of the Son of Man in heaven, as the sign of the end of this age, then the inscription (about which Pilate said, without knowing what truth he was saying: "What I have written I have written")[18] of the Divine Name on it is inseparable from it and has passed into the heavens of heavens, into the ages of ages. And the Lord Jesus rose from the dead with the same Name; or more precisely, the same Name passed through the gates of death and life, the gates of hell, remaining inseparably and unihypostatically with Him who "in the grave in the flesh, but in hell with Thy soul as God: in paradise with the thief, and on the throne with the Father and the Spirit wast Thou Who fillest all things, O Christ the Inexpressible."[19] And just as, after the deaths of their bearers, after their departure from this world, it is usual for names to share the fates of their bearers (which is expressed in the Church rite of remembrance by pronouncing names: a name *lives* its own special life; it outlives the bearer and is united with him in an inner mystical connection, constituting as before the nucleus of the personhood), so the holiest of Names remained inseparable from its Bearer, in Whom there is no change

---

18. John 19:22. — Trans.
19. From the Paschal Hours Troparion. — Trans.

and Who, too, will abide always, now, and forever, and in the ages of ages. That is why the Lord ascended to heaven in His Name, sitting at the right hand of God the Father, and will come with glory to judge the living and the dead: "this same Jesus, which is taken up from you into heaven, shall so come in like manner as ye have seen Him go into heaven" (Acts 1:11). And that is why we must "wait for His Son from heaven, Whom He raised from the dead, even Jesus" (1 Thess. 1:10). This, of course, must in no wise signify that Jesus is the *only Name of the God-Man;* on the contrary, it is conceivable that a *new* Name of Him will be revealed, about which the Apocalypse tells us directly, but this second and new Name cannot to any degree weaken or revoke the first Name, just as the Names "Son of God," "Son of Man," "Son of David," "Master," "Lord" did not revoke or weaken His proper Name, Jesus. Of course, the revelation of the new Name will be the greatest of religious events, the disclosure of a mystery, a new revelation, as it is portrayed in the Apocalypse (Rev. 3:12).

Thus, simple attentiveness and faithfulness to the whole Gospel story and to the Orthodox teaching prevents us from treating the most sweet Name Jesus with the blasphemous thoughtlessness displayed by our onomaclasts when they saw in this Name nothing more than an ordinary name among other ordinary names, an *instrumentum vocale*[20] (and, to make their view perfectly obvious, trampled and destroyed the letters representing the Name of God). The Name Jesus is in the heavens; it is written and lives in heaven and on earth, and it embraces the destinies of the world and of man; it is a human and Divine Name. Thus, in the Name Jesus we truly have (as our faith tells us, and all our faith is vain without this sweet truth) the pre-eternal Name of the Second Hypostasis, of the Word of God, of the Heart of God; and in conformity with the indivisibility and unity of the entire Holy Trinity, this Name that belongs to the Son also belongs to the Father and to the Spirit, to the entire Holy Trinity. And in distinction from the Divine Names as degrees of Divine revelation, the Name Jesus is not just one of the Divine Names but the Proper Name, the Name of God. And so, what attests to the great mystery of God? The Birth of Christ, the Incarnation, was for human beings a disclosure of the mystery of the Holy Trinity:

---

20. A "speaking implement," a term from Marxist polemics. — Trans.

the Son showed the Father and called for the Holy Spirit; the Theophany took place for the first time during the solemn Baptism of the Savior and it revealed another mystery of God: it revealed that *He has a Name* (or Names) and that this Name is Jesus (or that one of the Names is Jesus).

The Name of God, the naming and self-naming of Divinity, is, of course, an unfathomable mystery for us, before which we can only pray silently; however, this mystery is revealed and attested by the Name Jesus. God had names in the Old Testament. He revealed His Name Jehovah, but this was not a revelation of the mystery about God Himself; it was for humanity an act of the economy of our salvation. It was necessary *for man* to name God, just as the law was necessary for him, and although the entire law is a canopy erected over future goods, a canopy of the heavenly form, this canopy was impenetrable. The name itself and naming could have been considered a human invention (as the onomaclasts still consider it to be), existing only for man and in man. The Archangel's Annunciation of the Name of God, which is also a human name, revealed to the world and to humanity that the Name of God *is* and therefore (it must be concluded further) is also a human naming, because there are also Divine Names, an audacity of naming. The very faculty of name-creation, of naming, turns out to be ontologically grounded, loses its exclusively psychological aroma, and becomes a feature of the image of God in man, ontologically proper to him. In fact, it becomes clear why man is a name-bearer and name-creator, why he gives names to all and everything, and why he himself has a name. The name (and naming) is raised to an ontological height inaccessible to psychologistic critique: the name is the Image of God in man, belonging to his ontological makeup. And, conversely, God's inhumanization, whose purpose and consequence is man's deification, presupposes man's likeness to God as its preliminary condition. And among the many other features that characterize man (an immortal and free spirit, reason, will, love) we also find the feature that interests us: *man has a name* (and therefore gives names) as the nucleus of his personhood. The entire philosophy of naming and the name, which heretofore has been expounded abstractly-theoretically or analytically-anthropologically,[21] now

---

21. Bulgakov is referring to earlier parts of *The Philosophy of the Name.* — Trans.

acquires an objective reinforcement in facts, in revelation. The Name Jesus is a touchstone for the Christian philosophy of the name. It is clear why man gives and receives names: it is because he *has* the name as the potential of name-creation. And this imparts to naming a mysterious, profound, and realistic character. This affirmation, namely that the name enters into the image of God in man, that it is this image, i.e., that it belongs to the idea of man, to his mental being, this affirmation constitutes the most profound ontological basis of naming: thought collides here with the power of fact, before which all "why's" cease and become meaningless. Why does the Lord have a name? But this is no different from asking: Why is God trine in His Persons? One can endlessly explore the whole significance of this dogma, disclose all its consequences, and attempt to discover its imprint in all cosmic and human life, but all "why's" here are meaningless and even absurd. For thought, a similar primordial ground is represented by the revealed fact that the Divine Name exists. The rays of this Name can be found everywhere, but there is no need to try to ground its existence.

The Name Jesus is the Name of God, but it is also a human name. The Lord is the absolute, perfect, heavenly Man; the whole fullness of Divinity abides in Him bodily, but also the whole fullness of humanity is contained in Him celestially. All that is proper to man as a positive power (and therefore this excludes sin) has its foundation in Him and belongs to Him. One must understand not allegorically but completely realistically and ontologically those discourses of the Savior in which He identifies Himself with every human being. This signifies the union of all human beings in Christ, a union actualized in unified communion; and in this sense the Church is the Body of Christ. But this unity necessarily extends also to the name, in which is expressed the substantial nucleus of personhood. It would be unnatural and incomprehensible if human beings who are united with Him in all things should be separated from Him in this essential thing. In other words, this signifies that, essentially, dynamically, the great endless variety of names in the world forms one Name; or more precisely, all the names in the world are capable of entering into this one Name, of participating in It, of becoming one with It, of becoming Its rays emanating without separation from the sun. If Christ lives — or rather if

He can live and desires to live in every member of the faithful ("Behold, I stand at the door, and knock: if any man hear My voice, and open the door, I will come in to him")[22] — this in-dwelling of the Savior signifies not de-personalization, the dissolution of personhood, but its higher and uniquely true manifestation through illumination by grace; in every human being there must be imprinted Christ's most radiant Countenance,[23] or every human being must find himself in this Countenance and thereby see his own spiritual countenance, and all names substantially and dy-namically converge or emanate from the Name Jesus, for it is impossible to imagine anything that could belong to man but lie outside of Christ ex-cept the dark domain of sin, nonbeing, satanic evil.

The general anthropological and thus christological principle that all that is human should be known in Christ and through Christ, that all things should be seen in the light of the Hypostasis of the Son (a favorite idea of A. M. Bukharev,[24] which he served always and with great inspira-tion), this principle should without fail also be extended to the Name Jesus in its relation to human names. The most sweet Name Jesus, through the Son of Man, is inscribed in all of humanity, belongs to all of humanity. All of us, in spite of our unworthiness, participate in this great and Holy Name; in a certain sense we bear it and commune with it. Let it not be said that this is brazen audacity or blasphemy, for is there a measure to God's love and condescension, and will the Lord, who gives Himself, His Body and Blood in the sacrament of the Eucharist, deprive us of the grace-giving power of His Holy Name? That will never be! And just as the Lord took upon Himself all that is human (except sin), which is why every man can have in Him his personal Savior and Redeemer, so, in Him, in His most Holy Name, as their center, are united all human names, the substantial nuclei of all individualities. And if the Lord, in Whom all find themselves, is the all-individuality, then the Name Jesus is the *All-Name*, the Name of

22. Revelation 3:20. — Trans.

23. See previous note on *lik* on p. 59. — Trans.

24. Alexander M. Bukharev (1822-1871), Russian theologian, was one of the forerun-ners of the "Russian religious renaissance" that took place at the beginning of the twenti-eth century. In particular, he was a forerunner of the modern school of Russian Orthodox theology whose chief representatives are Pavel Florensky and Sergius Bulgakov. — Trans.

all names. There exists a hierarchy of names (as is directly attested by the Word of God: Heb. 1:4; Phil. 2:9-10), based on their dynamic correlation. And the names of all of humanity are only the manifested Name of the Heavenly Adam, and His Name is the true Name of all of humanity to the extent, of course, it finds itself in its essence, i.e., in God. The true humanity forms the Church; it is the Church. And only this humanity — of course not the sinful, temporal, empirical humanity — finds its names in the Name Jesus, and vice versa. The Name Jesus as a creative power, as the unified human principle, is the Church, i.e., the integral, Divine essence of man.

There is no doubt that this must be understood not linguistically (which would be totally meaningless) but mystically. Thus (here we use the distinctions established in our previous discussions) it is a question here not of the phoneme of the name, and not of the morpheme, but of the mystical syneme, of the individual energy that inheres and lives in every name, of the nucleus of the latter. These energies, these rays of color, are united in the rainbow of the Church and are contained in the white Tabor light of the Most Radiant Name Jesus. Such are the profoundest foundations of human names. The Name of all names is the Name Jesus.

But this Name is also a human name; moreover, Jesus is a concrete human name, one of many names, a common name widespread among His nation (the way the name Ivan is widespread among Russians). The mystery of the Divine condescension, of the kenosis, an unfathomable mystery before which one can only bow down with reverence, consists in the fact that the most radiant Name of God, becoming a human name, is clothed in the form of a servant, in rags of humility. But why is this a stumbling block for those who do not find a stumbling block in the appearance of God in the flesh, in the Divine kenosis? The Lord assumed a human body that was capable of being mortal, that was subjected to fatigue, hunger, and cold, that could be wounded; in other words, this body was not a phantom, it was not just the simulacrum of a human body; it was truly an ordinary human body, which only after the Resurrection, and at the moment of transfiguration, received and manifested another nature. And it is clear that the Incarnation could not have taken place in any other way if it was to be salvific and regenerative for the human nature; the manger, the cave of the birth, the abject poverty, the homelessness, the suffering and death — all this lay on the path of man's salvation. But, in that case, why do the onomaclasts find it such a stumbling block to accept that the Name of the God-Man, which therefore was also the Name of God, according to the human nature was just an ordinary human name? But this name — as the onomaclasts point out in their continued stumbling — was widespread, belonged, and even today belongs, to many men (the Mount Athos onomaclasts kept pointing the finger at some monk who bore the name Jesus, and used this as an occasion to blaspheme the Holy Name Jesus).[25]

But, of course, it is self-evident that no absolutely "proper" name exists, or can exist, as we explained above: all proper names are also common names, since they are *words* and therefore express an *idea,* i.e., something general. Nor can one regard as an exception names that have a special form according to their meaning or purpose, for they do not thereby lose the properties of words. Names are the qualities of human beings, the ideas of these qualities, and they inevitably can be repeated and will be repeated, and there is no power that could grant a monopoly over a name or guarantee its unrepeatability. Nevertheless, a name becomes a proper name only *in concreto,* i.e., on the one hand in combination with all the generic cognomens and agnomens, and on the other hand as a result of the connection established between it and its bearer. As far as the former is concerned one should not forget that in its concrete fullness a name bears only the central nucleus of the name, e.g., Jesus, John, etc.; it necessarily also joins in a concrete union with patronymic, surname, family tree. Therefore, a personal name, strictly speaking, is always complicated and concretized by the family name, by genealogy, which in this sense is nothing other than an extended name, the full name, the personal coefficient of a proper name. It is thanks to genealogy that a personal name truly acquires all its concreteness and individual unrepeatability. Therefore the onomaclasts, when finding the commonness of the name Jesus to be a stumbling block, should keep in mind that this concrete genealogical determinant of names, excluding all repeatability and mixing, is given also

25. Reference to the one of the uglier episodes in the Imiaslavie controversy. See the Appendix to the Translator's Introduction. — Trans.

in the Name Jesus: precisely such a determinant is "the book of the genera-tion of Jesus," the genealogy which, as is well known, is given in the Gos-pels of Matthew and Luke according to different schemes. In Matthew this is "the generation of Jesus Christ, the son of David, the son of Abraham"; we find here in descending order from Abraham the genealogy of Joseph the Betrothed. In Luke that genealogy is given in ascending order, and passes through the patriarchs to Adam and to God Himself. It is clear that all the names of the forefathers are, in an extended sense, also the names of the Son of David and the Son of Abraham, forming the photosphere of the name, its outward coverings. (So that the dishonorable slanders and blasphemous doubts of the Athos and non-Athos onomaclasts can be made powerless by a simple question: Does the Athos monk Jesus have a comparable genealogy, and therefore are the complementary colors of his name identical to those of the Name Jesus?) And let them not argue that all this genealogical expertise is usually absent, that a name is usually consid-ered apart from genealogy: the genealogy is potentially given in that indic-ative gesture, or agglutination, which unites the name with its bearer. For this reason (and only for this reason) one can say that proper names, though they are not proper but common, become singular in the concrete photosphere of the name, in its genealogy. But this connection that is es-tablished between the name and its bearer fills the name with individual color and fragrance, gives it living power proper to a given person, trans-forms it from a word-predicate into a name in the authentic sense, to which substance is proper. And in this case a name (even if we set aside all considerations relative to its concretization through genealogy), even if there is complete acoustic identity, appears and acts, in different cases of application, as different names. Here it is necessary to remember what we said above about the difference between phoneme (and morpheme) and syneme. If the phoneme is constituted by the acoustic body of the name (in the given case this includes its "internal form," i.e., the direct verbal meaning, which is of interest only for its genesis), the syneme of the name is constituted by its given bearer; the syneme is united with this bearer without separation. Therefore, to take abstractly the acoustic form alone, the body of the name without soul and power, to transform a name into a mere sound, as the onomaclasts do, is to fail to understand the essence of the name. The sounds Ivan, Peter, and other "proper names," when they are not referred to anything, are not names but mere words, predicates without subjects, ideas without actualization. About them it is, in general, impossible to make any judgment until they become names, i.e., until they acquire a concrete individual syneme. The onomaclasts find a stumbling block precisely in the abstractly taken phoneme of the name, which, as it turns out, does not differ in different cases of its application. But such was the fate not only of the name Jesus, owing to its commonness, but also of every other name: Napoleon, Nebuchadnezzar. After all, one could give a name like this to a dog, and both Napoleon the leader and Napoleon the dog are just *different* names, different words, in the same way that a "bat" meaning a stick and a "bat" meaning a flying animal are different words even though they have the same phoneme and even "internal form." The latter has significance for the genesis of the word and its historical understanding, but it does not abolish the existing distinctions between words. Therefore, generally speaking, identical names are not synonyms but have a species character: of families, ideas, tasks, in which the life of the bearer of the name passes. It is the common predicate in the case of different subjects, which are connected with it in their own way. However, it must be said that this connection, this resemblance or identity, can be paralyzed by the difference. Thus, this is the case also for the holy and divine Names of the Savior and of the Mother of God: Jesus and Mary. The Orthodox Church has established that the Names of the Savior and of the Mother of God cannot be shared by anyone, and if such sharing is sometimes practiced, it is an abuse; but at the same time the names Jesus and Mary given to various saints remain in the Orthodox calendar. Nevertheless, the Names of the Savior and of the Mother of God are considered to have an absolutely exclusive significance: it is as if they are not identical to their homonyms; it is as if they are not the same names as their homonyms but different, unique ones, not species names but individual ones, not family names but personal ones. Name-sharing is a secondary index in a name: in the genus expressed by a name, several families are distinguished that have a common forefather-saint. This introduces a specification into the name: $A^1, A^2, A^3, A^4 \ldots B^1, B^2, B^3$. Though the names Jesus and Mary enter according to their phoneme into their genus, nevertheless they are totally independent, not forming any family of those akin to or similar to them, and this is clearly because there can be no question here of kinship or similarity: they are like peaks which, though they belong to the same group of mountains, rise above all of them. However, this uniqueness, which is fully understandable, does not nullify the fact that, according to their phoneme, these Names belong to their genus. The Lord truly became incarnate and was truly in-humanized: He did not disdain the human name, but was in-humanized not only in His flesh but also in His Name, which was clothed in a humble human name common among pious Jews. Thus, the Name of the Lord Jesus is the Name of God, though it is also human. It is indissolubly connected with the human nature and the human name; and being immanent to the human nature, it introduces into the latter a Divine power — it is a Divine Incarnation in the Name as well.

Thus, the Name Jesus has for us a completely unique and exclusive closeness and accessibility: if the Name of God in the Old Testament is terrible and miraculous, the Name Jesus is sweet, though mighty: in it we commune with God's love, we partake of the grace of the Divine Name. If, as we have tried to show, Divine power is present in the Divine Names, in the Name Jesus this power is palpably close to man in a special way. As a Divine Name it contains Divine power and is a Divine energy, but it is also an energy of the human essence and belongs to the God-Man. Here we do not have that *transcensus*, that breakthrough from the immanent into the transcendent, from the world and from man to the not-world and to not-man — a breakthrough into the Divine domain. We have such a *transcensus* in the Old Testament, where only the high priest, protected by all manner of sacral means — by the solemnity of the liturgical moment, by his garments, by censing, by the holiness of the place — could enter into the Holy of Holies to proclaim the Name of God. But, as for the Name Jesus, all of us are called, in the capacity of the royal priesthood, to enter into the Holy of Holies of our hearts, to proclaim His Name there and to call Him, and He is present in His Name. For the ancient Jew the Name of God was like the peak of Sinai, shrouded in a darkness illuminated by lightning flashes, up to which only Moses could climb, and where almost every invocation of the Name of God (except liturgical invocations, legitimized ritually) was a sinful use of this Name in vain. By contrast, the Name Jesus allows itself to be invoked "at all times and in all hours" and to dwell unceasingly in a person's heart. It is necessary to become aware of and to feel all the power and acuteness of this difference, even this oppositeness, between the Name of the transcendent God, which (according to the perfectly definite testimony of the Word of God) was remote and terrible and dwelled only in the temple, and the Name Jesus, the temple for which is every human heart, and every member of the faithful, as having this Name imprinted in his heart, is a priest of this temple. Of course, this Name remains terrible and, as the greatest of holinesses, demands for itself tremulous veneration, for it is truly the Name of God. But it has become close, accessible, not separated from us by the ontological chasm that exists between the Creator and the creature. Over this chasm a bridge has been erected; the Divine and the human have become united without separation and without confusion: we repeat, only the priest or high priest (and only to the extent he was distinguished from the rest of humanity, to the extent he was transcendent to the present world, and only at the moments of greatest transcendence) had access to the majesty of the Name of God, whereas the Name Jesus is accessible and is given to everyone who "believes in His Name." And in this we already see the whole chasm that exists between the two Testaments; we see the power and salvific character of the Divine Incarnation. Of course, we do not wish to belittle the distinction between the priesthood and the laity that exists in the New Testament as well, for in this Testament, too, sacramental and priestly acts require conditions of transcendence and the fundamental *transcensus* of the person: ordination. But the points of this *transcensus* are shifted here. Thus, insofar as the Name Jesus is Divine-human, Divine and human, it receives all as its priests; it is accessible to all according to its human proximity; it is immanent to man. But insofar as it is Divine, it is the Name of God not in a lesser but even in a preeminent sense (in conformity with what was clarified above) in comparison with the other Divine Names: it is the terrible consuming fire of God's presence; it is the power and glory of God.

The onomaclasts are perplexed precisely by this closeness and accessibility of the most radiant Name and find in it a stumbling block: they are jealous of God's beneficence to human beings. It appears to them that God puts Himself at the disposal of those who invoke His Name, and that there is no barrier between Him and the person who invokes it. Yes, that is actually the case: such is God's love for human beings, such is the Divine condescension. But why are the onomaclasts so perplexed solely with regard to the Name of God? In every sacrament, and especially in the Holy Eucharist, the Lord gives Himself to human beings in conformity with their desire: the Divine consent and readiness are always given, as though they are something self-evident; the only thing required from man is the desire to use the grace of the sacrament. It is the same with the grace of the Holy Name of God, which is offered to everyone who invokes it with faith and in prayer. But here the onomaclasts are perplexed by two things: first, by what they consider an unseemly familiarity with the Holy Name (though it was their own behavior that was unseemly when they wrote over, tore to shreds, and even trampled on the Name Jesus), and, secondly, by the immeasurable significance that comes from invoking the Name of God.

The first doubt is easily resolved if we recall the foregoing discussion: a name has a phoneme and a syneme. First of all, the phoneme is different in different languages: e.g., Isus (Russian), Jesus (English), Iesous (Greek); secondly, it is not yet the name, but only its shell, its covering. As a word this phoneme may not yet represent a name; it may be only a predicate, not referring to the subject, and therefore alien to the subject and unfilled. Thus, the word "savior" or even "Jesus" is not yet the Name of the Lord. Or, more correctly, from this word, using it as a means, shell, or covering, this Name is *obtained*, being referred to its Bearer, being filled with His power, receiving the energy of the subject. The different verbal variations or modi of this word in different languages are so inessential because, though the Name, having full concreteness, has in every given case some verbal modus, it is not this modus, equivalent to every other modus, that makes the name the Name, but the whole fullness and saturatedness of it, the power living in it like fragrant myrrh in a poor vessel that can be polished or rough, painted in any color; this does not have any effect on the myrrh, but the vessel will necessarily have *some* concrete form, for without that it could not fulfill its function — it could not hold the myrrh contained in it.

The religious falsehood (and not just misunderstanding) of onoma-

clasm consists in its "psychologism," in the fact that here the efficaciousness of the Name of God is associated exclusively with mood: if a person
prays fervently and sincerely, the power of the Name of God will be palpable for him; if he does not, it will not be. The conditions of the reception of
grace and the character of this reception — which are connected with a
subjective element, with a person's mood — are transferred by the
onomaclasts to the objective meaning of what is taking place here, in exactly the same way that their Protestant predecessors denied the sacrament of the Eucharist, ascribing to it nothing more than a subjective significance, where, depending on mood, some commune while others do
not, as if any mood could offer the absent sacrament, could take the place
of the power of the Eucharist. Likewise, the power of the Name of God,
think the onomaclasts, is communicated by the mood of those praying, a
mood in virtue of which their prayer will be heard or not heard, as if God
needs to be cajoled and called before He will hear man. God hears everyone who calls Him, but not everyone who calls Him turns his heart toward Him and hears this hearing of God. And just as the Holy Gifts are the
Body and Blood of Christ equally for all communicants, whether they
commune in salvation or in judgment and condemnation, so the Name of
God is a power of God whatever our attitude toward it might be, one of
reverence or one of blasphemy. To imagine that the distance between
heaven and earth can be overcome by human will alone is to introduce
psychologism, anthropomorphism, subjectivism, and, in the final analysis, human-divinization into the very heart of religion, into its holy of
holies. Just as it is impossible to be saved by human power, so it is impossible to pray to God by human power if He does not condescend to this
prayer before we open our lips, if He is not present in it with the power
contained in His Name. Prayer becomes prayer to God and objectively signifies the union of man with God precisely through the presence of God
in the prayer itself, through the transcendent-immanent dwelling of the
Name of God in the prayer. The Name of God is the ontological foundation of prayer, its substance, power, and justification. This is why, in its essence, prayer is the invoked Name of God. And since the Name of God
contains divine energy and gives the presence of God, one can say (though
with great imprecision) that, practically and energetically, the Name of

God is God.[26] More precisely, in the Name of God is present the Power of God, which is inseparable from the Essence of God and in this sense is God Himself. Prayer would be impossible and incomprehensible without this condition. Every prayer is also a miracle, if *miracle* is defined as a discontinuity in the immanent, as the penetration of the transcendent into the immanent, and this miracle is the Name of God, which is God. From this we, of course, can see how insane, blasphemous, and sinful is our cold absentminded prayer, the invocation of the Name of God in vain, for in this Name we are always dealing with fire that burns us, though we are not conscious of this. Prayer becomes a joyous and terrible work, but also an immeasurably and extraordinarily significant one; it becomes a standing in the presence of God. Why should we be surprised if it turns out that the experience of the great ascetics of "noetic doing,"[27] of the Prayer of Jesus, and in particular of the great men of prayer of our own time, such as Father John of Kronstadt,[28] bears witness to the truth that "the Name of God is God Himself" and attests that this truth is an *axiom* and not a disputed theologeme, not a theological opinion or philosophical idea? One needs to read about this in its full context, for example in John of Kronstadt's religious diary, *My Life in Christ,* to see the entire obviousness of this truth. It is equally obvious that if God Himself is present in His Name, the Mother of God Herself and the saints themselves are present in their names.

If that is truly the significance of the Name of God in prayer in general, i.e., in private and personal prayer as well, it has such a significance to an even greater extent in liturgy, in cultic use. Strictly speaking, every prayer is a sacrament insofar as it is truly prayer, i.e., the addressing of God and the calling of Him by the Name of God. It might appear that, for us too, the decisive thing here is psychological *animus,* our mood, because without

26. The main thesis of the onomatodoxians. — Trans.

27. Reference to the Orthodox practice of mental, or "noetic," prayer, in particular of the Prayer of Jesus, which some ascetics repeat every moment of the day, both when awake and when asleep. — Trans.

28. Famous Russian Orthodox priest and elder (1829-1908), who had a large following among various strata of Russian society. He wrote the famous diary, *My Life in Christ,* regarded as one of the greatest spiritual and ascetic works of modern Orthodoxy. — Trans.

this the name will not be the Name of God but just a predicate or just a word. However, that is not the case: what is decisive here is not the psychological but the ontological element, the mystical intention that transforms the predicate into a subject, the verb into a noun. Although this intention does have a psychological aspect, its *how*, this does not abolish its proper nature, does not dissolve its nucleus. In this intention the living touching of Divinity takes place or, in other words, God Himself is present in the Name of God. After all, the simple vocative case contains an especially strong intention; it contains not only the presence of the one named, but a certain spiritual impetus is imparted to the latter, and of course this impetus is not just psychological. And this has force to an immeasurably greater degree in relation to the Spirit, who is not constrained by space, time, or outer shell: in each and every case when, invoking the Spirit, we name Him, we have His presence in the Name; and now it depends on us, on the transparence of our souls, how we will feel this presence: here we are truly oppressed and crippled by psychologism.

That is the way it is in private, personal prayer. However, in liturgy there is no place at all for psychologism; only ontology operates there: that which is said is enacted; and that which is enacted symbolically in the liturgy is enacted also in all the worlds, attaining to the heights of the heavenly and noetic altar. It is necessary to understand the true meaning of liturgy, i.e., its ontological objectivity, in virtue of which there is nothing that is merely mood but all things really take place, all things are symbolic, all things are illuminated and sanctified by the presence of God in the Name of God, which is precisely at the center of the liturgy. One can say that the whole liturgy is enacted "in the Name of God" — in the Name of the Holy Trinity, of the Lord Jesus Christ, of the Father, of the Holy Spirit; and this is not just a metaphor (as the onomaclasts wish to convince us) but a mystical reality. Liturgy is a continuous addressing of God, which He hears through His Name. And it is precisely in virtue of this hearing that the liturgy is enacted as a holy rite, full of real meaning and content; it is enacted not in virtue of the mood or psychological intensity of the priestly servants but by virtue of the Name of God, in which the Power of God is present. Without this condition of religious realism liturgy would be transformed into a theatrical performance on religious themes, into a mystery play well acted or poorly acted depending on these "moods." However, the mood determines only the measure in which we take in that which is enacted, the measure in which we use it for ourselves and assimilate it. To continue this analogy with a theatrical performance (however shocking such an analogy might seem), one must say that if an actor playing Napoleon were to become Napoleon in actual fact during the performance, not in virtue of his art but only in virtue of the fact that he was playing this role, it would depend on him and on the public to grasp his character in one measure or another; and without this condition we would have only fakes, even if they are talented; that is, we would have not Napoleon but only a "mood" occasioned by Napoleon, i.e., an empty nothing. Between a "theatrical performance" and the reality of the symbolism of the rite there exists a chasm — the same chasm that, in general, exists between being and nonbeing, between allegory and reality. And the foundation that fills with reality the holy liturgical rite is, without doubt, the Name of God, by virtue of which all things are enacted and sanctified here; and when they are sanctified, they themselves become full, authentic, and efficacious.

The Name of God is the foundation of liturgy, its heart, and the heart of the heart is the Name Jesus. For in connection with and in virtue of this Name we also have the most holy and majestic Name of the Father and of the Son and of the Holy Spirit, the revelation of the Holy Trinity, as well as the Name of the Mother of God and of all the saints. If hypothetically we were to take away this power of the Name Jesus, the whole liturgy, all the sacramental acts, would crumble into dust. The whole liturgy grows out of the Name of God as its seed. Thus, the Lord gives to the apostles and, in their persons, to the whole Church His Name as power and authority: "In My Name shall they cast out devils; they shall speak with new tongues," etc. (Mark 16:17; cf. Luke 10:17: "Lord, even the devils are subject unto us through Thy Name"; cf. Luke 16:18: "I command thee in the Name of Jesus Christ to come out of her"). And the first miracle of healing that manifested the apostolic power was accomplished by Peter and John over the lame man: "In the Name of Jesus Christ of Nazareth rise up and walk" (Acts 3:6; cf. 4:10). ". . . for there is none other name under heaven given among men, whereby we must be saved" (4:12). "And His Name through faith in His Name hath made this man strong, whom ye see and know" (3:16). (And this realism of the Name was clear to the pagans of Ephesus as well, about whom it is said: "and fear fell on them all, and the Name of the Lord Jesus was magnified" [19:17].) Thus, the evangelist says that "as many as received Him, to them gave He power to become the sons of God, even to them that believe on His Name" (John 1:12); or: "but ye are washed, but ye are sanctified, but ye are justified in the Name of the Lord Jesus, and by the Spirit of our God" (1 Cor. 6:11). And this Name as the power of God, as the real presence of the Lord Jesus Himself, was attested from their own experience by the practitioners of the Prayer of Jesus. Therefore we can say with the audacity of faith that our liturgy is not only service dedicated to God but also service done by God, in which Christ Himself is the High Priest and the priests are sanctified in His Name and manifest the power of His presence. In the Church sacraments, too, God is present and enacts them by the power of His Name. In general, the sacraments are power and reality affirmed by the Name of God.

Should one, like the onomaclasts, see a stumbling block in the fact that all this is *given* to man? If I desire, they say, I will call the Name of God and have God Himself. Yes, that is truly so; such is God's love and condescension. However, if they have in mind nothing more than the phoneme, an empty verbal shell deprived of content, then, of course, what they say is untrue. To accomplish the sacrament, what is needed, besides the objective conditions, is priestly grace as well as the animus — the desire to accomplish precisely the sacrament. And those who desire to experience the action of the Name of God must also desire to proclaim precisely the Name of God, and not just the sounds "Je-sus."

Thus, let us not be perplexed by the closeness and accessibility of God in His Name invoked with faith, and let us not regard it as a stumbling block; it cannot be otherwise, for the Lord is close to those who ask of Him. May His Name be blessed always, now and forever, and for ages of ages!

"The Name of God is God." This phrase of Father John of Kronstadt resounded in our days from the Caucasus wilderness and from Mount Athos and became the object of bitter wrangling and disputes, and of the most serious misunderstandings (of misunderstandings, it seems, more than anything else).[29] Some of the more fanatical "onomatodoxians" prefer the variant: "The Name of God *is* God *Himself*"; evidently, by underscoring the copula "is" they wish to establish full equality between the Name and God. But from this follows also the opposite conclusion (and this is something the onomatodoxians are perhaps not fully conscious of), not drawn by those who are led astray by this doctrine, namely the conclusion that "God = the Name of God" (which is why those who are led astray in this way call the onomatodoxians "name-of-Godders"). Therefore, it is first of all necessary to establish the *irreversibility* of this judgment: here the copula "is" does not by any means signify equality or identity. The judgment is, in principle, irreversible, for when the judgment is reversed, it becomes a completely new judgment, with a new subject and predicate. We clarified above that the predicateness, the quality of the subject, is connected with an ontological accent; the subject is always a noun, while the predicate, even if its form has the character of a noun, becomes, when dissolved in the copula, an adjective and verb, expresses not *ens* and not *res*, but an idea as quality, as universal; from this we get the irreversibility of the judgment. Those who make the judgment reversible do not take into account the adjectivalness of the predicate and are guided solely by formally grammatical, etymological characteristics, ignoring the syntax with its internal forms. Therefore, in the expression "the Name of God is God" the word "God" is the predicate (and perhaps — of course with a certain approximateness of meaning — it can be replaced by such terms as "divine," "divinity": *theion, theotēs*); in Greek, it must stand alone without an article, so that the expression has this form: *to tou Theou onoma Theos estin* (but not *ho Theos*).[30]

Therefore, totally inadmissible is the reverse judgment, which could approximately be expressed as: *ho Theos to tou Theou onoma estin*.[31] Such a truly "name-of-Godding" formula would signify not just a blasphemous heresy but even a complete absurdity. Thus, the predicate "is God" really signifies not substantial identity existing between the essence of God and

---

29. Bulgakov is referring to the Imiaslavie controversy. See the Appendix to the Translator's Introduction. — Trans.

30. "The Name of God is God (but not the God)." — Trans.

31. "The God is the Name of God." — Trans.

His Name, but the entering and presence of the Name of God in the domain of Divine being and power; this predicate signifies a manifestation of that which the Constantinople fathers called the *energy* of God.[32] And in this sense the Name of God occupies in the ontological hierarchy the same place as the light of Tabor, though of course this does not mean that the Name and the Light become identical in their phenomenon while remaining unisubstantial in their noumenon. One can safely make the following juxtaposition: the Name of God is God, the light of Tabor is God (to this one can add: the grace of God sacramentally bestowed upon men is God); in all these cases the predicate "is God" does not by any means establish an identity with God's *hypostatic* essence; it only leads us into the Divine domain and marks the quality of Divinity: metals or stones that pass through fire absorb the light and heat of this fire and themselves become transformed into fire, but nevertheless they differ from the original fire which is the source.

In accordance with its direct meaning and in conformity with the very nature of words and sentences, the formula "the Name of God is God" does not, and cannot, signify anything more than this. Those delirious "name-of-Godding" ravings that frighten and perplex the onomaclasts are simply not permitted here by language, by the nature of words, and it would be better for the essence of the matter and for the realm of the Church if this formula did not concentrate undue and premature attention upon itself. In any case, in and of itself this formula does not give an exhaustive answer to the question raised, nor does it constitute a dogmatic definition; it must be developed or completed, because Divinity ("is God," *Theos ēstin*) insufficiently defines the specific character of the case examined and, as we have already indicated, it also characterizes other forms of Divine energy, of the self-revelation of God. It follows that the formula "the Name of God is God" cannot by any means be regarded even as an attempt at a dogmatic definition of the Name of God, for it gives only the most general doctrine (and when it is understood correctly, this doctrine does not by any means provoke those reproaches of "name-of-Godding" which, in their own way, were even justly directed against it);

32. A reference to the doctrine of Gregory Palamas. — Trans.

this general doctrine must clarify precisely *in what* sense the Name of God "is God," i.e., precisely in what sense It is Divine. Thus, in our understanding and in our interpretation, the formula "the Name of God is God" signifies only that the Name of God is Divine, that it enters into the sphere of God, of His energies. This, of course, does not in any way diminish the fact that, during the ontological invocation of the Name of God in prayer (using the vocative or nominative case, in the sense of subjectivity or substantiality), the Lord Himself is present with His power, with His simplicity, with His indivisibility, and the invocation of the Name of God in prayer is unceasing communion with God, who is simple and indivisible. But this presence of God in His Name, which compelled the pious man of prayer to cry out in astonishment, "the Name of God is God," this presence does not in any way signify that God is the Name itself; it does not introduce a fetishism of the Name; rather, it reveals to us the eternal and unfathomable mystery of the Divine Incarnation and the Divine condescension, the mystery of the presence of God in His Name, a presence of which we become certain in the sacrament of prayer.

Post Scriptum to "The Name of God": A Sophiological Interpretation of the Dogma of the Name Jesus

I

The Name of God, in conformity with the nature of every "proper name," has its origin in naming as a complete sentence, which the subject (that which is named) is united with the predicate (the name) through the copula *(is)* as logical and verbal agglutination: A (the one named) is B (the name). The link between the one named and the name, the agglutination, becomes so strong that, to a certain extent, the name loses its meaning (the "internal form of the word"); it partly stops being a syneme, and becomes, as it were, nothing more than a phoneme, a pronominal sign, a logical or even onto-logical (and therefore also psychological) gesture. Things do not always go to the extreme of the total loss of meaning of the "proper name," to the loss of its original verbal meaning, as a result of the strength of agglutination or forgetting; however, one comes closer to this extreme the more "proper" a name becomes, the more it becomes saturated with the power of being, the more ontic it becomes. It indeterminately approaches a pronoun, an inter-nal indicative gesture, a nonverbal word: a "pro-nomen," a word that is in place of a name. Such is the power of the *proper* name. Such is its character.

Bulgakov wrote this *post scriptum* in 1942, many years after he had completed the main text of *The Philosophy of the Name.* — Trans.

However, in spite of all its "properness," it is still a naming; it never loses the character of predicateness, at least in intention. Insofar as the proper name is dual in character, it unites in itself subject and predicate. If as the subject one "pronominally" thinks I, you, he, we, you (plural), they (and one invariably and inevitably thinks this), then in this character of the proper name one can perceive not only the nature of the word as something said about something, but also a mode of *hypostatic* being expressed in every judgment: A (the one named) is B. This is a universal mode of being, which is always objective, but it also has its verbal revelation, its word, which is precisely objectified in the proper name. Such is the *duality* according to meaning that characterizes the proper name insofar as it remains a *word* as a naming but also has the significance of a nonverbal pronominal gesture.

The Name of God does not formally differ from other proper names; like them, it is a naming that in a special manner coalesces with its subject and to that extent is identified with it. This subject itself, i.e., in the given case God's hypostatic being, is (according to the intuition of Pseudo-Dionysius) nameless because it is above all names. It can be expressed either by a silent mystical gesture or through the NOT (*a privativum*) of "negative theology" in the capacity of the subject, though here it is expressed in an indeterminate series of names that differ in their predicateness but are equivalent in the intention of correlatedness to one subject. Anonymity is combined here with polyanomy — that is the fundamental idea of the Pseudo-Dionysian onomatology, which has been assimilated both by Christian dogmatics (confronting the same sort of fact) and by Biblical revelation.

However, such polyanomy has its limits even apart from the general anonymity of negative theology. In the Bible (as well as in theology) out of the total set of Divine Names there are distinguished a few most important Names, "great" Names, which are regarded as more "proper," as it were, than the others. Of these Names there are seven, and among them is the holiest and most majestic of all the Old Testament Names of God, the Name revealed and given by God Himself to Moses on Sinai: Jehovah, I AM THAT I AM. However, this Name too, in spite of all the exclusiveness and solemnity of its revelation, bears distinct signs of the dual character that generally characterizes proper names: on the one hand they are words that have not lost their semantic, verbal meaning (I AM THAT I AM), and on the other hand they are words that have acquired a "pronominal" usage and to that extent have lost their direct meaning, i.e., they are words that have been transformed from phoneme into syneme. To that extent one can say that even Jehovah is not the "proper" Name of God but only a common name, one of the many names, though one that has become unique by its application. "And I appeared unto Abraham, unto Isaac, and unto Jacob, by the name of God Almighty, but by my name JE-HOVAH I was not known to them" (Exod. 6:3 [the King James Version has been slightly modified here]). To that extent its proper meaning is not lost but distinctly resounds and radiates in this Name, is clearly contained in it, though it is a hypostatic Name, I AM THAT I AM, Jehovah. Here the subject is clearly united with the predicate, and the predicate with the copula.

What is the relation of this revelation of the Name I AM THAT I AM to the revelation of the Holy Trinity as I-WE, which already exists in the Old Testament as a kind of cryptogram (e.g., the tale of the creation of the world and of man, the appearance of God to Abraham, the confusion of languages at the Tower of Babel, and other texts)? Is this I of the Divine tetragrammaton a unihypostatic I (and if it is, precisely of what hypostasis?), or is it the trihypostatic I in its triunity? There is no direct guidance about how to answer this question. In different contexts the Old Testament revelation which speaks about God's person is applicable to different hypostases in conformity with the overall meaning, but the Name Jehovah is used only in relation to God's hypostatic being in general. Does this usage not compel us to refer in general this Holy Name precisely to the triunity of the Divine hypostases, in which three Divine hypostatic lights merge ("one in Trinity and Trinity in one," according to the words of the great canon)? Does the holy cryptogram not contain revelations about God's personhood, which is revealed in the fullness of Divine being: I AM THAT I AM? If this theological-exegetical conjecture is justified, then the scope and content of the revelation about the Name of God Jehovah should be understood as simultaneously including the whole fullness of ontological naming. This provides guidance toward a sophiological explanation of the Name of God, which unites a personal character, the hypostasis, without separation and without confusion, with the Divine essence, the ousia, in its self-revelation, in its wisdom as well as its glory. (The latter is clear from the text in which it is said that God, in revealing His Name to Moses, also reveals to him His glory [Exod. 33:19] in their biunity and ontological inseparability, in their identity with difference.) Therefore, Jehovah, I AM THAT I AM, signifies the Divine trihypostaticity in its sophianicity, in the Wisdom and Glory of God. The Name of God signifies both its hypostatic Bearer and the Divine Sophia; it expresses not only the hypostatic but also the sophianic being of God, though this expression has a preliminary, indistinct, Old Testament character. To this it should be added that it also has a supramundane, transcendent character, though one that, through revelation, becomes immanent to man's being. However, in spite of this touching and meeting of the transcendent and the immanent, which characterizes all revelation in general, the latter nevertheless remains more directed toward God's supramundaneness than toward creaturely being. If one expresses this idea in terms of sophiology, the Name Jehovah refers more to the Divine Sophia than to the creaturely Sophia.

In the New Testament revelation about the Name of God the Name Jehovah cedes its place to the Name Jesus, which eclipses and abolishes it as it were, the way a concrete thing abolishes an abstract thing. Nevertheless, the former name is presupposed by and even included in the latter name, but it loses its significance as the "proper name" par excellence. First of all we must ask: What is the hypostatic significance of this New Testament Name? That which is named here, is it the one, though trihypostatic, Divine I, the Divine triunity, as in the case of Jehovah; or is it the hypostasis alone, precisely the Second one, so that the entire Holy Trinity remains here nameless or above name, and the Name Jesus thus belongs only to the Second Hypostasis? Or is this not the case? Is it the case, instead, that the moment of **tri**hypostaticity in the Name Jesus is not absorbed in the unity of the directly named Second Hypostasis but is contained in the concreteness of the meaning of this Name in a special, appropriate manner? The second is clearly the case. The Name Jesus belongs directly to the Second Hypostasis, but in and through the latter it names the entire Holy Trinity; and in this sense this Name Jesus is analogous and has a similar meaning to the Name Jehovah, I AM THAT I AM. This meaning of this

Name has its origin in the personal character of the Second Hypostasis, which is also the Word of God and, in this capacity, the Word of the Father and the Word of the Holy Spirit, proclaimed by Them and revealing Them. The Father, the Principle, abides in transcendence even in the Holy Trinity. He Himself is silent — but His word about Himself, His self-naming, is the Word of God pre-eternally begotten by Him, and this Word is not only the word of all words, the all-predicate, but also the proper Name of God, the all-subject, speaking all about all. In this sense, as the Word of the Father, the Name of the Son names the Father too in the one principle of the Holy Trinity; it belongs to the Father too, though not as His proper word. And the same thing can be said about the Holy Spirit, who, not having His proper name, reposes upon the Son of the Father and, as the Spirit of Truth, manifests the word as existent truth. To that extent the Name of the Son belongs to the Holy Spirit too as a "nonproper" name of the Latter. Therefore the Name Jesus is the one Name of the Holy Trinity in Its unity as concrete trine self-consciousness. Just as the Second Hypostasis Itself is not separated from the triunity of the Holy Trinity through Its hypostatic properties, but is only distinguished in this triunity, so Its Divine Name, while belonging to the entire Holy Trinity, also belongs to each of the hypostases, and to each of them in a special sense. However, these are not three different names, but one name. Moreover, it is not even a name that is common to the three and that, in this capacity, could be isolated in brackets, as a triply repeating name. It is not common in this sense and is not repeated; rather, it sounds in its own manner for each hypostasis, in the Divine triunity: it is not three completely identical names, A_1, A_2, A_3, but the triune Name, the trine context of the one Divine Name Jesus. It is, therefore, both the "proper" Name of the Son alone and the "nonproper," but trine, Name of the entire Holy Trinity. In this "nonproper" but trine Name each hypostasis manifests its relation to the Name: the Father manifests His unnameability or supranameability as the Principle, the initial hypostasis; the Holy Spirit too is unnamed, since He does not have His proper word and name, but only that of the Son; finally, the Son has a name and gives it through Himself to all three hypostases in triunity. Therefore, it is impossible to answer the arithmetically formulated question: "How many names does the Holy Trinity have, three or one?" It has not three and not one, but is triune or, rather, unitrine, as are all the definitions pertaining to It.

To this one should add that the three hypostatic namings of the First, Second, and Third Hypostases — the Father, the Son-Word, and the Holy Spirit — are *not* proper names but only namings that express their hypostatic properties, or character. They can also be used in the capacity of the proper namings of each of the hypostases, and they are actually used in this capacity, though together with other namings that are not as exclusive in their meaning, but this does not make them proper names in the exact sense. One must add that, in this common-name character of theirs, they nevertheless remain trinitarian or triune, concealing the trine context that is full of its significance: the Father is the Father of the Son, upon Whom reposes the Holy Spirit, proceeding onto the Son; the Son is the Son of the Father, begotten of the Father and overshadowed from Him by the Holy Spirit; finally, the Holy Spirit proceeds from the Father onto the Son and reposes upon Him. Thus, each of these hypostatic names can also be disclosed as the trine Name when it is taken only in some one initial definition or aspect. Manifested here is a trine interrelation. But this does not occur in the "proper" Name of Jesus itself, though in its meaning it too is disclosed in a trine aspect, originating, however, in the already given hypostatic character, which establishes their interrelation.

II

In the sophiological interpretation of the Name of God in general — both in the case of the Old Testament Name Jehovah and in the case of the New Testament Name Jesus — there arises the following fundamental question: To what does the Divine revelation contained in the Name of God refer? Does it refer only to the hypostasis, to the Divine Person, or also to the essence, the nature, the "energies," the wisdom, the glory, the Divine Sophia? The most primary and direct significance of the Name of God refers to the Divine hypostasis.

The name is a synonym, or power, of the pronoun, of the personal hypostatic I, spoken by the Word, and not just an ontological gesture, which in essence is nonverbal. As a proper Name, pronominal, it lacks all verbal content, all predicateness; nothing is said in it about its bearer, Who, though He is the foundation of being, its noumenon, cannot Himself be expressed in exhaustive phenomenality. From this we get the conclusion that the Name as "subject" is, as it were, located outside of its own sophianicity, though it is inseparable from its own ontic photosphere. And this leads to the paradoxical and, of course, contradictory conclusion that, in the Name, the Person of God is named outside, without, or apart from the Divinity, that it is asophianic. Clearly, at the basis of such a conclusion there is a misunderstanding that it is necessary to remove.

In western theology of the eleventh century,[1] in connection with the teaching of Gilbert de Poirée, which was condemned at the Council of Reims, there arose the question of whether the hypostatic God is distinguished from Divinity *(Divinitas)*, and if so, what the distinction is. Gilbert distinguished them and seemed to oppose them, whereas the Council identified them. In essence the question clearly concerned the relation between the hypostasis and the ousia, or self-revelation in God. The question was not brought to complete theological and sophiological clarity, and was not so much resolved as stifled, and of course all discussions of it were then prohibited, prematurely. One can agree fully with neither of the sides. Hypostasis and ousia, the divine person and the divine person's self-revelation, differ from each other, but they are not opposed to each other in such a way as to allow duality in God. God is hypostatic in His being, but His being (nature, essence, self-revelation) is always hypostatized and cannot be nonhypostatic. The connection between hypostasis and ousia is such that they cannot be separated and opposed, just as it is impossible to fuse or identify them. Here we have two different sides of one Divine hypostatic being. This distinction is expressed in the dogma of trinity as the trihypostaticity and consubstantiality of one self-identical Divinity. Thus, the question does not admit rationalistic resolution (either/or), but requires the antinomic identity of the two definitions (both-and).

This same distinction/identification is applicable in the question of the Name of God. The name, as a mystical gesture or symbol, does not

---

1. See my essay, "Chapters on Trinitarity," Part I, Excurses.

name but only indicates what is named, the subject; however, it does this predicately. It itself is a predicate that has become a subject, an antinomy of identity. This is perfectly clear with regard to the Old Testament Name Jehovah, I AM THAT I AM (as well as with regard to all the Names of God that express divine "properties," and this in human language, immanently). They are as much names as Namings with a definite content and, thus, with a sophiological character. But is the case not different with regard to the New Testament Name, the Name of the God-Man Jesus? Is it not the proper Name par excellence? As the Divine-Human Name, at the same time it is also the Name of God that is pre-eternally existent in the heavens and brought to earth from God through the archangel at the Divine Incarnation, and it is thus transcendent in a special sense. Along with this significance which is semantic according to its very character in the absence of a special "internal form," in any case its direct significance fails to correspond to its uniqueness to such an extent that in no wise can it be regarded as adequate to it. It even rather produces the impression not of the Name in the precise sense but of an ordinary name. Therefore, the Name Jesus can be apprehended as the proper Name par excellence, deprived of its special significance or content. Both considerations pose the question of its sophianic significance: How are *Deus* and *deitas* related in it? Is the Name Jesus sophianic, as is in general the Name of God? Is the Name Jesus a predicate for the Divine subject, or not?

Clearly, in this application of naming as a "secret" name, we have the fusion of the subject and the predicate, of the one named and the name. In virtue of this fusion the Name of God expresses the unity of the hypostatic subject and the sophianic predicate or definition in their fusion and indistinguishability, but also in their distinction from one another. The Name as a "proper" Name expresses the hypostasis, has a pronominal significance, precisely that of a personal pronoun, but it also has the significance of content, which retains its power as a self-revelation of the hypostatic God. Depending on context, on one or another semantic combination, the accent in the Name refers either to its first or to its second significance — to the subject or to the predicate. The Name itself, in the fullness of its significance, is not only first or second, but their duality and inseparability. Even in the Divine Name of the Holy Trinity, this nuance is manifested in the Names of the three hypostases: In the First Hypostasis, that of the Father, is inscribed the Name of God as the "proper" Name in the precise sense. The Father is the One who reveals Himself, the hypostasis par excellence, the subject in the entire trine self-revelation and self-definition of God. Therefore the logical accent falls here on the hypostatic significance of the name. In contrast, the Son, the Word of the Father, revealing, showing, and doing the will of the Father, is the hypostatized predicate, and He is thus named the Word of God, the Wisdom of God. Similarly, the Holy Spirit names the Divine Being, Life, and Power, this too in a hypostatized manner but with the significance, par excellence, of the link between the Father and the Son. It is thus proper for the Third Hypostasis to express also the Glory of God, of the Father in the Son. Based on this, we can understand that Old Testament usage according to which the Name of God is identified to such a degree with the Glory of God, as we read in Exodus: "And the Lord said, I will make all My Glory pass before thee, and I will proclaim the Name of Jehovah before thee" (33:19).[2] One can therefore say that the proper Name, the divine I (= God the Lord), belongs to the First Hypostasis, the One that reveals Itself, and that in relation to It the Second and Third Hypostases have a Name that is preeminently "common": they are the hypostases that reveal God's essence, Glory, and Wisdom, and in this sense they are preeminently the sophianic names, though with a hypostatic application.

Such is this distinction in the trine Name of the Holy Trinity. But how is it defined in the Name of Jesus, of the God-Man? It is one not only for the Second Hypostasis, that of the God-Man, but in it is also secretly contained the Name of the entire Holy Trinity; it is the sacred cryptogram of the Latter. The essence of the matter does not change even here, in these secret depths. The dual meaning of the Name of God is fully retained in the Name Jesus too, since this Name appears in the proper Name of the Second Hypostasis, of the God-Man, and in it and through it the entire Holy Trinity is named in Its trine interrelation; at the same time it also expresses the power, depth, and self-revelation of Divinity revealed in Wis-

---

2. The King James Version has been modified to conform with the Russian version used by Bulgakov. — Trans.

dom and Glory, i.e., it is a sophianic self-definition. And its first meaning as the proper hypostatic Name is united without separation with its second meaning, its sophianic and ousianic meaning, in the entire power and fullness of Divinity. Jesus is also the Logos, the Word of all words about all things: "All things were made by Him."[3] Jesus is the univocal and all-containing universal Name, but this Name also signifies Divine Power, Wisdom, and Glory. It is, as it were, the Divine "Title" of all Being, which in the Old Testament language is given as "I AM THAT I AM," and in the New Testament language as "Jesus." This is the universally symbolic Name of the Divine Sophia, pre-eternally existent in the heavens and disclosing Herself in creaturely becoming as "to be," "to become existent," in appearance out of nothing in creatureliness.

From this we draw the general conclusion that the Name of God and the Name Jesus, proclaiming God's hypostatic being, is also a sophianic name. It must be understood not only trinitarianly-theologically but also sophiologically, theophanically, anthropologically, and cosmologically, with application to all the definitions of Divine and creaturely being. This corresponds also to the dual character of the Name: as the silent hypostatic subject on the one hand and as sophianic self-revelation, the ontic predicate, on the other. In itself it implies: "I AM THAT I AM" but also "In the Beginning [in Divinity, Sophia] was the Word [the hypostatic *ho logos*], and the Word was with God [the Father, *ton Theon*], and the Word was God [divine, *Theos*]," and as the Divine essence, nature, wisdom, glory, being in beauty, the existent name. The Names Logos and Jesus are identical in their power, just as they are self-identical in their hypostatic correlatedness.

This identity of the meaning of the Name Jesus can also be expressed in terms of the Chalcedonian dogma of one Divine-human hypostasis and two natures. The Name Jesus, as a hypostatic name, is one: it is the Name of the Son of God and the Son of Man come down from heaven (John 3:13), of the Heavenly First Man. But this Name is proper to the two natures and in that sense it is dual, belonging both to His divinity and to His humanity. Thus, this Name is uni-dual, in accordance with the entire Chalcedonian definition. Nevertheless, it remains one, like the God-Man Himself.

3. John 1:3. — Trans.

In conclusion, it is necessary to confirm once more that the "Name of God" is not only a word, a Divine word, in the entire profundity and inexhaustibility of its meaning, but also the Divine power and essence. "The Name of God is God" in the sense of the Divine presence, of Divine energy. This is its most essential meaning, and this is how it must be understood in prayer and in life. This Name is inscribed in the entire universe and in all of humanity, as well as in the world of angels. Not closed for this Name are all the worlds and all their abysses, all the heavenly, earthly, and nether places. This Name penetrates everywhere, for "all things were made by Him; and without Him was not any thing made that was made." It is the naming that bears within itself the Name of God.

Glory to It in the ages of ages.

Index